Sensory Environmental Relationships

Between Memories of the Past and Imaginings of the Future

Dr Blaž Bajič and Dr Ana Svetel
University of Ljubljana, Slovenia

Series in Anthropology

VERNON PRESS

www.vernonpress.com

In the Americas:	*In the rest of the world:*
Vernon Press	Vernon Press
1000 N West Street, Suite 1200	C/Sancti Espiritu 17,
Wilmington, Delaware, 19801	Malaga, 29006
United States	Spain

Series in Anthropology

Library of Congress Control Number: 2023938705

ISBN: 978-1-64889-916-4

Also available: 978-1-64889-693-4 [Hardback]; 978-1-64889-763-4 [PDF, E-Book]

Table of Contents

List of Figures

Foreword:
On Recent Turns and Revolutions in the Humanities and Social Sciences, and on their Sensory Part

Rajko Muršič

University of Ljubljana, Slovenia

We can say we have lived for decades in times of turns in the humanities and social sciences, but the overall impression is that turning ways of knowledge do not show much progress. Following the constant flow of ever-new "turns," can we say that we know societies – past and present, domestic and far away, seemingly simple and complex, recently established and ancient – are actually substantially better? Or do we need revolutions (Howes 2006)? Revolutions, in which sense? In its original sense, derived from the movement of celestial bodies, returning to their initial position in their orbiting around the Sun? Are we waiting for "revolutionary" Kopernik in the humanities and social sciences, denying revolutionary thinkers from the past? Or are we waiting for a revolution in a social sense, an overthrow, or a coup in present-day (pre)dominant scholarship? Following the manifold turns in recent times and fashionable utterings of continuously redressed vocabularies, isn't it time to pose the question about the emperor's new clothes?

Let me mention just some turns in social sciences and the humanities, following perhaps the initial, postmodern turn: the linguistic turn; the literary turn; the spatial or topographic turn; the cultural turn; the individualist turn; the postcolonial turn; the moral/ethical turn; the ontological turn; the corporeal turn; the hierarchical multi-turn; the mobilities turn; the affective turn; the historical turn; the neoliberal turn; the multispecies or animal turn; the performative turn; the symbolic turn; the metaphorical turn; the walking methodology turn (perhaps my private invention), or, simply put it, the whatever turn. None of them is, I guess, essentially a "paradigmatic" turn in Kuhn's sense (1962), and they are obviously not supposed to be.

In the humanities and social sciences, based on hermeneutic methodology and not on the hypothetical-deductive one, the progress is different than in "paradigmatic" sciences. It is a progress in understanding, a progress in degrees, a progress in gradation, forming clines of knowledge. In neoliberal times, under the pressure of quantitative assessment of scholarly merits, scholars are forced to follow the same logic as writers in the sciences. Standardization in academic publishing dictates not only the development of academic discourse but also the shape of whole disciplines. Furthermore, sinking deep into the information age, the humanities and social sciences are facing another crisis: a statistical crisis. The unpredictability of human future is just one aspect of general unpredictability in a random universe (Clegg 2013). Exponentially rising computation facilities provide statistical and algebraic tools for complex social systems. Modernist dreams of social scientists becoming "true scientists" are within reach, despite the obvious and simple fact that human societies were always fighting unpredictability with rules and laws. And rituals. And magic.

Are these above-mentioned recent turns a symptom or a cure? Or are they magical acts to determine luck? Or are they perhaps cyclical rituals to impose rules into threatening disorder?

The so-called sensory turn might be a good example to consider. It is deeply embedded in the history of empiricism, which started with claims that observation is the beginning of all knowledge, theories follow observation, and congruity of observation and theoretical explanations should provide the final sense of knowledge. Nevertheless, it was only in the 1980s when human (i.e., social/cultural) sensoria became an object of specific scholarly concern in social sciences and humanities (if we ignore studies of sensual perception in psychology). Social dimensions of sensoria were obviously not important for the development of social sciences and humanities, despite the fact that improved observation of natural phenomena grounded the very development of science. Extension of sensory perception (telescopes, microscopes, thermometers, scales, colliders, etc.) released unprecedented dimensions of human apperception, but its practical everyday tuning in social environments was not an important issue for the humanities and social sciences.

What was then missing, and what initiated all these turns? It seems that, in contrast to hypothetical-deductive sciences, which certainly advance with paradigmatic turns after their inevitable crises, when facing essentially new observations, the humanities and social sciences are circling around the same issues for ages, redressing their data, interpretations and orientations.

One of the reasons for pretending that turns provide a solution by circling around the same topics is the social aspect of knowledge production. Any newcomer must critically assess the knowledge produced so far and provide a radically new twist. Although it is a mere rhetorical figure to become successful in research and scholarly writing, it may initiate the effects of classical modernist rejections of tradition. It typically occurs in denial or sharp criticism of the founding fathers, and the ritualist radical criticism constantly calls for a new rhetorical fashion. Providing a new turn is but a career development in neoliberal academia.

Nevertheless, regarding studies of the social/cultural formation of the senses and the variety of approaches in sensory studies, there is still a lot to do. It is impossible not to recognise challenges for further developments in ethnography.

Ethnography as a method that emerged from many different sources. Ironically, it does what *theoroi* did in Ancient Greece: its aim is to observe and report about processions in other places. Theory is close a kin of ethnography, not only etymologically. One of the earliest sources of ethnographic research in modern times is "description of the people" (or the peoples), i.e., *Volksbeschreibung* and *Völkerbeschribung*, developed in the late 1730s in far-east Russia (see Vermeulen 2015). Decades later, at the end of the eighteenth century, various scholars introduced neologisms "ethnology" and "ethnography." These early ethnographic activities, and descriptions of the life of common people, at home and abroad, were part of the state statistics. During the Enlightenment, the rulers and their administration prepared questionnaires to collect records of manifold activities of ordinary people. Questionnaire-based and expedition-organised observations were important in the development of the ethnographic method. But only with the "revolutionary" (see Jarvie 1964) introduction of participant observation did the experiential part (or foundation) of ethnography with long-term fieldwork became the standard. If we take a participant-observant and a researcher, as "the instrument for both data collection and analysis through your own experience" (Bernard 1994, 144–145), it becomes obvious that we must calibrate the instrument. The necessary condition of its calibration is to take the researcher's senses seriously and calibrate them with the sensualities of the people the researcher studies. In a way similar to the observed people themselves, the researcher must learn to use her senses socially.

Sensory "turn" is thus embedded into the very essence of ethnography as *praxis*. It became even more so due to the recent challenges in using well-developed human-computer interfaces. With the advent and development of digital technologies, all human perception entered new dimensions. All sensory perception, i.e., aesthetic perception, is no more emerging from unquestioned (Kantian) categories of space and time. The new categories brought twists into these basic categories much like hypertext transformed text in something more. The new social worlds exist beyond inherited sensualities and, at the same time, provide for their partial extension. This is why the 1980s, exactly the decade of the introduction of personal computers, marks the above-mentioned "turns" towards experience, including the sensory turn.

Sensory anthropology (its early example is Stoller 1989) is an important contributor to sensory-based approaches in other branches of the humanities and social sciences (Howes and Classen 2014), integrating into a very wide field of sensory studies. After decades of their development, they still provide new perspectives in urban studies, studies of the environment, and even in studies of virtual worlds and hyper-modernity. They initiated methodological experimentation, especially in recently (re)discovered walking methods (O'Neill and Roberts 2020; Springgay and Truman 2019); they inevitably problematise relationship of *techné, poiesis, praxis* and *colere* (Bakke and Peterson 2018; Muršič 2021), and they provide for a rethinking of the intersection of urban life, memories, technologies, and trans-generational dialogue (Murray and Järviluoma 2023). As the following texts show, sensorial approaches are not a methodological magic wand. They are an integral part, though perhaps too neglected in the past, of any research of human beings and groups (up to humanity itself) in their myriad occurrences around the planet, past, present and future. They are the most fruitful for ethnographic studies in the present and they may reveal some important hidden aspects of the past or announce unexpected perspectives for the future.

References

Bakke, Gretchen, and Marina Peterson, eds. 2018. *Between Matter and Method: Encounters In Anthropology and Art*. London, Oxford, New York, New Delhi and Sydney: Bloomsbury Academic.

Clegg, Brian. 2013. *Dice World: Science and Life in a Random Universe*. London: Icon.

Howes, David. 2006. "Charting the Sensorial Revolution." *The Senses and Society* 1(1): 113-128.

Howes, David, and Constance Classen. 2014. *Ways of Sensing: Understanding the Senses in Society*. London and New York: Routledge.

Jarvie, Ian Charles. 1964. *The Revolution in Anthropology*. London: Routledge.

Järviluoma, Helmi, and Lesley Murray, eds. 2023. *Sensory Transformations: Environments, Technologies, Sensobiographies*. London and New York: Routledge.

Kuhn, Thomas S. 1962. *The Structure of Scientific Revolutions*. Chicago: The University of Chicago Press.

Muršič, Rajko. 2021. "Between aisthēsis and colere: sensoria, everyday improvisation and ethnographic reality." *Amfiteater* 9(2): 136-155. Available at https://www.slogi.si/wp-content/uploads/2021/12/Amfiteater_9_2_Raz_09_Mursic_EN.pdf, accessed March 25, 2023.

O'Neill, Maggie, and Brian Roberts. 2020. *Walking Methods: Research on the Move*. London and New York: Routledge.

Springgay, Stephanie, and Sarah E. Truman. 2019. *Walking Methodologies in a More-than-Human World: WalkingLab*. London and New York: Routledge.

Stoller, Paul. 1989. *The Taste of Ethnographic Things: The Senses in Anthropology*. Philadelphia: University of Pennsylvania Press.

Vermeulen, Han F. 2015. *Before Boas: The Genesis of Ethnography and Ethnology in the German Enlightenment*. Lincoln and London: University of Nebraska Press.

Chapter 1

Introduction

Ana Svetel and Blaž Bajič

University of Ljubljana, Slovenia

More than a decade ago, the French urban sociologist Jean-Paul Thibaud (2011) called for research focusing on the relationships between space, time, and multisensory perception. Since then, sensory anthropology concentrating on memories of the past and on experiences of the present proliferated, while those centring on the imaginings of the future remain few and far between (cf. Pink 2021). Recognising the epistemological, methodological, empirical and social conjunctions – or, the sensory revolution, as dubbed by the anthropologist David Howes (2006) – that engendered (and are advanced) by sensory anthropology, *Sensory Environmental Relationships: Between Memories of the Past and Imaginings of the Future* stages an ethnographic encounter between changing spatialities, distinct temporalities and multiple sensory modalities. Yet at the same time endeavours to introduce new, hopefully, productive issues and questions, including those related to the future. We hope to show how our sensory environmental relationships – a notion borrowed from the Finnish soundscape and cultural studies scholar Helmi Järviluoma-Mäkelä (2017) – remain necessarily contingent, open, and disjunctive, a facet which we desire to endorse and expand. Hence, this volume stages an encounter, rather than a dialogue (cf. Žižek 2012, xix-xxii) between the diverse theoretical starting points, methods utilized, temporal perspectives, and different cultural and ecological contexts encompassing all corners of Europe.

The main questions and the thematic scope of the volume are based on the panel 'Sensory Environmental Relationships – Between Memories of the Past and Imaginings of the Future', which was held at the Congress of International Union of Anthropological and Ethnological Sciences (IUAES) in Šibenik in 2021. The panel invited papers addressing the question of how embodied and emplaced practices of sensing and moving in and through diverse environments inform the processes of remembering the past, experiencing the present, and imagining the future. It, therefore, stressed also the importance of different types of mobilities, though walking was recognised most frequently in both thematic and methodological senses. A proliferation of "ethnography on foot" (Ingold and Vergunst 2008) and other walking-based approaches is more or less explicitly present in all the chapters and offers an overarching leitmotif, transcending temporal, spatial and methodological differences.

While the first chapter aims to rethink some conceptual coordinates and explore them theoretically, the contributions that follow 'translate' these thoughts into a more spatiotemporally specific and ethnographic manner. In other words, the following chapters take the theoretical points developed in the first one as "opportunities and hindrances" and recalibrate them in accordance with their own thematic, conceptual, and intellectual scope. Both geographically (covering different parts of Europe, from the English seaside to the neighbourhoods of New Belgrade, from the Utterslev marsh at the outskirts of Copenhagen to the Mythical Park in southern Slovenia) and historically (touching, for example, the modernization of Ljubljana in the early twentieth century, the near-pasts of the pandemic, and the environmental futures of other-than-human beings) diverse, the chapters offer rich, thematically varied and ethnographically sound directions. As one aim of this volume is to show that the relations between senses, temporalities and environments are by no means predetermined and that any schematizations might lead to unnecessary limitations, we acknowledge that the contributions offer many more entry-points – many affordances, so to say – than the ones outlined here and, even more importantly, resonate with each other in a myriad of ways, which we invite the readers to explore. In the following pages, we, therefore, present the chapters constituting this volume without, however, proposing a unifying epistemic and interpretative framework.

In the first chapter, *Affordances for/of the Future: Relating/Reconfiguring Environments, Temporalities, and People*, Blaž Bajič and Ana Svetel theoretically explore the main questions of the volume. What defines human-environment relationships? How to conceptually tackle sensorial experiences? What kind of temporalities emerge from memories, practices, and visions? Where do these questions collide? In order to address these, two points are particularly emphasised: the sensory anthropology's dealings with language, on the one hand, and the future with its multiple faces of agency, on the other. Here, the idea of affordances can serve as an entry point to address the relations between the environment, senses, and time in human lives. "If we approach the sensory-environmental relationships through the conceptual lens of the affordances," Bajič and Svetel (*this volume*) argue, "we can acknowledge the finitude and the potentials of the 'world,' recognize the attachment to language and at the same time avoid the deterministic 'sensory captivation' (and vice versa)." Thus, the idea of futural affordances enables us to conceive how people might (or not) envision the future when relating to the(ir) environment.

In the chapter *Grieving with Utterslev Marsh: Commoning and More-than-human Temporalities,* Linda Lapiņa offers a nuanced multi-layered exploration of the entanglements between different personal and environmental losses, through which she rethinks the notions of time and temporalities, geographical distances, intimate relations with her close-ones, and more-than-human presences. By bringing together her ethnographic and autoethnographic accounts from Denmark and Latvia, memory work, poetry, dance and visual materials, as well as the reflections on the pandemic (im)mobilities, she shows how the sensory engagements with(in) the surroundings can serve as a way of approaching grief, re-membering, responsivity and reciprocity. Not only do grief-work and more-than-human ecologies, elaborated by Lapiņa, oppose the idea of time as exclusively linear but also hold "the potential to re-assess liveliness" (Lapiņa *this volume*).

Much like Lina Lapina's chapter, the contribution by Helmi Järviluoma, Inkeri Aula, Eeva Pärjälä, Sonja Pöllänen, Milla Tiainen, and Juhana Venäläinen zeros in on the mutually constitutive relationships between artistic creativity and the(ir) living environment while locating their exploration in urban landscapes of Brighton and Turku. Moreover, the chapter titled *The City as Art and Artists in the City: Intra-actions of Art and the Environment on Sensobiographic Walks* highlights a sensobiographic and generational dimension of the process, showing the intra-activity of artists' and cities' lives. Järviluoma, Aula, Pärjälä, Pöllänen, Tiainen, and Venäläinen can do so thanks to their experiments with sensobiographic walking conducted with people of different age groups. Importantly, however, by utilizing sensobiographic walks, they do not aim to provide an account of an artist's career but create a situation where "[s]ensations and memories intertwined with personal experience are communicated, evoked, verbalised, and co-produced intra-actively" (Järviluoma et al. *this volume*). Perhaps most importantly, following Deleuze and Guattari, they show that beyond the flashy, "major" artification (and, one could wager, gentrification), a "minor" artification is taking place, an artification of "coincidental and hidden or selectively shared aesthetic experiences" (Järviluoma et al. *this volume*) that gives urban lives their flavour and texture.

Against the backdrop of the historical contextualisation of the modernisation processes in the first half of the twentieth century Ljubljana, that is to say, continuing on the idea of sensory and urban transformations, Sandi Abram's chapter *Modernisation of the Senses: Sensory Transformations of Ljubljana in the Early Twentieth Century* offers, *inter alia*, vivid sensory memories of

Franščiška, one of his research participants. Her sensobiographical narrative not only sheds light on the interplay between the personal (childhood) remembering and the societal, infrastructural, and political changes in the pre-Second World War Ljubljana but also represents "a window into the transformations in the urban sensorium" (Abram *this volume*). The modernization processes, described by Abram, were closely interlinked with the hygienization and aestheticization, including the new ideas on cleanliness, which led to the regulation of urban smellscape. The novelty of the chapter lies in the fact that all these wider currents, brought forth by the historical and historiographical sources, including newspaper reports from that time, are furthered and "personalised" by the intimate memories and sensory experiences of Franščiška.

The chapter *Temporalities of the Mythical Park: Reassessing the Past for the Future* by Katja Hrobat Virloget and Saša Poljak Istenič thoroughly deals with the question of (intangible) heritage, which is approached through the lenses of both anthropology and folklore studies. The latter has traditionally considered collective practices, skills and knowledge as embedded in a particular environmental or spatial setting, for example, through the concept of place-lore. But not only is the heritage (and heritagization processes) "placed," it is also inevitably linked to the future, albeit it might seem contradictory at first. Through the case-study of the Mythical Park Rodik in Southern Slovenia, they ethnographically display Judith Okely's (2001) differentiation between seeing and looking. The chapter does not, however, present the Mythical Park as a *fait accompli*. Rather, it focuses on the process of its creation and can also serve as an analysis of how research on embedded folklore narratives may develop into more applicative directions. The very fact that the locals were actively involved in the process of creating the park "gave rise to the self-reflection of their (different) future(s)" (Poljak Istenič and Hrobat Virloget *this volume*).

Combining a historical overview and ethnographic examples, the chapter *Environmental Relationships in Transhumant Pastoralism in Bohinj, North-Western Slovenian Alps* by Jaka Repič shows how structural and experiential levels of the environmental relations can be analytically differentiated but affect and co-create one another. One of the crucial contributions of the chapter is, therefore, the elaboration of the notion that "environmental knowledge, skills, or habituated practices serve to constitute affordances for the development of new practices, thus providing possibilities for imagining futures and coping with the changing world" (Repič *this volume*). Furthermore, the author argues that environmental relationships (including those between humans and non-humans) are constantly in the making. These various actors, as illustrated by the ethnographic accounts, while moving along, create the meshwork of places, roads, pastures, and paths, which together form the alpine environment, its representations, and its imaginations.

Bethan Prosser's chapter *Lockdown Listening: Moving and Sensing the Urban Seaside Environment through Pandemic Times* draws on walking methods to elaborate the "lockdown listening" method or, in other terms, a socio-sonic-mobile method (Prosser *this volume*). Through this tripartite methodological approach, combining walking and listening and social theory, Prosser researched how the residents of the English urban coastal environment "hear" different, intertwined temporalities, how these "sound sparks" entwine with existing narratives and, by placing the research within the pandemic era, explored the ways it co-shaped the relations between sense, time and place. Following Burdsey's (2016) concept of coastal liquidity, Prosser shows how the non-linear experiences of time by the residents were felt when referring to individual and collective pasts, presents, and futures. Furthermore, three types of sounds, namely the returning, absent, and imagined sounds, identified through the analysis, closely correspond with the messy presents, contested pasts and uncertain futures.

While the majority of the chapters explore the multiplicity of the senses in her chapter *Burning Tires, Sauerkraut and Dung: The (Classist) Boundaries of an Olfactory Landscape* Sara Nikolić shows how focusing on the sense of smell can unravel the processes of Othering and multiple social positionalities of the residents of Blok 45 in New Belgrade. Building from two successive methodological steps, olfactory mapping and smell walks, the author shows that "olfactory constructions play a significant role in how collective identities are tacitly (re)produced" (Nikolić *this volume*). Specifically, three culturally conditioned olfactory categories, the external others, the internal others, and the double others, are further discussed and contextualized, showing that the olfactory landscapes can function as a fruitful entry point for understanding not only individual tastes and preferences but also class- and race-based attitudes that tend to reproduce the past through the present into the future.

Now, while all the other chapters rethink moving as a constituent of environmental relations (cf. Ingold and Vergunst 2008) or methodologically employ walking and other mobile research techniques, the contribution by Veronika Zavratnik approaches the themes of movement, its environmental and sensorial aspects by focusing on an item of "mundane technology" (Michael 2000) ostensibly too trivial to normally warrant attention, namely footwear. The chapter *Worn-out and Wanted: Footwear and its Temporalities* leads the reader "through narratives about footwear that revolve around the footwear as a part of the material culture that is central to our bodily engagements with the world and through which we experience the world, both physically and representationally" (Zavratnik *this volume*). Combining the conceptualizations of the material culture scholars, especially Daniel Miller, and her long-term ethnographic research on shoes, she shows that not only can the materiality of the footwear be the entry point to understanding social relations, individual temporalities, and identities, but also that the footwear shapes the relations between the body and the environment and influences how people sense the surroundings.

As all the chapters are grounded in ethnographic work and, therefore, strongly resonate with their particular times and places; the texts show the methodological inventiveness and, we claim, the experimental vitality of contemporary anthropological research approaches. We may speculate that the reason for the multiplicity of the methodological orientations found in this short volume is related to the thematic direction towards such elusive concepts as future(s) and senses. The need not only to constantly rethink the temporal, environmental and sensual dispositions theoretically, as shown in the first chapter, but also to continuously "retune" them ethnographically, as the following chapters confirm, might seem an obvious condition for anthropological validity, but perhaps needs to be nevertheless acknowledged. We believe that the ensuing contributions indeed achieve this.

References

Burdsey, Daniel. 2016. *Race, Place and the Seaside: Postcards from the Edge.* Basingstoke: Palgrave Macmillan.

Howes, David. 2006. "Charting the Sensorial Revolution." *The Senses and Society* 1(1): 113-128.

Ingold, Tim, and Jo Lee Vergunst. 2008. *Ways of Walking: Ethnography and Practice on Foot.* London and New York: Routledge.

Järviluoma-Mäkelä, Helmi. 2017. "Art and Science of Sensory Memory Walking." In: Marcel Cobussen, Vincent Meelberg and Barry Truax, eds. *The Routledge Companion to Sounding Art.* New York: Routledge. Pp. 191-204.

Michael, Mike. 2000. "These boots are made for walking ...: Mundane technology, the body and human-environment relations." *Body & Society* 6(3-4): 107-126.

Okely, Judith. 2001. "Visualism and landscape: Looking and seeing in Normandy." *Ethnos* 66 (1): 99-120.

Pink, Sarah. 2021. "Sensuous futures: Re-thinking the concept of trust in design anthropology." *The Senses and Society* 16(2): 193-202.

Thibaud, Jean-Paul. 2011. "A Sonic Paradigm of Urban Ambiances." *Journal of Sonic Studies* 1(1): 1-14.

Žižek, Slavoj. 2012. *Organs without Bodies: On Deleuze and Consequences.* London and New York: Routledge.

Chapter 2

Affordances for/of the Future: Relating/Reconfiguring Environments, Temporalities, and People

Blaž Bajič and Ana Svetel
University of Ljubljana, Slovenia

Abstract

In the first chapter, the authors and the editors theoretically explore the main questions of the volume. What defines human-environment relationships? How to conceptually tackle sensorial experiences? What kind of temporalities emerge from memories, practices, and visions? Where do these questions collide? In order to address these, two points are particularly emphasised: sensory anthropology's dealings with language on the one hand and the future and the multiple faces of its agency on the other. Here, the idea of affordances can serve as an entry point to connect the relations between the environment, people, senses, and time. If we approach the sensory-environmental relationships through the conceptual lens of affordances, we can acknowledge the finitude and the potentials of the "world," recognize the attachment to language, and, at the same time, avoid the deterministic captivation of experience. Thus, the idea of futural affordances enables us to conceive how people might (or not) envision the future when relating to the(ir) environment.

Keywords: human-environment relationships, future, senses, language, affordances

* * *

Introduction

Senses are indispensable to our lives; they are essential to the ways we relate to the environments in which we live, ourselves and one another. It almost goes without saying that we smell, touch, taste, hear, and see whatever is present in the world. And – since we did just the same in the past – be it yesterday or ages ago – we often remember these experiences, sometimes vividly and viscerally.

It may even feel as if our sensory memories transport us through time and space back to the very events and places from which they emerged. Less obvious, however, is how, if at all, we can relate through our senses to the future, to something which has thus far not occurred (and might not even occur at all) and is not there yet (if it will ever "be there").

Obviously – discounting second sight, if one at all grants credibility to this alleged (extra-)sensory capability to literally see the events to come – senses cannot penetrate into the future. Yet, our senses do play a role when we imagine, anticipate, or predict the future. However, to fully recognize this interplay, we must move away from any notion of senses as providing an immediate, "full" access, a sensuous-certainty, in the first place and see them as always-already decentred, subverted, due to our entrance into the language (and symbolic order, more broadly). Thus, we must conceive them as open to and permeated by our imaginings and fantasies. In this chapter, then, we firstly point out some of the ways in which researchers have related the themes of the environment, time, and the senses. While comparatively scarce, we draw attention in particular to those ethnographic and theoretical "buds" that sketch a possible framework for understanding how people "sense the future." Secondly, we briefly, although critically, rehearse the crucial points in the (sub)discipline's formation thus far. It seems that with its pivotal emphasis on "the sensory" at the expense of "the linguistic", a major, perhaps even defining feature of the sensory itself was largely disregarded by most of the field. Our point here is indeed a simple one: the sensory and the linguistic must be taken together in their antagonistic underpinning of one another, even if they do not coincide and ultimately remain incommensurable (Dolar 2008; 2017).

We suggest the category of sensory environmental relationships to designate a kind of a *carte blanche* of the ways in which people perceive, experience, and conceive their surroundings. Hence, the sensory environmental relationship should not be understood as pertaining to a clearly defined and defining "link" between individuals and collectives and the(ir) environments, but rather a "heuristic machine" (Holbraad and Pedersen 2017, 280) for the manifold ways in which the (dis)junctions between the sensory and the linguistic play out across different times and spaces, a "machine" accommodating the diversity of ethnographic situations, without prejudicing how such relationships might unfold and what might they entail for those involved. Because of this, it is a "machine" whose successful operation calls for conceptual flexibility and inventiveness to consider the polyphony of sensory modalities, spatial processes, and temporal orientations, not to mention the wider cultural, social, political, and economic contexts.

There are, however, two related reasons why the notion of sensory environmental relationships appears important today. On the one hand, it lays bare the arguably trivial but nevertheless crucial and all too often overlooked fact that sensory perception serves as an indispensable "tool" in how we, in our everyday lives, interact with our environments (Grasseni 2007; Howes and Classen 2014; Ingold 2000), even if there are reasons to doubt it as a sufficient means to know the world in which we live (Le Breton 2017, 19-22). Moreover, our perception is nowadays shaped, decentred, sometimes self-consciously manipulated and enjoyed in new, often technologically engendered ways (Allen-Collinson and Hockey 2010; Bajič 2014; Bajič 2020; Howes 2005). On the other hand, the notion in question draws our attention, albeit tacitly, to the increasingly urgent environmental issues insofar as these stem from the ways in which we relate, practically, affectively and conceptually, to the environment and its future, as the much-discussed notions of Anthropocene and Capitalocene and ideas about the Modern alienation from nature suggest (see, for example, Latour 1993; Mathews 2020; Moore 2016).

With this in mind, we now turn to the crucial notions and themes defining sensory environmental relationships, wherein we – knowing very well that diverse scholarly disciplines approach the issues with their own specificities – focus on the considerations and reflections from cultural anthropology. So, what, then, are we talking about when we talk about sensory environmental relationships?

Conversations with Themes

The relations between people(s) and environments lie, in multiple ways, at the centre of anthropological enquiry (Benediktsson and Lund 2010; Dove and Carpenter 2008; Haenn and Wilk 2006; Kopnina and Shoreman-Ouimet 2013; Kopnina and Shoreman-Ouimet 2017). Following Phillipe Descola and Gísli Pálsson's (2004, 18) emphasis on the irreducibility of these relations, we understand the environment as a material multiplicity of living and non-living, human and non-human components which people inhabit. Consequently, we recognize that environments are conceptualised, translated (Di Giminiani and Haines 2020), practised and perceived (Ingold 2000; Le Breton 2017, 1-19), as well as remembered and anticipated, in specific historical and cultural, or some would say, ontological, contexts (Descola and Pálsson 2004, 15). Thus, as mentioned, environmental relationships inevitably include complex temporal dimensions and constellations (Hicks 2016; Ingold 2000, 189-208; Kozorog 2017; see also chapters in this volume), from memories of the past to imaginings of the future (and everything in-between).

When dealing with the environment, whether taken from the perspective of ecology, (un)sustainability, environmental, and climate change (Crate and Nuttall 2009; Hastrup and Skrydstrup 2013; Hoffman, Eriksen and Mendes 2020; Orlove et al. 2014; Simonetti 2019; Taddei 2013), or, as already suggested, under the rubric of the Anthropocene or Capitalocene (Brightman and Lewis 2017; Moore 2016; Persoon and van Est 2000; Zee 2017), questions of the future, and thus imagining of the future, play a critical part, perhaps inevitably so (Barnes 2016). Even if different forms of changeability are immanent to the environment (Ingold 2000, 20), Thomas Hylland Eriksen (2016) argues that, due to the workings of global capitalism, we now live in an era of "accelerated change" not only of the environment but of our ways of life. We are faced with increasing precarity, with "instability, uncertainty, and unintended consequences in a broad range of institutions and practices, [which] contribute to a widely shared feeling of powerlessness and alienation" (Eriksen 2016, 16). Nevertheless, "people perceive, understand, and act upon the changes in widely differing ways, depending on their position in their local community and on the characteristics of the locality, as well as its position within regional, national, and transnational systems" (Eriksen 2016, 16) which can lead to specific forms of resilience.

Thus, as Mark Nuttall suggests, "[o]ne critical task for anthropology is to understand how people not only respond to, manage, and live with such change but how they reflect upon past changes to negotiate present circumstances and anticipate future conditions" (2017, 219). Anthropology needs to engage with contested and multiple futures and forms of changeability, emerging through various sensory, practical, and imaginative entanglements with and in concrete environments, together with constitutive geomorphic, zoological (Mathur 2015), vegetational, meteorological (Barry, Borovnik and Edensor 2021; Ingold 2011; Vannini, Waskul and Gottschalk 2012), seasonal (Krause 2013; Olwig 2005; Palang, Sooväli and Printsmann 2007) and diurnal dynamics and effects (Chartier, Lund and Jóhannesson 2021; Dunn and Edensor 2021; Edensor 2017; Galinier et al. 2010; Morris 2011).

If, nowadays, in its different permutations and mixtures, sensory anthropology explores the ways in which people in different times and places experience, integrate, and make sense (or do not) of sensory perception, it should be noted that, nevertheless, it is normally conceived as an embodied and emplaced, enskilled (Downey 2005; Grasseni 2007), and explorative experience and action, intimately intertwined with knowing, remembering, and imagining (Ingold 2000; Le Breton 2017; Pink 2015). Often, sensory perception is seen as linked to affect, that is to say, as pre- or non-conscious/subjective intensities variously (de)activating bodies, permeating times, places, and events (Anderson 2010; Brennan 2004) and, lately, with "things" such as atmosphere, ambience, mood, or *Stimmung*. More precisely, the latter have been employed to elucidate precisely the intersection between the sensory, the affective and, more often than not, the spatial and the environmental (Riedel 2020, 4; Svetel 2022).

Thematically, as well as methodologically, sensory anthropology privileged the past, or rather remembering, and the present, that is to say, an immediate experience in the here and now, but conspicuously overlooks the future and imagining of times to come (cf. Pink 2015, 45-47; 2021). Anthropologists have, for example, studied the ways in which sensory memories and sensory biographies are produced individually and collectively (Bajič 2020; Desjarlais 2003; Järviluoma and Murray 2023; Seremetakis 1994). Typically, the past is seen as "an active immanence /.../ in the body that informs present bodily actions in an efficacious, orienting, and regular manner," as Edward Casey (2000, 149; see also Connerton 1989) succinctly put it, and as forming the bedrock of what Pierre Bourdieu (1977) classically described as habitus (see Vannini, Waskul and Gottschalk 2012). As such, our pasts condition our present "ways of sensing" (Howes and Classen 2014); that is to say, the plurality of sensory practices and conjunctions, together with the various materialities, practices, and narratives that structure and make it meaningful (Bajič 2020). In turn, ways of sensing may "provoke the future" (Stoller 1997, 55) – a claim to which we will return shortly.

It was particularly after the turn of the millennium that in the wake of the September 11 attacks, global financial and economic crisis, and accelerating climate and environmental change, when anticipating, planning, and imagining the future became increasingly difficult (Adams, Murphy and Clarke 2009) – when history hurt us enough for us to realize that it has in fact not ended –, and anthropology developed a sustained, in-depth engagement with the future (Bryant and Knight 2019, 9–10; Salazar et al. 2017). Most recently, the Covid-19 pandemic further complexified any and all future plans (e.g. Kozorog 2021; Svetel and Zavratnik 2021), not to mention armed conflicts and wars and their far-reaching and unforeseeable consequences. Countless interventions that further anthropological theory on time and temporality by conceptualising future-oriented propensities have appeared (Bryant and Knight 2019; Collins 2008; Fortun 2012; Pels 2015; Petrović-Šteger et al. 2020; Rabinow et al. 2008; Strzelecka 2013; Zeitlyn 2015).

Interest in the future expanded in just about any sub-field of the discipline imaginable (but sensory anthropology), adding to the observation that distinct spheres of activity seem to imply their own temporalities and spatialities, however frail they may be (Bryant and Knight 2019; Lefebvre 2004). Nevertheless, many ethnographic accounts seem to chime well with Heiddegger's (1962, 378) assertion that "the primary phenomenon of primordial and authentic temporality is the future." For instance, Rebecca Bryant and Daniel M. Knight (2019, 16) recently suggested that without recognizing the future by and of itself, "the present ceases to exist as such." Thus, to grasp imagining of the future, we must account for both the specific temporalities and spatialities and for how we, individually and collectively, actualize them when finding our temporal and spatial bearings.

Now, given that despite the long-established research interest in time and temporality (see Adam 1990; 1998; Brumen 2000; Evans-Pritchard 1940; Gell 2001; Makarovič 1995; Munn 1992), anthropology has until rather recently disregarded the study of "the future as a cultural fact" (Appadurai 2013; however cf. Maruyama and Harkins 1978; Rihtman-Auguštin 1976; Riner 1991; Textor 1995), lack of interest in the future in sensory studies should not come as too much of a surprise. Yet, in sensory anthropology, there is, we argue, the additional issue that the way in which sensation was normally conceived (namely as bound to what was and what is "available" to sensory perception) hinders the idea that sensation and imagining the future might be linked. The issue, we claim, stems, partially at least, from the way in which language was, in sensory anthropology, simultaneously accepted and rejected (Porcello et al., 2010).

In order to elucidate these questions, we now (re)turn to the history of sensory-anthropological thinking, the ways in which it, on the one hand, "excommunicated" the linguistic and, on the other hand, incorporated new approaches to sensory experiences and reality.

The unbearable lightness of the senses

So, how did we get here, and how did it all begin? In the late 1980s and early 1990s, an increasing number of scholars grew increasingly dissatisfied with what they deemed to be an overindulgent emphasis on text and language or, at the very least, with treating potentially any aspect of cultural life as if it was a text or (a) language. Moreover, a realization emerged that the two main alternatives proposed – to focus on the body and to centre on visual culture – despite their crucial move away from language, remain ultimately unsatisfactory. The former was considered insufficient due to its reliance on the classic liberal notion of the individual, even if transubstantiated into flesh, the latter due to its embeddedness in the Western ocular-centric hierarchy of senses (Howes 2003, 28-58; see also Classen 1997, 401; Cox 2018; Porcello et al. 2010; Stoller 1989). Additionally, many strived to go beyond established forms of fieldwork and academic writing (Stoller 1989; Stoller 1997). Proponents of then-nascent sensory anthropology argued that, instead, the humanities should recognize how cultural life is indelibly sensory, that the senses may or may not "synchronise" with one another, and that the senses are to be understood as "cultural constructs" defined by specific "sensory model[s]" (Classen 1993, 135-7). These epistemological postulations were, with their culturally-relativistic charge, to "denaturalize" the senses and to enable us to understand the plethora of ways in which the senses are arranged and thought about, "experienced", and "used." Given the newfound importance of the senses, it is not surprising that they have also been accorded the capacity to transfer and create meaning. Language, on the other hand, was recast as some sort of neutral medium of expression of "sensory meaning," which the West "forgot" about, precisely due to its dualist "verbocentrism." Crucially, however, a similar shift was taking place at a methodological level, where, in anthropology, for example, instead of the ocular-centric practice of participant observation, a decidedly multisensory exercise of participant sensation was argued for (Howes 2006, 121; see also Cox et al. 2016). In addition, at a representational level, multimodal techniques and procedures began to be considered.[1] So, by forefronting the senses, in all stages of research, the humanities, from anthropology and history to design and architecture, were again (or so the proponents of the alleged sensory revolution claim), after decades of losing themselves in empty words, in the position to touch on the realities of cultural life.

As many became sceptical of what is usually designated as dualist thinking (Latour 1993), as well as the accompanying "epistemologies of purification," the senses, as conceived in the early 1990s, too, came to be viewed as products of such approaches. Namely, as divorced from thinking, on the one hand, and as experiences turned in on themselves, on the other (Ingold 2000, 283-284). Such a view contributed to the development of "an interdisciplinary approach"

---

[1] While there should be no doubt about the importance of the senses in social and cultural life, and while sensory-methodological and sensory-representational endeavours can indeed prove to be successful in addressing people's experiences, and enormously rewarding for the researcher, there is tendency to – to borrow a nearly half a century old observation about fieldwork by Eric Wolf (1997: 13) – "convert merely heuristic considerations of method [and representation] into theoretical postulates about society and culture."

(Pink 2010, 331), drawing from anthropology, science and technology studies, diverse philosophical strains, psychology, and cognitive science, which focuses on experience and perception understood as inseparable from action. Accordingly, much attention has been devoted to methodological and representational innovations attuned to capturing these fluid, ephemeral happenings, from experiments with new technologies to resorting to the most mundane practices, like walking, as vehicles for knowledge production and exchange. At its most radical, sensory anthropology suggested that the Western, dualist epistemological procedures underpinning most of the endeavours in the humanities need to be reversed to ultimately dissolve the very distinction between the (sensing/perceiving) subject and the (sensed/perceived) object, in order to uncover the primary flow of sense-substance. Here, perception, insofar as perception presupposes a minimal difference between the perceiver and the perceived, is strictly speaking, not possible (see Jay 1994: 93). Instead, a sensation without a sensing subject, a "perception with" (Ingold 2011, 88; Ingold 2013, 91-108; Ingold 2015, 94-100), affords us to assert nothing less than a direct and complete immersion into reality itself. Sense-substances – sometimes termed "sensory atmospheres," sometimes "affective atmospheres" – are not, it is argued, "mediated," insofar as mediation, too, presupposes pre-formed subjects and objects (Manning, Munster and Thomsen 2019), mediated, let alone overdetermined, by language, or any other such purported abstraction (for a critical appraisal of such a position see Bajič 2016, 22-23; Howes 2019, 23-24). Rather, sense-substances are seen as always-already seamlessly flowing into one another without beginning or end, effectively making the entirety of the process of becoming, through its infinitesimal variation, wherein the very possibility of a difference that makes a difference dissipates – making sense-substances, strictly speaking, inconceivable.

While there is much more to be said about sensory anthropology, not only the two waves outlined (Pink 2010; cf. Cox 2018) but other, more "casual" contributions as well, their presuppositions and implications, we now turn to its dealings with language. We do so because, we believe, it tends, with its anti-dualist impetus, to conflate our seeing, hearing, smelling, touching, and tasting with the narratives we, individually and collectively, make, be it retroactively, concurrently, or anticipatorily. As Thomas Porcello and others put it emphatically, sensory anthropology's "recurring feature … is its rejection of language" (2010, 59).[2] Thus, it "flattens" what experience, space, and time may mean for cultural analysis: approximating experience to something like a cultural or quasi-natural captivation, space to an a-topic backdrop or a metaphysical, substantialized "fluid space" (see Bajič 2016, 24), and time to something akin to "homogenous, empty time" (Benjamin 2007) or pure duration (cf. Gell 2001, 319). Obviously, this is crucially important when thinking about sensory environmental relationships and their articulations in memory, experience, and imagination. If we are to recognize peoples' autonomy fully, regardless of how relative, partial, and thwarted it may be, in these processes, the minimal (cf. Badiou 2007, 55-57) difference between sense and sense[3] must be maintained.

How and why, then, do the two waves obfuscate language, or more precisely, what dimension of language do they negate? Despite their differences, the two approaches concur that based on a dualist "split between the thinking mind and the executive body" (Ingold 2011, 77) – whether introduced by Plato, Descartes, or Kant, to name just the usual suspects – anthropology, too, came to separate sense from sense erroneously. As suggested above, this move, on the one hand, enables the kind of "verbocentrism" against which sensory anthropology protests from its very beginning and, on the other hand, presupposes a reifying epistemology of one sort or another. If, then, anthropological thinking lost sight of the junction between language and sensation, sensory anthropology posited native point(s) of view as potentially aiding us in noticing the coincidence once again.[4] Indeed, the search for such a point, a signifier with which language and sensation would unequivocally pass into one another, is effectively what, for instance, Paul Stoller looks for with his "different mode of expression" (1989, 54) needed to produce "tasteful ethnographies," inspired, in his example, by the Songhay (cf. Majid and Levinson 2011). One is even tempted, then, to take the term "sensory meaning"

---

[2] This does not say that researchers have not dealt with how the senses are represented in oral and written records (see, e. g. Classen 1993), merely that they have denied its "sensuous-supra sensuous" nature, if we appropriate from Marx, that is, it denied the arbitrariness of the sign, the autonomy of the signifier (see below) – an autonomy conditioning our thinking and imagining.

[3] The difference between, to put it simply, (linguistic) meaning and (perceptive) feeling, between concept and precept.

[4] Even if one or another group holds that there is no opposition between the linguistic and the sensory, that language is counted among the senses, it in no way justifies our uncritical incorporation of such a position into our epistemological endeavours.

literally. However, if the problem is defined not simply as one of a lacking meeting point between otherwise distinct spheres but rather as of the very separation itself, a possible solution, then, is to be found in a "world" ontologically prior to their differentiation. Such a line of thought is paradigmatically showcased by Tim Ingold's notion of "stories," wherein, similarly, animist notions of "relationality" represent the crucial impetus for its forming. Stories stem from our complete and total immersion into reality, always-already being a part of the aforementioned flows of sense-substance.

So, to be exact, it is not language as some sort of neutral medium that is targeted, but language as *langue* where any identity is reducible to difference, as part and parcel of the symbolic order, an agent fundamentally sustaining and decentring our experience. Language, then, is rejected because it shatters any conception, any ontology, if you will, which admits only to purely positive, here sensory causes and effects (cf. Žižek 2012, 31-32) – it explodes the kind of entities presupposed by sensory anthropology; rather it is accepted as just another sensory "practice," as just another sense. Any notion of difference is attributed to false, dualistic epistemology that fails to grasp how language is either a mere excrescence of, or indeed non-distinct, from sensations. Efforts to reconnect (a diluted conception of) language and sensation (see Majid and Levison 2011; cf. Porcello et al. 2010, 60-61), or rather recover the supposed "natural" link or even non-distinction between the two, that is to say to (re)discover what Georg W. F. Hegel (2018, 60-68) termed sensuous-certainty, are thus a "necessary" component of sensory anthropology. Insofar as sensuous-certainty in its different, usually ethnographically tinged guises underpins sensory anthropology, a marked possibility for essentialization remains. In other words, it leads, in its cultural-relativistic mode, to substantialising, i.e. totalizing and closing in the multiple cultures of its purview, and, in its realistic form, to positing a singular "meshwork" of flows as a fundamental, immutable structure of reality. Moreover, sensory anthropology, in the first case, essentialises via a "subject supposed to believe," an ethnographic proxy, and, in the second case, directly, by incorporating native positions directly into its very substance. Thus, sensory anthropology establishes either a locally-bounded specimen or one global instalment of a kind of sensory totalitarianism, to paraphrase Michael Carrithers (in Venkatesan 2010, 160), each with its adjacent (a-)temporality and (a-)spatiality. In this way, it can avoid the aporia between the certainty (the factual, positive, etc. dimensions) and ambiguity (the interpretative, evocative, etc. dimensions) otherwise characteristic of anthropology (Carrithers 2014). Therein, perhaps, lies an answer as to why "the future as a cultural fact" was largely overlooked in sensory anthropology – insofar "the senses" or "flows" captivate us, determine or steer everything, including thinking and imagining, the future, strictly speaking, cannot be envisioned, nor can it happen. There can merely be a perpetuation of the present.

Now, we are by no means arguing for a wholesale rejection of sensation as a pertinent issue for anthropological inquiry. On the contrary, we claim that we can only do it justice, firstly, by regarding it as a problem, not a solution, and, secondly, by recognising the epistemic limits of a sensory approach. The reason is simple: while our experiences and social processes are conditioned by "the life of the senses," the former cannot and must not be reduced to the latter (and something similar could, of course, be said apropos language). Although it is a crucial first step, it is thus not enough to assert that it is "more productive to treat discourse as part and parcel of processes of embodiment and knowledge and sense-making" (Porcello et al. 2010, 61). The difficult problem is, rather, how to think about the relationship between language and sensation if neither of them can be reduced to the other. Somewhat ironically, a clue is provided by the central tenet of structuralism – one of those paradigms discarded in sensory anthropology as irredeemably dualist and "a-sensory." It posits that, while in themselves senseless, signifiers, in their mutual (sensory) differences, (literally) make sense. It is this dialectic (dis)junction between sense and sense that can ground our thinking about sensation's relationship(s) with other "aspects" of experience, providing a form with which to conceive sensory-environmental relationships in terms of attunement rather than cultural or quasi-natural captivation; it recognizes their mutual interdependence and incommensurability, without conflating or obscuring either of them.

Now, it should be added that despite our suggestion's seeming incompatibility with sensory anthropology in just about any of its guises (cf. Le Breton 2017), it, in fact, trails sensory anthropology's lead in its dealings with technology. Language, like technology, not only "develops" and "strengthens" our senses (as the classic McLuhanesque thesis would have it), but also "fragments" and "confuses" them. It co-creates the circumstances within which the "enskillment" and diverse practices take place; it is a *sine qua non* of perceptual-cum-conceptual affordances (cf. Ingold 2000; Holbraad and Pedersen 2017; Keane 2018). Furthermore, it may appear that in proposing such a "form", we contradict our previous assertion that we must not preconceive how relationships might unfold. Yet such a reading would overlook how the (dis)junction of sense and sense, in fact, provides for the very diversity of ethnographic situations and their indeterminacy. In other words, it is a condition of possibility for a multiplicity of interpretations, narratives, negotiations, dialogues and encounters, meanings that we weave into our sensory environmental relationships. To put it simply, (dis)junction between sense and sense is a prerequisite for understanding the senses as open, situational, partial, non-deterministic and relational.

With this, while losing its distinguishing certitude, sensory anthropology can (re)gain the kind of openness we mentioned in the beginning and, through ethnography, provide ever-new, even if necessarily tentative and fragmented perspectives. In fact, despite some rather totalising suppositions and implications of sensory anthropology, it, with its numerous (re)arrangements and (re)inventions at methodological, epistemological, and even ontological levels over the past thirty years, exhibits precisely such a drive and continues to inspire – as the following chapters attest. However, how can, in light of "new-found" uncertainty and arbitrariness, but also irreducible heterogeneity and (implicit) emancipatory possibilities (cf. Venkatesan 2010), future be brought into the purview of sensory anthropology? How, in short, can we account for instances when our senses, to again refer to Paul Stoller's memorable phrasing, "provoke the future"?

In search of lost time

Sensory anthropology, as suggested, rarely "touched" the future, second sight – a sixth sense if ever there was one (Howes 2009) – notwithstanding. Sensory perception, with its bodily, material grounding, cannot, by its very nature, reach what is not there. Nevertheless, as Sarah Pink's (2021, 3) auto-ethnographic vignette about experiences of pain shows, "how performing bodily movements and being reminded of sensations involve ways of knowing, remembering, and imagining which enable us to sense or feel other moments in our past or possible lives." Sensing the future, then, is not about actualised reality *per se* but the potential futures our senses prompt us to imagine. Here, in particular, it is crucial to understand sensations not (only) as objects formed by a particular sensory model or a substance, binding to what is (or was), but as relations, open to contingency and necessity, difference and identity, change and permanence, that predicate anticipation, imagination and perhaps even "making" of that-which-is-not.

To grasp how we, individually and collectively, imagine the future, notions such as "orientations" (Bryant and Knight 2019; Lyon and Carabelli 2016) and "method of hope" (Miyazaki 2004; see also Jansen 2016; Kleist and Jansen 2016) have been proposed, while others have stressed that the future is produced, entailing that we think of the multiplicity of ways in which people as "future-makers" encounter, manage, and anticipate the future (Appadurai 2013, 285-286). Yet, while all these notions presuppose what is customarily termed agency, Stoller (2017) importantly suggests that contingency, humility, risk, and negative capability traverse most future-making undertakings, possibly abeying agency (Miyazaki 2004) and limiting such endeavours in scope and to the "near future" (Guyer 2007). Others still have been critical of "defuturing," that is, "the systematic destruction of possible futures by the structured unsustainability of modernity" (Escobar 2018, 112), and argue that the very possibilities for future-making, or "futuring", as Arturo Escobar terms it, need to be re-established, especially in view of environmental and climatic change.

On the other hand, "our orientations to the future matter a great deal for how we inhabit the present" (Lyon and Carabelli 2016, 431). They "entail planning, hoping for, and imagining the future, [yet] they also often entail the collapse or exhaustion of those efforts: moments in which hope may turn to apathy, frustrated planning to disillusion, and imagination to fatigue" (Bryant and Knight 2019, 18-19). In other words, the future affects us (Anderson 2010), and thus "confuses linear temporality, so that the future is not (only or so much) a distinct and/or far off temporality, separate to the present (and past), but is (also) experienced and felt 'in' and as the present" (Coleman 2017, 527). In fact, Vincanne Adams, Michelle Murphy, and Adele E. Clarke (2009, 257) argue that "regimes of anticipation /.../ provoke affective and sensory states as well as practical responses in the present." So, to reiterate, that-which-is-not, the future as an epitome of present absence and certain uncertainty is a source of action and its suspension, (cruel) optimism (Berlant 2011) and of (courageous) hopelessness (Žižek 2017). Consequently, when thinking about how sensory environmental relationships pertain to the ways in which we may (or may not) envision the future, it is crucial to account for the multi-directionality of the process, that is to say, not only how our perceptions "feed into" our anticipations of the future (Gell 2001, 237), but also how new visions of the future may "retroactively" change (our perception of) the present (and the past).[5]

---

[5] Incidentally, such thinking of time, or rather historicity, is made possible by recognizing the autonomy of the signifier, insofar as it decenters our temporal experience (Lacan 2006).

Figure 2.1: Visitors to Logar Valley digitally mediating "their" sensory-environmental relationship, Solčavsko. Photo by Blaž Bajič, 12 June 2021.

Following Webb Keane (2018) and Miha Kozorog (2021), we suggest the notion of futural affordances to account for how we might, based on our sensory environmental relationships, imagine the future. The notion of affordances, first introduced by James Gibson, designates the perceived properties of "things" that lend them to action. They are, as Tim Ingold (2018, 39) succinctly put it, "opportunities and hindrances." Affordances, then, direct us towards the future (Kozorog 2021). While "classically" the notion referred to the sensed environment, some recently argued for its expansion into the conceptual domain. For example, Martin Holbraad and Morten Axel Pedersen (2017, 199-241), in their endeavours to "give a voice" to things (Bajič 2017), suggested the notion of "conceptual affordances" of materials, while Webb Keane (2018, 31) discussed how affordances "contribute to the emergence of meaning within a world of [material] causality" and how in immaterial objects (emotions, bodily movements, affective atmospheres, etc.), too, affordances can be found. Ultimately, they returned – to quote Ingold's (2018, 42) critical estimate – "an unsatisfactory compromise between a realist and a relational ontology." That is to say, to an uneasy compromise pertaining to the dilemma of whether an affordance is a property of reality "out there" or is relative to our perception, a dilemma arguably immanent to the very notion itself. However, it is precisely this ambiguity, or a (dis)junction between the "material" fluxes and flows, "sensory differences in time," on the one hand, and the "immaterial" meanings and senses, created not only "on the spot," but also appropriated from globalized imagery and ideologies, on the other, that leaves sensory environmental relationships "open," making affordances not only good to act with but also good to think with. And, given the ever-changing technological meditations (on which late capital insists) and which continuously open new possibilities whilst setting up new obstacles, it seems that (the notion of) affordances will remain pertinent. One can think of such "mundane technologies" as shoes (Michael 2000; see also Zavratnik, *this volume*) or digital media and technology (Järviluoma et al., *this volume*). The implications that drones, GPS trackers and positioning apps, digital augmentation, and the algorithms we live by (to paraphrase George Lakoff and Mark Johnson) might have for our perceptions and conceptions, our sensory environmental relationships, and hence for the incessant re-formation of our capabilities for action, both in an immediate environment as well as in wider social context, are enormous.

To sum up, if we approach the sensory-environmental relationships through the conceptual lens of the affordances, we can acknowledge the finitude and the potentials of the "world" (cf. Merleau-Ponty 1962, 303-304), recognize our attachment to language and at the same time avoid a deterministic "sensory captivation" (and vice versa). Thus, the idea of futural affordances pertains to the ways people might (or not) envision the future when relating to the(ir) environment and how these visions might engender or abey action in a specific setting. If nothing else, anthropology and cognate disciplines – particularly those that authorise their knowledge on ethnographic engagements with people in their daily lives in concrete locales (albeit lives and locales strongly affected by events from halfway around the globe) – need to recognize something of the sorts simply due to the fact the environments and weather patterns are changing (changing itself related in complex and convoluted ways to climate change). People notice these changes and, drawing on diverse bodies of knowledge and experience, make sense of and act on them. For example, in Solčava in the Kamnik-Savinja Alps, where we have been conducting fieldwork, farmers have been noticing that, due to increasingly hot summers, various drought-resistant types of grass, such as butterbur, have started to grow in large numbers. The problem for the farmers is that cattle and sheep will not eat them. On top of that, farmers also believe that the increasingly hot and dry summer months contribute to the diminishing production of milk. Perhaps the most pressing change, however, is related to the increasing number of carnivorous wild animals that roam the mountain ridges in search of food. To address these, some farmers consider introducing goats or bringing in shepherd dogs to the area.

What becomes evident through this example is the fact that there are several forms of change, from climate and environmental to economic and technological and others, that manifest and become interrelated in this specific environment. All the new species of plants and animals call for different techniques and technologies of cultivation – and preservation – of the landscape. Observation of, and adaptation to, these changes is, therefore, what preserves the cultivated landscape, that is to say, making it suitable for dwelling for present and future generations. These places will, otherwise, according to some interlocutors, become uninhabitable and empty. In short, what the farmers in Solčava see, hear, taste, smell, and touch in the environment informs how they envision and provoke, that is, call forth the future, and these visions, in turn, provide them with affordances for imagination and action.

Proceeding from the observations suggested in recent years about the significance of the future, or rather imaginings of the future, for social life and, hence, social analysis, we argued in this chapter that for this aspect, too, we must take our senses, and perceptions of our environments, seriously. However, for such a suggestion to add up, we contend, senses must be understood as radically open to and permeated by our imaginings and fantasies and – more fundamentally – language. For this, we have maintained that simply claiming that "senses make sense," as the overused adage goes, is not enough; thus, we have suggested thinking of the relation – not a continuity – between sense and sense as one of (dis)junction, that is a relationship where the two sides support one another, cannot do without its other, yet do not coincide, or "mesh." It is such a (dis)junction that conditions and needs to be acknowledged if we are to account for the ineradicable diversity, changeability, and – lest we forget – creativity in the ways people relate to their environments. Conceived this way, sensory-environmental relationships can provide support for diverse imaginings of the future, together with what we have termed futural affordances, which in turn may motivate (or abey) and provide a footing for action here and now. Understanding how we relate to our immediate environments is of critical importance in a time when they are changing at an increasing pace, becoming a challenge in and for our everyday lives; only by fully understanding our sensory-environmental relationships, including their outermost workings, can we understand how social life in the past, the present, and the arduous progress towards the future.

Figure 2.2: Cattle grazing in Roban Cirque, Solčavsko. Photo by Ana Svetel, 22 September 2021.

Acknowledgment

Project DigiFREN is supported by MIZŠ, Slovenia; NCN, Poland; AKA, Finland; HRZZ, Croatia and RCN, Norway under CHANSE ERA-NET Co-fund programme, which has received funding from the European Union's Horizon

2020 Research and Innovation Programme, under Grant Agreement no. 101004509.

References

Adam, Barbara. 1990. *Time and Social Theory*. Oxford: Polity Press.

Adam, Barbara. 1998. *Timescapes of Modernity: The Environment and Invisible Hazards*. London: Routledge.

Adams, Vincanne, Michelle Murphy, and Adele Clarke. 2009. "Anticipation: Technoscience, Life, Affect, Temporality." *Subjectivity* 28: 246-265.

Allen-Collinson, Jacqueline, and John Hockey. 2010. "Feeling the Way: Notes toward a Haptic Phenomenology of Distance Running and Scuba Diving." *International Review for the Sociology of Sport* 46(3): 330-345.

Anderson Ben. 2010. "Preemption, Precaution, Preparedness: Anticipatory Action and Future Geographies." *Progress in Human Geography* 34(6): 777-798.

Appadurai, Arjun. 2013. *The Future as Cultural Fact: Essays on the Global Condition*. London, New York: Verso.

Bajič, Blaž. 2014. "Running as Nature Intended: Barefoot Running as Enskillment and a Way of Becoming." *Anthropological Notebooks* 20 (2): 5-26.

Bajič, Blaž. 2016. "Gospoda Timothyja Ingolda prevrat znanosti." *Glasnik SED* 56(3-4): 17-30.

Bajič, Blaž. 2017. "Staro za novo." *Glasnik SED* 57(3-4): 33-37.

Bajič, Blaž. 2020. "Nose-talgia, or, Olfactory Remembering of the Past and the Present in a City in Change." *Ethnologia Balkanica: Journal for Southeast European Anthropology* 22: 61-75.

Barnes, Jessica, ed. 2016. Environmental Futures. Special Issue. *JRAI* 22(S1).

Barry, Kaya, Maria Borovnik, and Tim Edensor, eds. 2021. *Weather: Spaces, Mobilities and Affects*. New York and London: Routledge.

Benediktsson, Karl, and Katrín Anna Lund, eds. 2010. *Conversations With Landscape*. Farnham: Ashgate.

Benjamin, Walter. 2007. "Theses on the Philosophy of History." Hannah Arendt, ed. *Illuminations*. New York: Schocken. Pp. 253-264.

Berlant, Lauren. 2011. *Cruel Optimism*. Durham: Duke University Press.

Bourdieu, Pierre. 1977. *Outline of a Theory of Practice*. Cambridge: Cambridge University Press.

Brennan, Teresa. 2004. *The Transmission of Affect*. Ithaca, NY: Cornell University Press.

Brightman, Mark, and Jerome Lewis, eds. 2017. *The Anthropology of Sustainability: Beyond Development and Progress*. London, New York: Palgrave.

Brumen, Borut. 2000. *Sv. Peter in njegovi časi: socialni spomini, časi in identitete v istrski vasi Sv. Peter*. Ljubljana: Založba /*cf.

Bryant, Rebecca, and Daniel Knight. 2019. *The Anthropology of the Future*. Cambridge: Cambridge University Press.

Carrithers, Michael. 2014. "Anthropology as Irony and Philosophy, or the Knots in Simple Ethnographic Projects." *HAU: Journal of Ethnographic Theory* 4(3): 117-142.

Casey, Edward. 2000. *Remembering: A Phenomenological Study.* Bloomington: Indiana University Press.

Chartier, Daniel, Katrín Anna Lund, and Gunnar Thór Jóhannesson, eds. 2021. *Darkness: The Dynamics of Darkness in the North.* Montreal and Reykjavík: Isberg and Research Centre in Geography and Tourism at the University of Iceland.

Classen, Constance. 1993. *Worlds of Sense: Exploring the Senses in History and across Cultures.* New York: Routledge.

Classen, Constance. 1997. Foundations for an Anthropology of the Senses. *International Social Science Journal* 49(153): 401-412.

Coleman, Rebecca. 2017. "A Sensory Sociology of the Future: Affect, Hope and Inventive Methodologies." *The Sociological Review* 65(3): 525-543.

Collins, Samuel Gerald. 2008. *All Tomorrow's Cultures: Anthropological Engagements with the Future.* New York and Oxford: Berghahn.

Connerton, Paul. 1989. *How Societies Remember.* Cambridge: Cambridge University Press.

Cox, Rupert. 2018. "Senses, Anthropology of." In: Hilary Callan, ed. *The International Encyclopedia of Anthropology.* New York: Wiley-Blackwell. Pp. 5411-5422.

Cox, Rupert, Andrew Irving, and Christopher Wright. 2016. *Beyond text? Critical Practices and Sensory Anthropology.* Manchester: Manchester University Press.

Crate, Susan A., and Mark Nuttall, eds. 2009. *Anthropology and Climate Change: From Encounters to Actions.* London: Routledge.

Descola, Philipe, and Gísli Pálsson. 2004. "Introduction." In: Descola, Philipe and Gísli Pálsson, eds. *Nature and Society: Anthropological Perspectives.* London, New York: Routledge. Pp. 1-21.

Desjarlais, Robert. 2003. *Sensory Biographies: Lives and Deaths among Nepal's Yolmo Buddhists.* Berkeley, Los Angeles and London: University of California Press.

Di Giminiani, Piergiorio, and Sophie Haines, eds. 2020. Translating Environments: Translation and Indeterminacy in the making of Natural Resources. Special Issue. *Ethnos* 85(1).

Dolar, Mladen. 2008. "Touching Ground." *Filozofski vestnik* 29(2): 79-100.

Dolar, Mladen. 2017. *Heglova Fenomenologija duha.* Ljubljana: Društvo za teoretsko psihoanalizo.

Dove, Michael R. and Carol Carpenter, eds. 2008. *Environmental Anthropology: A Historical Reader.* Malden: Blackwell.

Downey, Greg. 2005. *Learning Capoeira: Lessons in Cunning from an Afro-Brazilian Art.* Oxford: Oxford University Press.

Dunn, Nick and Tim Edensor, eds. 2021. *Rethinking Darkness: Cultures, Histories, Practices.* London and New York: Routledge.

Edensor, Tim. 2017. *From Light to Dark: Daylight, Illumination, and Gloom.* Minneapolis: University of Minnesota Press.

Eriksen Thomas H. 2016. *Overheating: An Anthropology of Accelerated Change.* London: Pluto Press.

Escobar, Arturo. 2018. *Designs for the Pluriverse: Radical Interdependence, Autonomy, and the Making of Worlds.* Durham and London: Duke University Press.

Evans-Pritchard, Edward E. 1940. *The Nuer.* Oxford: Clarendon Press.

Fortun, Kim. 2012. "Ethnography in Late Industrialism." *Cultural Anthropology* 27(3): 446-464.

Galinier, Jacques, Aurore Monod Becquelin, Guy Bordin, Luarent Fontaine, Francine Fourmaux, Julliette Roullet Ponce, Piero Salzarulo, Phillipe Simonnot, Michele Therrien, and Iole Zilli. 2010. "Anthropology of the night: Cross-disciplinary investigations." *Current Anthropology* 51(6): 819-847.

Gell, Alfred. 2001. *The Anthropology of Time: Cultural Constructions of Temporal Maps and Images.* Oxford and Washington: Berg.

Grasseni, Christina, ed. 2007. *Skilled Visions: Between Apprenticeship and Standards.* Oxford and New York: Berghahn.

Guyer, Jane. 2007. "Prophecy and the near Future: Thoughts on Macroeconomic, Evangelical, and Punctuated Time." *American Ethnologist* 34(3): 409-421.

Haenn, Nora, and Richard Wilk, eds. 2006. *The Environment in Anthropology. A Reader in Ecology, Culture, and Sustainable Living.* New York: New York University Press.

Hastrup, Kirsten, and Martin Skrydstrup, eds. 2013. *The Social Life of Climate Change Models: Anticipating Nature.* London: Routledge.

Hegel, Georg W. F. 2018. *The Phenomenology of the Spirit.* Cambridge, Cambridge University Press.

Heiddegger, Martin. 1962. *Being and Time.* London: SCM Press.

Hicks, Dan. 2016. "The Temporality of the Landscape Revisited." *Norwegian Archaeological Review* 49(1): 5-22.

Hoffman, Susanna, Thomas. H. Eriksen, and Paulo Mendes, eds. 2020. *Cooling Down: Local Responses to Global Climate Change.* New York and London: Berghahn.

Holbraad, Martin, and Morten Axel Pedersen. 2017. *The Ontological Turn: An Anthropological Exposition.* Cambridge: Cambridge University Press.

Howes, David. 2003. *Sensual Relations: Engaging the Senses in Culture and Social Theory.* Ann Arbor: University of Michigan Press.

Howes, David. 2005. "Hyperesthesia, or, the Sensual Logic of Late Capitalism." In: David Howes, ed. *Empire of the Senses.* Oxford: Berg. Pp. 281-302.

Howes, David. 2006. "Charting the Sensorial Revolution." *The Senses and Society* 1(1): 113-128.

Howes, David, eds. 2009. *The Sixth Sense Reader.* London and New York: Routledge.

Howes, David. 2019. "Multisensory Anthropology." *Annual Review of Anthropology* 48: 17-28.

Howes, David, and Constance Classen. 2014. *Ways of Sensing: Understanding the Senses in Society.* London: Routledge.

Ingold, Tim. 2000. *The Perception of the Environment: Essays on Livelihood, Dwelling and Skill.* London: Routledge.

Ingold, Tim. 2011. *Being Alive: Essays on Movement, Knowledge and Description.* London: Routledge.

Ingold, Tim. 2013. *Making: Anthropology, Archaeology, Art and Architecture.* London and New York: Routledge.

Ingold, Tim. 2015. *The Life of Lines.* London and New York: Routledge.

Ingold, Tim. 2018. "Back to the Future with the Theory of Affordances." *HAU: Journal of Ethnographic Theory* 8(1-2): 39-44.

Ingold, Tim, and Jo Lee Vergunst, eds. 2008. *Ways of Walking: Ethnography and Practice on Foot.* Surrey: Ashgate.

Jansen, Stef. 2016. "For a Relational, Historical Ethnography of Hope: Indeterminacy and Determination in the Bosnian and Herzegovinian Meantime." *History & Anthropology* 27(4): 447-64.

Jay, Martin. 1994. *Downcast Eyes: The Denigration of Vision in Twentieth-Century French Thought.* Berkley, Los Angeles, London, University of California press.

Järviluoma, Helmi, and Leslie Murray, eds. 2023. *Sensory Transformations: Environments, Technologies, Sensobiographies.* London, New York: Routledge.

Keane, Webb. 2018. "Perspectives on Affordances, or the Anthropologically Real: The 2018 Daryll Forde Lecture." *HAU: Journal of Ethnographic Theory* 8(1-2): 27-38.

Kleist, Nuaja and Stef Jansen. 2016. "Hope over Time: Crisis, Immobility and Future-making." *History & Anthropology* 27(4): 373-392.

Kopnina, Helen, and Eleanor Shoreman-Ouimet, eds. 2013. *Environmental Anthropology: Future Directions.* London and New York: Routledge.

Kopnina, Helen and Eleanor Shoreman-Ouimet, eds. 2017. *Handbook of Environmental Anthropology.* London and New York: Routledge.

Kozorog, Miha. 2017. "Threads from the 'Spinning Wheel Mountain': A Critique on Temporality of Landscape Process." Unpublished manuscript.

Kozorog, Miha. 2021. "Uncertain Times and the Optimism of Affordances" *Glasnik SED* 62(1): 45-50.

Krause, Franz. 2013. "Seasons as Rhythms on the Kemi River in Finnish Lapland." *Ethnos* 78(1): 23-46.

Lacan, Jacques. 2006. "Logical Time and the Assertion of Anticipated Certainty." *Ecrits: The First Complete Edition in English.* London: W. W. Norton and Company. Pp. 161-175.

Latour, Bruno. 1993. *We have never been Modern*. Cambridge: Harvard University Press.

Le Breton, David. 2017. *Sensing the World: An Anthropology of the Senses*. London: Bloomsbury.

Lefebvre, Henri. 2004. *Rhythmanalysis: Space, Time and Everyday Life*. London: Continuum.

Lyon, Dawn, and Giulia Carabelli. 2016. "Researching Young People's Orientations to the Future: The Methodological Challenges of Using Arts Practice." *Qualitative Research* 16(4): 430-445.

Makarovič, Gorazd. 1995. *Slovenci in čas: odnos do časa kot okvir in sestavina vsakdanjega življenja*. Ljubljana: Krtina.

Manning, Erin, Anna Munster, and Bodil Marie Stavning Thomsen. 2019. *Immediation I*. London: Open Humanities Press.

Maruyama, Magoroh and Aarthur M. Harkins, eds. 1978. *Cultures of the Future*. Berlin: De Gruyter Mouton.

Mathews, Andrew. 2020. "Anthropology and the Anthropocene: Criticisms, Experiments, and Collaborations." *Annual Review of Anthropology* 49(1): 67-82.

Mathur, Nayanika. 2015. "'It's a Conspiracy Theory and Climate Change": Of Beastly Encounters and Cervine Disappearances in Himalayan India." *HAU* 5(1): 87-111.

Michael, Mike. 2000. "These Boots Are Made for Walking ...: Mundane Technology, The Body and Human-Environment Relations." *Body & Society* 6(3-4): 107-126.

Miyazaki, Hirokazu. 2004. *The Method of Hope: Anthropology, Philosophy and Fijian Knowledge*. Palo Alto: Stanford University Press.

Moore, Jason W. ed. 2016. *Anthropocene or Capitalocene? Nature, History, and the Crisis of Capitalism*. Oakland: PM Press.

Morris, Nina. 2011. "Night Walking: Darkness and Sensory Perception in a Night-Time Landscape Installation." *Cultural Geographies* 18(3): 315-342.

Munn, Nancy. 1992. "The Cultural Anthropology of Time: A Critical Essay." *Annual Review of Anthropology* 21: 93-123.

Nuttall, Mark. 2017. "Climate, Environment, and Society in Northwest Greenland." In: Helen Kopnina and Eleanor Shoreman-Ouimet, eds. *Handbook of Environmental Anthropology*. London and New York: Routledge. Pp. 219-229.

Olwig, Kenneth R. 2005. "Liminality, Seasonality and Landscape." *Landscape Research* 30(2): 259-271.

Orlove, Ben, Heather Lazrus, Grete K. Hovelsrud and Alessandra Giannini. 2014. "Recognitions and Responsibilities: On the Origins of the Uneven Attention to Climate Change around the World." *Current Anthropology* 55(3): 1-27.

Palang, Hannes, Helen Sooväli and Anu Printsmann, eds. 2007. *Seasonal Landscapes*. New York: Springer.

Pels, Peter. 2015. "Modern Times: Seven Steps toward and Anthropology of the Future." *Current Anthropology* 56(6): 779-796.

Persoon, Gerard A. and Diny M. E. van Est. 2000. "The Study of The Future in Anthropology in Relation to the Sustainability Debate." *Focaal* 35: 7-28.

Petrović-Šteger, Maja, Sanja Potkonjak, Ivan Rajković and Felix Ringel. 2020. "On the Side of Predictable: Visioning the Future in Serbia." *Etnološka tribina: godišnjak Hrvatskog etnološkog društva* 50(43): 3-31.

Pink, Sarah. 2010. "The Future of Sensory Anthropology/the Anthropology of the Senses." *Social Anthropology* 18(3): 331-333.

Pink, Sarah. 2015. *Doing Sensory Ethnography*. London: Sage.

Pink, Sarah. 2021. "Sensuous Futures: Re-Thinking the Concept of Trust in Design Anthropology." *The Senses and Society* 16(2): 193-202.

Porcello, Thomas, Lousie Meintjes, Ana Maria Ochoa, and David W. Samuels. 2010. "The Reorganization of the Sensory World." *Annual Review of Anthropology* 39: 51-66.

Rabinow, Paul, George E. Marcus, James D. Faubion, and Tobias Rees. 2008. *Designs for an Anthropology of the Contemporary*. Durham and London: Duke University Press.

Riedel, Friedlind. 2020. "Atmospheric Relations. Theorising Music and Sound as Atmosphere." In: Friedlind Riedel and Juh Torvinen, eds. *Music as Atmosphere: Collective Feelings and Affective Sounds*. London and New York: Routledge. Pp. 1-42.

Rihtman-Auguštin, Dunja. 1976. "Pretpostavke suvremenog etnološkog istraživanja." *Narodna umjetnost* 13: 1-25.

Riner, Reed. 1991. "Anthropology about the Future: Limits and Potentials." *Human Organization* 50(3): 297-311.

Salazar, Juan, Sarah Pink, Andrew Irving, and Johannes Sjöberg, eds. 2017. *Anthropologies and Futures: Researching Emerging and Uncertain Worlds*. London: Bloomsbury.

Seremetakis, Nadia C., ed. 1994. *The Senses Still. Perception and Memory as Material Culture in Modernity*. Chicago and London: University of Chicago Press.

Simonetti, Cristián. 2019. "Weathering Climate: Telescoping Change." *JRAI* 25: 241-264.

Stoller, Paul 1989. *The Taste of Ethnographic Things: The Senses in Anthropology*. Philadelphia: University of Pennsylvania Press.

Stoller, Paul. 1997. *Sensuous Scholarship*. Philadelphia: University of Pennsylvania Press.

Stoller, Paul. 2017. "Afterword: Flying toward the Future on the Wings of Wind." In: Juan F. Salazar, Sarah Pink, Andrew Irving and Johannes Sjöberg, eds. *Anthropologies and Futures: Researching Emerging and Uncertain Worlds*. London: Bloomsbury. Pp. 243-248.

Strzelecka, Celina. 2013. "Anticipatory Anthropology – Anthropological Future Study." *Prace Etnograficzne* 41(4): 261-269.

Svetel, Ana, and Veronika Zavratnik, eds. 2021. Special Issue: Covid-19. *Glasnik SED* 61(2).

Svetel, Ana. 2022. "Nevidne prisotnosti: Atmosferske in materialne dispozicije koncepta hygge v luči idealizacije 'nordijskega' načina življenja." In: Rajko Muršič, Blaž Bajič and Sandi Abram, eds. *Občutki mest: antropologija, umetnost, čutne transformacije.* Ljubljana: Znanstvena založba FF. Pp. 173-202.

Taddei, Renzo. 2013. "Anthropologies of the Future: On the Social Performativity of (Climate) Forecasts." In: Helen Kopnina, and Eleanor Shoreman-Ouimet, eds. *Environmental Anthropology: Future Directions.* London and New York: Routledge. Pp. 246-265.

Textor, Robert B. 1995. "The Ethnographic Futures Research Method: An Application to Thailand." *Futures* 27(4): 461-471.

Vannini, Phillip, Dennis Waskul, and Simon Gottschalk. 2012a. *The Senses in Self, Society, and Culture: A Sociology of the Senses.* London: Routledge.

Vannini, Phillip, Dennis Waskul, Simon Gottschalk, and Toby Ellis-Newstead. 2012b. "Making Sense of the Weather: Dwelling and Weathering on Canada's Rain Coast." *Space and Culture* 15(4): 361-380.

Venkatesan, Soumhya. 2010. "Ontology is just another Word for Culture: Motion Tabled at the 2008 Meeting of the Group for Debates in Anthropological Theory, University of Manchester." *Critique of Anthropology* 30: 2010, 152-200.

Zee, Jerry. 2017. "Holding Patterns: Sand and Political Time at China's Desert Shores." *Cultural Anthropology* 32(2): 215-41.

Zeitlyn, David. 2015. "Looking Forward, Looking Back." *History and Anthropology* 26(4): 381-407.

Žižek, Slavoj. 2012. *Less than Nothing: Hegel and the shadow of dialectical materialism.* London, New York, Verso.

Žižek, Slavoj. 2017. *The Courage of Hopelessness: Chronicles of a Year of Acting Dangerously.* London: Penguin.

Chapter 3

Grieving with Utterslev Marsh: Commoning and More-than-Human Temporalities

Linda Lapiņa

Roskilde University, Denmark

Abstract

In this chapter, I explore how environmental sensing can be a practice of commoning through embodied re-membering and grief work that are simultaneously localised and expansive with regard to a sense of time, place, and relationality. I examine the interconnectedness of environmental and personal grief emerging in my fieldwork by Utterslev marsh, a series of interconnected lakes in Northwestern Copenhagen. Through sensory engagements across seasons, changing weather, and unfolding events, embodied memories surface into the present and resonate with/in the ecologies of the marsh. In my fieldwork, I use dance, poetry, performative writing, autoethnography, and memory work inspired by feminist and indigenous approaches to knowledge production. I assemble a framework for conceiving and being-with more-than-human relational time, building on indigenous perspectives and feminist ecological critiques of anthropocentric temporalities. Finally, I discuss how grief work offers potential for commoning and ecosocial transformation: more reciprocal and caring ways of being-together-with(in) environments undergoing loss and destruction.

Keywords: embodied re-membering, more-than-human temporality, affective methodology, dance, grief

* * *

As a child

I believed in black amber

>*The black lumps turned out to be oil waste*

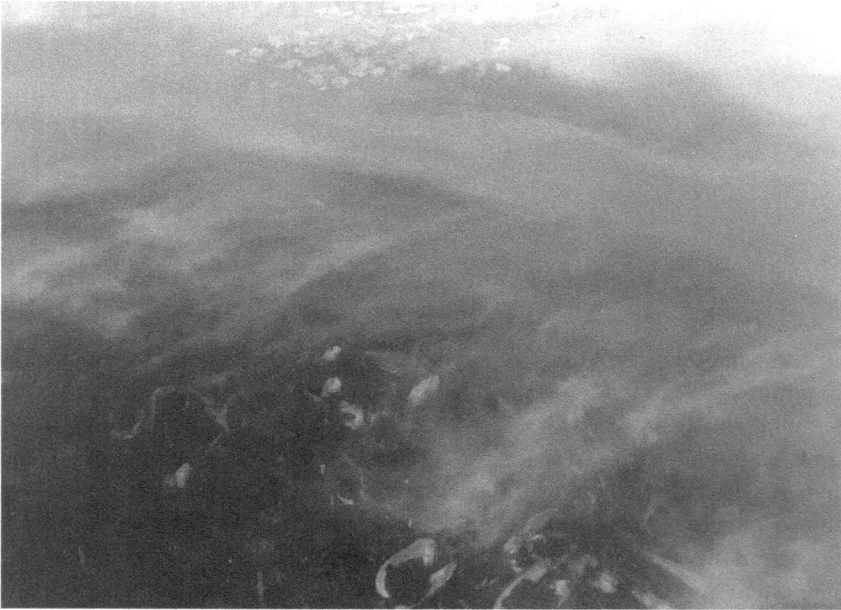

Figure 3.1: Empty mollusc shells below the water surface.

Introduction

This chapter explores the entangled temporalities emerging in my fieldwork by Utterslev marsh, a series of interconnected, shallow lakes in Northwestern Copenhagen. I examine how ongoing sensory relationships with the marsh and its ecologies rupture experiences of linear time and geographical distance. Through sensory engagements across seasons, changing weather, and unfolding events, embodied memories surface into the present and resonate with the ecologies of the marsh. Future, past, and present events, seemingly separate in space and time, are sensed as entangled. This practice of embodied re-membering brings together intergenerational memories and biographical events with listening to the multispecies presences and temporalities of the Utterslev marsh, facilitating knowledge of ongoingness and cyclicity rather than linear time.

I illustrate these temporal effects by discussing how my sensory relationships with the marsh during COVID-19 lockdowns in Denmark coincided with grief-work in the wake of my grandmother's slow slipping away due to progressing dementia and her death in 2021. These relationships highlight the interconnectedness of environmental and personal grief, showing the entanglement of emotions, temporality, materiality, social relations, and natural phenomena. By analysing these enmeshed human and more-than-human temporalities, I aim to offer ways of thinking "differently about how human and other life and materials are mutually embedded while at the same time accounting for clear evidence of different power relations within such assemblages" (Head 2018, 10).

The chapter draws on my work with affective methodologies, where I aim to build a methodological sensitivity that aims to listen to human and more-than-human presences in order to "work with traces, gaps, absences, submerged narratives, and displaced actors in order to shape a form of mediated perception" (Blackman 2015, 25). This approach is inspired by decolonial and indigenous movements, as my aim in foregrounding embodied experience and emotions in research is to transcend the divisions between mind and matter, thoughts and feelings, nature and culture that are central in Western knowledge traditions (de Oliveira 2021; Santos 2016). Instead of these dualisms, I work with relational ontologies: being and becoming- with more-than-human agencies (Bawaka Country et al. 2016; Kimmerer 2013; Rose and Dooren 2017). Through sensory engagements, my fieldwork comes to constitute a practice of commoning: nurturing affective bonds, interdependence and being-in-common (Breshihan 2015; Frederici 2019; Singh 2017) with the more-than-human ecologies of the marsh.

I draw on multiple methods in order to build relationships and listen to human and more-than-human agencies. Elsewhere, I have written about how dance, which is also central in my fieldwork by the Utterslev marsh, can provide ways to practice embodied re-membering in relation to urban nature-cultures and the built environment (Lapiṇa 2021). In addition to these explorations of dance, the chapter draws on my ongoing work with autoethnography and memory work, with a focus on researcher positionality (Lapiṇa 2018; 2020b). My approach to autoethnography and memory work is informed by feminist theory, emphasizing how everyday lived experiences are embedded in and testify to sociopolitical processes and inequalities (Haug 2008; Hinton 2014). Rather than solidifying the researcher as an independent self, working with autoethnography and memory work can enable addressing entanglements of matter and being, time and history. Finally, I also draw on my earlier work with arts-based methods, including poetry, performance, images and audio works (Lapiṇa 2020a). I use performative writing, including excerpts from poems inspired by my ongoing relationships with the ecologies of the marsh.

Engaging with nature-cultures of Utterslev marsh under lockdown

I took up dancing in the early mornings on a wooden platform by the marsh in March 2020, during the first COVID-19 lockdown in Denmark. With the city largely shut down, restless running and walking human bodies, moving in circles, were populating the path system around the bog. These paths had been laid out as part of a welfare state activation project for unemployed people in the 1940s. Water birds – geese, swans, ducks, seagulls, grebes – inhabited the middle of the lakes, their voices intermingled with the sound of cars from the nearby highway, somewhat lulled due to the decrease in traffic under lockdown. The sky was conspicuously vacant, emptied of planes. From the platform, I would witness the gradual onset of light, the morning landscapes of clouds reflected in the water; the empty mollusc shells below the water's surface, submerged in the mud at the bottom of the lake. In those months, the platform was like a liminal space, in-between the circular, high-paced flow of human bodies along the paths and the often conspicuously calm water surface of the marsh.

Figure 3.2: A spring morning on the platform.

Dancing on the platform attuned me to Utterslev marsh as an urban nature-culture shaped by seemingly contradictory spatiotemporal logics. On the one hand, it was a nature preserve where birds seemed to reign, traversing and at home in this body of water, with human bodies relegated to the relatively narrow surrounding system of paths. I watched swans, protected and esteemed in their status as Denmark's national birds, swim majestically on the water surface, remembering the outrage following attacks on swans in the lakes in central Copenhagen some years ago. On the other hand, the lake and the movements around it could offer a metaphor for Denmark's tackling of the COVID-19 crisis – an image of a protected system enclosed upon itself while the world around it was burning and had been ablaze for a long time. Yet, despite appearing peaceful and sheltered, the lake was itself in the midst of an ongoing crisis: a polluted ecosystem, a site of recurring mass death of fish and birds.

While dancing by the marsh enabled sensing and being-with polluted and dying natures, it was also a response to conditions of separation and distance in space and time. As the lockdown started, I found myself at a distance from human bodies. I did not touch a mammal for months. My family in Latvia, my friends, students, and colleagues were present to me as seemingly disembodied voices in my headphones- or talking heads on my computer screen. Separation from family by nation-state borders and living alone acquired a different reality. Even more than before, dance became a way of enacting connectedness from a location of longing, a directedness towards bodies out of reach: the water surface, the birds, the sky, people I loved.

> I have never touched this water
> > Never immersed myself into it
> Never swallowed it
> > Never smelled it
> Never wiped it from my skin

The COVID-19 lockdown coincided with the increasingly rapid ageing and dementia of my grandmother, who had been my primary caregiver while I grew up in Riga, Latvia. At the beginning of the 1990s, a time of sociopolitical ruptures after the fall of the Soviet Union and the ensuing rapid transition to capitalism, she gave up her now suddenly low-paid work as a historian to take care of my brother and me. She lived with us and took care of the household while my mother was working multiple jobs. Talking to my grandmother through the screen in 2020, I realised it was a question of time before she would not be able to recognize me anymore. More and more often, language failed us, me unable to understand her words, her unable to hear me. I sang to her, songs she had taught me when I was a child. I moved with her, trying to reach out to her through the screen. Even so, I felt that we were becoming pixelated ghosts to each other. I mourned being apart from her. I mourned her dying slowly. I mourned not being able to hold her. Yet, it was as if I was holding her as I moved by the water's surface. As if the bog was holding grief that was greater than mine, and we could somehow enter a space of holding together, a space for grief-work.

My grandmother died in a nursing home in late October of 2021, around one and a half years after I had started dancing by Utterslev marsh. I (re-)turn to the event of her death in the last part of the chapter. First, though, I propose a framework for conceiving more-than-human relational time.

More-than-human relational temporalities

In this section, I engage with ways of conceiving time that provide alternatives to linear, unidirectional temporalities. This is not a theoretical exercise in a narrow sense of the word: these ways of conceiving time also comprise ways of being (with)in and relating to time that inform my fieldwork by the marsh. In other words, this section addresses ways of *sensing time* as much as it engages with *thinking about* time.

A predominant way of perceiving – and performing – time in the West is that of a linear, externalized and "objective" line, moving from past through present to future: the time of progress and Western modernity. However, this notion of time has been challenged and nuanced from multiple directions in the past decades: from Hannah Arendt's (1958) critique of linear history as linked to the notion of mastery over nature through postmodern and poststructuralist theories since the 1960s and subsequent temporal turns in anthropology (Bear 2016), cultural geography and other disciplines. Critical time studies have emerged as an independent research field dedicated to investigating time as multiple, relational, and/or discordant (see, for example, Bastian, 2014; Birth, 2017; Huebener et al., 2017; Sharma, 2014), made through everyday practices and shaping how we relate to others (Bastian 2011).

In this chapter, I am interested in ways of conceiving and experiencing time that de-centre the human, as these are relevant for environmental sensing and its relational ontologies – processes of being – and becoming with more-than-human natures. Therefore, it is most relevant to look at two strands of thought that challenge linear time: interdisciplinary scholarship based on an ecological critique of anthropocentric temporalities inspired by feminist new materialisms (Bastian 2009; Neimanis and Walker 2014; Puig de la Bellacasa 2015), and indigenous knowledges (Bawaka Country et al. 2016; Kimmerer 2013; Whyte 2017).

The Anthropocene demands ways of thinking about time that "make strange our understanding of pasts, presents, and futures" (Craps et al. 2018, 502). More-than-human temporalities can destabilize taken-for-granted ways of being in time, instead enabling us to "embrace the multiple, relational, ambivalent, incompatible, fragmented, ephemeral, discontinuous, and dissonant in order to see, hear and feel differently" (Rossini and Toggweiler 2017, 6). Furthermore, re-thinking time can offer new perspectives on what counts as an agency within the Anthropocene (Bastian 2009, 100), revealing a diversity of eco-temporalities (Puig de la Bellacasa 2015; Reinert 2016; Rose and Dooren 2017) that move beyond timeframes often applied to think of human lifespan (Barad 2017; Colebrook 2017). Here, I will briefly present one such critique of anthropocentric time inspired by feminist new materialisms, moving on to consider three lenses for engaging with time informed by indigenous knowledges.

In their article "Weathering: Climate Change and the 'Thick Time' of Transcorporeality" (2014), Astrida Neimanis and Rachel Walker propose the notion of 'thick time': a trans-corporeal stretching between present, future, and past (Neimanis and Walker 2014, 561). The authors build on the notion of trans-corporeality that emphasizes the entanglement of human and more-than-human bodies and natures (Alaimo 2010). 'Thick time' thus captures the embeddedness of all bodies in the unfolding of time, weather and climate, highlighting how these phenomena are, in fact, relationships. Neimanis and Walker (2014) aim to revise the temporal narratives of climate change discourse through thinking and performative writing about the embodied unfolding of 'thick time' as a way of developing sensitivity. Their primary goal is not methodological sensitivity, as advocated by Blackman (2015), whom I referred to earlier in this chapter. Rather, Neimanis and Walker (2014, 560) focus on relationality and ethics, seeking to develop a feminist ethos of responsivity. This resonates with Haraway's (2016) conceptualization of response-ability as embeddedness in a web of interdependent relationships in a thickening present.

The sense of embeddedness of human and more-than-human bodies is central to indigenous perspectives on time. In one of the chapters in her book *Braiding Sweetgrass: Indigenous Wisdom, Scientific Knowledge and the Teachings of Plants* (2013), Robin Wall Kimmerer revisits the wild strawberries of her childhood. She writes about how the strawberries raised her, creating her sense of the world and her place in it. She writes of the Strawberry Moon, *ode'mini-giizis*, the time of the year when school would end for the summer and she would lie on her stomach in her favourite patches, watching the berries grow sweeter and bigger under the leaves (Kimmerer 2013, 23). She also writes about how the children would eat the sour, unripe berries, "impatient for the real thing." In the course of the chapter, this impatience is reframed- no longer just a childish trait; it becomes a way of being and relating to settler capitalism and, hereby, also Western modernity. She writes: "I knew the long-term results of my short-term greed, but I took them anyway," situating these actions in the commodity economy that has been around for four hundred years, "eating up the white strawberries and everything else" (Kimmerer 2013, 32). She juxtaposes this short-term greed with learning to wait, gaining knowledge that transformation is slow and that everything we consume is or has been alive.

I interpret Kimmerer's encounters with strawberries as illustrating different ways of being with(in) relational time. The affective dimensions of impatience and greed, of taking something prematurely, are contrasted to self-restraint and reciprocity, "living in gratitude and amazement at the richness and generosity of the world" (Kimmerer 2013, 31). This gratitude and appreciation for what presents itself results in a different way of exercising agency – it makes one hold back; take less rather than more. Instead of rushing ahead to reach what can be attained now, to maximize, the strawberries teach us to wait for signs from the environment; to take what is given, and to receive with gratitude. These are lessons in listening and responsivity. The sense of time that emerges is built on reciprocity with multiple beings and can thus not possibly be a linear line.

This approach resonates with the temporalities that emerge in the writings of Bawaka Country et al., a research collective of land, scholars and indigenous people in northern Australia. In an article from 2016, they write about co-becoming with the land through the practice of harvesting *ganguri* roots:

> *Yolŋu* women get out their digging sticks when they know it's a good time to dig *ganguri*. How do they know this? They pay close attention to what's happening around them and listen carefully to the messages that are sent out. As the messages emerge, we emerge, we co-become. (...) The seasons emerge through ongoing, material processes of co-becoming, including through lived experiences of the everyday. (...) *Midawarr* begins when the flies tell us and when the calmness of the sea sends its message. (Bawaka Country et al. 2016, 462-63).

Time, both the changing seasons and the everyday time, emerges through attunement to more-than-human kinships, listening to messages, and engaging responsibly with the bodies that the collaborative research encounters. This way of being with/in time can be thought of as a practice of commoning- embodying a stance of interdependence and being-in-common with more-than-human ecologies (Singh 2017).

Kimmerer (2013) and Bawaka Country et al. (2016) foreground more-than-human time as an exercise of connectedness, with notions of futurity emerging through the practice of reciprocity and responsivity. The final lens for inhabiting and co-creating temporality I would like to include in this chapter comes from an indigenous Anishinaabe perspective, foregrounding the affective dimension of ongoing loss (Whyte 2017). Writing about indigenous conservation and restoration efforts, Whyte contextualizes the Anthropocene as a "historically brief, highly disruptive moment," "today's dystopia of our ancestors" (Whyte 2017, 209). He writes about how, with this intergenerational knowledge, the Anthropocene is not experienced as an acute, all-encompassing crisis in the same way as from a settler perspective, since settler colonialism has already destroyed the livelihoods of indigenous peoples, severing their relationships with plants, animals and the land. Climate destabilization adds to and amplifies these losses, but 'the crisis,' dying and violence have been ongoing. This locates one at a junction: "at the convergence of deep Anishinaabe history and the vast degradation caused by settler colonial campaigns in such a short time." (Whyte 2017, 209).

For my thinking of temporality and experiencing time by Utterslev marsh, this perspective contributes with a felt insight into how "the present" is a coming-together, indeed a junction, of different time-lines and time-frames: a meeting point for intergenerational and biographical memory; the agencies of the weather and the seasons; the rhythms of more-than-human life – of rusting objects, water birds, algae and dragonflies.

In addition, this way of being with/in time is informed by already having lived through loss (Whyte 2017, 213). It reminds me of Povinelli's (whose scholarship draws on decades-long collaborations with indigenous people in Australia) writing on endurance and ongoing loss in conditions of suffering that do not acquire the status of an event (Povinelli 2011). This is indeed not a catastrophic time (Colebrook 2017), a time punctured by grand events, but a time that accommodates and acknowledges ongoing loss, slow violence (Nixon 2011) and dying.

In this section, I have sketched ways of conceiving and being (with)in time that frame my relationship with Utterslev marsh in temporal terms. I have noted how more-than-human relational time entails reciprocity and response-ability; trans-corporeality as a mode of embodiment; being-with and receiving that which unfolds in a junction of different relational rhythms and timeframes.

I now bring these sensitivities and arts of noticing (Tsing 2017) to my fieldwork by Utterlsev marsh to explain how these ways of being with/in time inspire embodied re-membering and grief-work as a mode of environmental relating.

Embodied re-membering as environmental relating

the first autumn leaves
green broken into by exclamations of orange. yellow. red. brown.
        it dawns while I walk to you.
the lost smell of damp-dark chilly autumn mornings, frost stiff fingers
reaching out
        to you
        it was- it is- still dark.
walking to you, backwards and forwards in time
i reach out to you while reaching for unspoken memories
decaying leaves unfold spaces at the back of my mind, back of my spine.
a language left behind me, dormant inside me, unspoken.
you become a landscape of loss that birthed us.
you teach me to move besides time.
you pull me
apart and beyond

My first encounter with 're-membering' was through my work as a clinical psychologist. I learned about it as a technique in narrative therapy, working with experiences of loss and grief. Used in this way, re-membering challenges the idea of loss as a finite event. Instead of moving through stages of grief, from shock, anger, and sadness through acceptance to letting go and moving on, re-membering explores the continued presence of that which might seem lost to us. A therapist inspired by this technique might ask, for example, how the courage and stubbornness the client possessed as a young adult, and which seem to have left them, manifest in the present; or how a relationship with someone no longer physically present continues to matter in the client's life, perhaps having become a part of what they know about themselves. Re-membering refuses to locate loss in the past as something to be gotten over.

Instead, it renders visible how traces of events and relationships continue to saturate the present, refusing to ascribe to the progress of linear time.

This resonates with how re-membering appears in the work of feminist posthumanist and new materialist scholars, often inspired by the work of Haraway (1988; 1991). Notably, Barad (2017, 63) writes of the "embodied practice of re-membering" as "the material reconfiguring of spacetimemattering in ways that attempt to do justice to account for the devastation wrought as well as to produce openings, new possible histories by which time-beings might find ways to endure."

In my engagements with Utterslev marsh, embodied re-membering unfolds as resonance with the surroundings. Time becomes enfleshed and thickens through acknowledging the presence of the rusty bikes at the bottom of the lake, the empty mollusc shells, and the wood used for making the platform on which I stand as I dance by the water. As shown in the poem cited in full above, these engagements with the matter-of-now enliven traces of what otherwise might seem distant in space and time:

"i reach out to you while reaching for unspoken memories

decaying leaves unfold spaces at the back of my mind, back of my spine."

Embodied re-membering is not *about* activating forgotten memories or re-surfacing that which might seem absent. While this might be one of the effects of the practice, the sensory engagements with the ecologies of the marsh teach me to move, (be)hold and listen *with*, learning to apprehend our embeddedness in a more-than-human web of relations (Bawaka Country et al. 2016; Kimmerer 2013; Pitt 2016). Kimmerer (2013) learned about her place in the world from the wild strawberries. I learn about my entanglements with the world through being-with a polluted body of water. Watching and smelling the algae grow in the summer in the shallow waters of the marsh, I re-encounter the algae in the waters of the Riga gulf of my childhood. My dad carried me over the strip of seaweed, dirt and garbage so I could play in the shallow water before I learnt to swim. When I did learn to swim, my mom called me a baby seal. Picking mushrooms in the autumn with my grandmother, we often saw seal corpses washed up on the shore. Embodied re-membering connects these entangled histories of ongoing destruction and slow violence, materialising the mutual embeddedness of human and other lives and bodies (Head 2018) on a sensory level.

Thus Barad's seemingly abstract above-quoted thoughts on embodied re-membering as material reconfiguring of spacetimemattering (Barad 2017) become very concrete in my sensory engagements with the marsh. The local impact of pollution, multispecies loss and slow violence, which I witness by the marsh, become interwoven with grief and loss linked to memories of being-with polluted environments as a child, as well as the unfolding death of my grandmother. Through these encounters, I no longer experience grief as something that belongs to me, related to events of "my" life. Instead, mourning enacts larger ecologies of endurance, living, and dying.

In a way of concluding. Grief-work as communing

In this final section of the chapter, I explore how grief-work, ongoing through my sensory encounters with Utterslev marsh, comprises a practice of commoning temporalities: co-creating and inhabiting more-than-human senses of time. I build on notions of grief that diverge from the idea that mourning involves getting over loss and moving on, which is inspired by early psychoanalysis (Mortimer-Sandilands 2010) and aligned with ideas of progress and linear time of Western modernity. Instead, the scholars I draw on, mostly situated within feminist theory and environmental humanities, explore the political, transformative and disruptive potential of grief. I pose that grief, conceived and practised in this way, can enable deeper relating and sensing of shared-while-differentiated vulnerabilities within the ecologies we are part of. To illustrate this, I re-turn to the event of my grandmother's death in the autumn of 2021.

When my grandmother died in late October 2021, Latvia was once again undergoing a strict COVID-19 lockdown. A funeral ceremony would have had to take place outside a crematorium in a rented plastic tent, with a maximum of ten people present, wearing masks in the November cold. After speaking to my family, I decided to postpone going to Latvia until another kind of ceremony would be possible. At the event of her death, I once more found myself (be)holding the loss of my grandmother, and the grief of my mother and brother, at a distance.

At the same time, dancing by the marsh, I also found just how much she continued to be with me. Unable to witness her death and share the grief with my family in direct proximity, I immersed myself in the smells of the lake, the decaying leaves, and the surface of the still, rancid water. I sensed that I was carrying her in my body.

In the book *Precarious life: The Powers of Mourning and Violence*, Judith Butler highlights the transformative potential of loss and grief:

> (...) one mourns when one accepts that by the loss one undergoes one will be changed, possibly forever. Perhaps mourning has to do with

agreeing to undergo a transformation (perhaps one should say *submitting to transformation*) the full result of which one cannot know in advance. (Butler, 2006, 21, my emphasis)

I propose that this submission to transformation in the face of loss can contribute to disrupting an experience of being a bounded self, distant and distinct from the surroundings – a form of selfhood that is engrained in Western modernity's emphasis on separation (de Oliveira 2021; Santos 2016). A surrendering stance and openness to transformation disrupt an idea of mastery and seeking control.

Falling
Coming open
Torn open with/in grief
Unbecoming, being undone

Seeing mourning as transformative of one's sense of oneself and 'the other' as separate entities highlight the political potential of grief. Building on Levinas, Derrida (1995, 46), who is an inspiration for Butler, writes of how grief for 'the other' enables one to perceive that one's responsibility (and hereby, I would argue, also responsivity) is not tied to oneself but "derived from the other." While for Derrida, 'self' and 'other' remain somewhat bounded entities, this perspective emphasizes a becoming and timeliness through relating, as highlighted in the indigenous perspectives on being and time that I presented earlier in this chapter. In experiences of grief, we bear the other in us; and at the same time, loss contains "a movement of renunciation which leaves the other alone, outside, over there, in his death, outside of us" (Rae 2007, 16). This blurring of boundaries between what is inside and outside, self and the other, highlights how grief resonates, pulsating and animating spaces in-between that might otherwise appear as boundaries.

In my sensory engagements with Utterslev marsh, the grief for my grandmother is fused with grief for the slow violence and dying that I witness in my immediate surroundings. Being with(in) the ecologies of the marsh through dance enables attentiveness to how multiple, layered timeliness emerges from the surroundings. The grebes' efforts at building a nest that remains empty and is later abandoned. The slippery layer of frost on the wooden platform, even into March. The brightness and heat of the morning sun, already in May. Shimmering dragonflies over the water's surface. Through listening to messages from my surroundings, I learn that my pain is not my own. It is not exceptional or separated from the suffering of more-than-human others. The loss I am sensing does not unfold in a secluded present but stretches across time

> to the seal corpses I witnessed on Garciems beach as a child;
>   the lumps of oil waste I collected, thinking it was black amber.

Grief, practised through embodied re-membering, is thus a way of ma(r)king time and kin with more-than-human others, and an act of recognition. Ahmed (2004, 191) notes how grief constitutes "some others as the legitimate objects of emotion," establishing a "distinction between legitimate and illegitimate lives." I pose that rather than separating between legitimate and illegitimate lives, grief-work in more-than-human ecologies holds the potential to re-assess liveliness. For one, it extends grievability (Butler 2006) to "forms of suffering and dying, enduring and expiring, that are ordinary, chronic, and cruddy rather than catastrophic, crisis-laden and sublime" (Povinelli 2011, 11). It enables one to attend to acts of living and dying that might otherwise never acquire the status of having taken place. Moreover, grief offers a way to recognize and be-with complicity. This recognition of implicatedness is part of the modes of responsivity that can be cultivated through grief-work and part of its transformative political potential. Environmental grief is thus conducive to "emergence of political communities in the context/s of economies of abandonment, racial formations of exclusion, expropriation and slow death," allowing one to assess and re-negotiate "production of vulnerability, precariousness and disposability in specific contexts" (Haritaworn et al. 2013, 558).

Branching out across linear time, physical distance, species boundaries and what is conceived of as animate or not, grief-work constitutes a practice of commoning time and subjectivity, nurturing a sense of interdependence with more-than-human ecologies of the marsh. Through sensory encounters with the marsh, I become witness, cultivating responsivity that "holds on to a curious attentiveness to the lives and deaths of others" (Rose and Dooren 2017, 126). This responsivity connects ongoing complicity and commonality in a web of relationships with more-than-human beings. It offers a way of moving towards different imaginaries of what the different beings that inhabit a given ecology – water, birds, trees, rusting metal, algae – can mean for each other, how they can hold, extend towards, and form part of one another (Reinert 2016, 101), embedded in non-linear temporalities.

Writing about the widespread failure to grasp and counter-act everyday environmental destruction in the global North, Jones, Rigby and Williams

(2020) propose that mourning can be resistant; that collective grieving can activate ecosocial transformation. This might seem like a lot to hope for. And yet, as I have shown in this chapter, environmental sensing can enable embodied re-membering and grief-work that are spatiotemporally specific *and* expansive regarding the sense of time, place, and relationality. Through broadening the scope of responsivity, these practices can pave the ways for more reciprocal and caring ways of being-together-with(in) environments undergoing loss and destruction.

Figure 3.3: Morning fog.

Acknowledgements

I feel very grateful to all the beings I have gotten to know, spend time with, and learn from by the Utterslev marsh.

References

Ahmed, Sara. 2004. *The Cultural Politics of Emotion*. Edinburgh: Edinburgh University Press.

Alaimo, Stacy. 2010. *Bodily Natures: Science, Environment, and the Material Self*. Bloomington: Indiana University Press. Bloomington: Indiana University Press.

Arendt, Hannah. 1958. *The Human Condition.* Chicago and London: University of Chicago Press.

Barad, Karen. 2017. "Troubling Time/s and Ecologies of Nothingness: Re-Turning, Re-Membering, and Facing the Incalculable." *New Formations* 92: 56–86.

Bastian, Michelle. 2009. "Inventing Nature: Re-Writing Time and Agency in a More-than-Human World." *Australian Humanities Review* 47: 99-116.

Bastian, Michelle. 2011. "The Contradictory Simultaneity of Being with Others: Exploring Concepts of Time and Community in the Work of Gloria Anzaldúa." *Feminist Review* 97: 151–67.

Bastian, Michelle. 2014. "Time and Community: A Scoping Study." *Time & Society* 23 (2): 137–66.

Bawaka Country, Sarah Wright, Sandie Suchet-Pearson, Kate Lloyd, Laklak Burarrwanga, Ritjilili Ganambarr, Merrkiyawuy Ganambarr-Stubbs, Banbapuy Ganambarr, Djawundil Maymuru, and Jill Sweeney. 2016. "Co-Becoming Bawaka: Towards a Relational Understanding of Place/Space." *Progress in Human Geography* 40 (4): 455–75.

Bear, Laura. 2016. "Time as Technique." *Annual Review of Anthropology* 45 (1): 487–502.

Birth, Kevin K. 2017. *Time Blind. Problems in Perceiving Other Temporalities.* Cham, Switzerland: Palgrave Macmillan.

Blackman, Lisa. 2015. "Hauntologies: Exploring an Analytics of Experimentation." In: Britta Timm Knudsen and Carsten Stage, eds. *Affective Methodologies: Developing Cultural Research Strategies for the Study of Affect.* London: Palgrave Macmillan. Pp. 25–44.

Bresnihan, Patrick. 2015. "The more-than-human commons: From commons to commoning." In: Samuel Kirwan, Leila Dawney and Julian Brigstocke, eds. *Space, Power and the Commons.* London: Routledge. Pp. 93-112.

Butler, Judith. 2006. *Precarious Life: The Powers of Mourning and Violence.* London: Verso.

Colebrook, Claire. 2017. "Anti-Catastrophic Time." *New Formations* 92 (May): 102–19.

Craps, Stef, Rick Crownshaw, Jennifer Wenzel, Rosanne Kennedy, Claire Colebrook, and Vin Nardizzi. 2018. "Memory Studies and the Anthropocene: A Roundtable." *Memory Studies* 11 (4): 498–515.

Derrida, Jacques. 1995. *The Gift of Death.* Chicago and London: The University of Chicago Press.

Federici, Silvia. 2019. *Re-Enchanting the World. Feminism and the Politics of the Commons.* Toronto: PM Press.

Haraway, Donna. 1988. "Situated Knowledges: The Science Question in Feminism and the Privilege of Partial Perspective." *Feminist Studies* 14 (3): 575–99.

Haraway, Donna. 1991. *Simians, Cyborgs, and Women. The Reinvention of Nature.* London: Free Association Books.

Haraway, Donna. 2016. *Staying with the Trouble. Making Kin in the Chthulucene.* Durham and London: Duke University Press.

Haritaworn, Jin, Adi Kuntsman, Silvia Posocco, and Elizabeth Povinelli. 2013. "Obligation, Social Projects and Queer Politics." *International Feminist Journal of Politics* 15 (4): 554–64.

Haug, Frigga. 2008. "Memory Work." *Australian Feminist Studies* 23 (58): 537–41.

Head, Lesley. 2018. *Hope and Grief in the Anthropocene. Re-Conceptualising Human–Nature Relations.* London: Routledge.

Hinton, Peta. 2014. "'Situated Knowledges' and New Materialism(s): Rethinking a Politics of Location." *Women: A Cultural Review* 25 (1): 99–113.

Huebener, Paul, Susie O'Brien, Tony Porter, Liam Stockdale, and Rachel Y. Zhou. 2017. *Time, Globalization and Human Experience. Interdisciplinary Explorations.* London and New York: Routledge.

Jones, Owain, Kate Rigby, and Linda Williams. 2020. "Everyday Ecocide, Toxic Dwelling, and the Inability to Mourn." *Environmental Humanities* 12 (1): 388–405.

Kimmerer, Robin Wall. 2013. *Braiding Sweetgrass, Indigenous Wisdom, Scientific Knowledge and the Teachings of Plants.* London: Penguin Random House.

Lapiņa, Linda. 2018. "Recruited into Danishness? Affective Autoethnography of Passing as Danish." *European Journal of Women's Studies* 25 (1): 56–70.

Lapiņa, Linda. 2020a. "Re-membering Desire. Visual Tracings of a Billboard." In: Charles Drozynski and Diana Beljaars, eds. *Civic Spaces and Desire.* London: Routledge. Pp. 160–76.

Lapiņa, Linda. 2020b. "Sexual Harassment or Volunteer Work? Affordances of Differentiated Whiteness." *Intersections. East European Journal of Society and Politics* 6 (3): 97-115.

Lapiņa, Linda. 2021. "Dancing with a Billboard: Exploring the Affective Repertoires of Gentrifying Urban Spaces." *Ephemera: Theory and Politics in Organization* 21 (1): 229–53.

Mortimer-Sandilands, Catriona. 2010. "Melancholy Natures, Queer Ecologies." In: C. Mortimer-Sandilands and B. Erickson, eds. *Queer Ecologies: Sex, Nature, Politics, Desire.* Bloomington: Indiana University Press. Pp. 331–58.

Neimanis, Astrida, and Rachel Loewen Walker. 2014. "Weathering: Climate Change and the 'Thick Time' of Transcorporeality." *Hypatia* 29 (3): 558–75.

Nixon, R. 2011. *Slow Violence and the Environmentalism of the Poor.* Harvard: Harvard University Press.

de Oliveira, Vanessa Machado. 2021. *Hospicing Modernity: Facing Humanity's Wrongs and the Implications for Social Activism.* North Atlantic Books.

Pitt, Hannah. 2016. "An Apprenticeship in Plant Thinking." In: Michelle Bastian, Owain Jones, Niamh Moore, and Emma Roe, eds. *Participatory Research in More-than-Human Worlds.* London: Routledge. Pp. 92–106.

Povinelli, Elizabeth A. 2011. *Economies of Abandonment.* Durham and London: Duke University Press.

Puig de la Bellacasa, Maria. 2015. "Making Time for Soil: Technoscientific Futurity and the Pace of Care." *Social Studies of Science* 45 (5): 691–716.

Rae, Patricia, ed. 2007. *Modernism and Mourning*. Bucknell University Press.

Reinert, Hugo. 2016. "About a Stone." *Environmental Humanities* 8 (1): 95–117.

Rose, Deborah Bird, and Thom Van Dooren. 2017. "Encountering a More-than-Human World. Ethos and the Arts of Witness." In: Ursula Heise, Jon Christensen, and Michelle Niemann, eds. *The Routledge Companion to the Environmental Humanities*. London: Routledge. Pp. 120–128.

Rossini, Manuela, and Mike Toggweiler. 2017. "Editorial: Posthuman Temporalities." *New Formations* 92 (May): 5–10.

Santos, Boaventura de Sousa. 2016. *Epistemologies of the South: Justice against Epistemicide*. London and New York: Routledge.

Sharma, Sarah. 2014. *In the Meantime. Temporality and Cultural Politics*. Durham and London: Duke University Press.

Singh, Neera. 2017. "Becoming a Commoner: The Commons as Sites for Affective Socio-Nature Encounters and Co-becomings." *Ephemera: Theory and Politics in Organization* 17 (4): 751-776.

Tsing, Anna Lowenhaupt. 2017. *The Mushroom at the End of the World: On the Possibility of Life in Capitalist Ruins*. Princeton: Princeton University Press.

Whyte, Kyle Powys. 2017. "Our Ancestors' Dystopia Now. Indigenous Conservation and the Anthropocene." In: Ursula Heise, Jon Christensen, and Michelle Niemann, eds. *The Routledge Companion to the Environmental Humanities*. London: Routledge. Pp. 206-15.

Chapter 4

The City as Art and Artists in the City: Intra-actions of Art and the Environment on Sensobiographic Walks

Helmi Järviluoma, Inkeri Aula, Eeva Pärjälä, Sonja Pöllänen, Milla Tiainen, and Juhana Venäläinen

University of Eastern Finland, Finland

Abstract

In this article, we analyse changes in urban sensescapes brought to the fore by sensobiographic walks conducted with artists. The sensed and experienced urban environment is not just a collection of mechanical or static features. It is intertwined with individuals and groups living in the urban area in question, who perceive, interpret, recall, and co-produce their living environment in multisensory ways. We focus on artists of different ages and their experiences of changes in the urban sensescapes of two medium-sized European cities – Turku and Brighton. This article outlines and contributes to the latest cultural studies' approaches to urban research based on our five-year research project, *Sensory Transformations and Transgenerational Environmental Relationships in Europe, 1950–2020* (SENSOTRA). The starting point is that cities and the artists living in them influence each other by way of mutual intra-action. Our article also contributes to recent and emerging research on artists, providing new perspectives on the relationship between artists and their environments.

Keywords: urban studies, sensory ethnography, sensobiographic walks, intra-action, research on artists

* * *

Introduction

The sensed and experienced urban environment is not just a collection of mechanical or static features. It is intertwined with individuals and groups living in the urban area in question, who perceive, interpret, recall, and co-produce their living environment in a multisensory and dynamic way. In this article, we scrutinise changes in urban sensescapes that were brought to the fore by sensobiographic walks conducted with artists. The starting point is that cities and the artists living in them influence each other by way of mutual *intra-action* (Barad 2007). We focus on artists of different ages and from different artistic fields, examining their experiences of changes in the urban sensescapes of two medium-sized European cities – Turku in Finland and Brighton in the United Kingdom. Researchers of the five-year SENSOTRA project approached city residents of different generations and socio-cultural backgrounds about their experiences of urban habitats, not only in Turku and Brighton but also in Ljubljana in Slovenia, utilising a research method we called sensobiography. Half of the research participants were artists from different fields. In this article, we do not define artists – or, for that matter, other research participants – as 'sensory witnesses,' to elaborate on the term 'earwitness' coined by the soundscape researcher R. Murray Schafer. However, we do consider whether artists have special ways and skills to perceive urban environments and their changes through the senses – and if this is the case, how might these special habits or abilities manifest themselves.

Sensobiographic walks and the discussions between the participants that emerge during them are central to the sensobiographic research method. This sensory ethnographic method has its roots in European research on soundscapes and soundwalks (Järviluoma 2021; 2017; Järviluoma and Vikman 2013). During the SENSOTRA project, we conducted sensobiographic walks with participants from two age groups: one born in the 1930–1940s, the other in the 1990–2000s. One participant from each age group was present in each of the almost 180 walks. The research design emphasised both intergenerational information exchange and the historical nature of the cities and the participants' experiences of them. At the same time, the researchers found an opportunity to analyse the commensurability – or the lack thereof – of the ways the city is sensed and experienced by different participants.

The sensobiographic walks of SENSOTRA were conducted by pairing two participants, who represent different generations, to walk in the city together with one or more researchers. Each of the research participants chose a walking route in turn. During the walks, sensations and sensory memories incited by the walk and its environments were discussed. We will return to the method shortly, but it should be noted that the participants' comments, observations, and reminiscences tended to focus on their experiences of environmental changes and how the ways of living in and "using" the city have changed over the years, while everyday technologies, such as digital gadgets, have also evolved and become part of our daily experience.

Biographical methods in the humanities came to be seen as outdated during the 1960s. They were considered obsolete in the wake of new theoretical trends, such as the linguistic and constructivist turn and *the death of the author*, which question the individual nature of human activities. However, in recent decades the significance of and possibilities afforded by biographical approaches have been critically reassessed from perspectives sometimes referred to as the biographical turn (see, e.g. Caine 2010, 1–2; Hakosalo et al. 2014, 11; Leskelä-Kärki 2012, 28; Renders, de Haan and Harmsma 2016, 6–11, 17–18, 250–255). A few decades ago, feminist researchers, such as Liz Stanley, began to call for a qualitative renewal of (auto)biographical research. They stressed the need to discard the unified narratives of previous biographies and to shift the attention toward processes by which it is possible to interpret past lives (and their representation) from today's perspective (cf. Järviluoma, Moisala and Vilkko 2003, chapter 3; Stanley 1992, 3, 6–11, 17–18, 250–255). Inspired by this biographical turn and other research approaches, such as the topobiographical methodology outlined by Pauli Tapani Karjalainen (2009), we focus our analysis especially on how artists experience their living environment and its metamorphoses (cf. Benjamin 1989; Jennings 2008, 9–17).

The sensobiographic method amounts to "life writing" (Gr. *bios* + *graphein*) via two intertwined meanings: on the one hand, by outlining a personal life history and on the other by charting socio-historical changes in the urban environment and the "life of the city." According to Anna Logrén (2015), who has studied conventional discourses on artists, the starting point of much research about artists (in Western culture) has its roots in the biographies of Renaissance artists. Biographical research still has its place in the history of the arts (Logrén 2015, 20). However, sensobiographic walks do not aim to provide an account of the career or artistic identity of the artists participating in our study. Instead, artists – from musicians to theatre set designers and from sculptors to architects or poets – share a unique situation with researchers during these walks. Sensations and memories are constitutive of personal experience and are communicated, evoked, verbalised, and co-produced intra-actively.

Before the breakthrough of (post-)structuralist theories in the humanities, artists were typically approached in studies of the arts and culture as exceptional creative individuals. However, according to post-structuralist understandings, individual actions are always conditioned by meaning-making systems and socio-cultural practices that exceed the individual. Research trends drawing from this thinking – such as deconstruction, discourse analysis, critical studies of representation, and feminist theory – turned researchers' attention from the artist's person towards the cultural and ideological meanings to be found in art. On the other hand, researchers also developed an interest in how the art world, the artists themselves and the wider publics maintain various stereotypical and mythical views of the artist (see, e.g. Battersby 1990; Lepistö 1992; Rossi 1999; Tiainen 2005).

Recently, new methodological and thematic priorities have appeared in the study of artists, providing interesting perspectives on the relationship between artists and their environments. Certain studies expand the earlier understanding of artists' work and identity by examining how these are formed in multidimensional relationships with other people and institutions (e.g. museums and art galleries), but also with various material and non-human factors, such as materials of art, technologies, and particular physical spaces (see, e.g. Kontturi 2018; Tiainen 2017). One of the key themes in artistic research, which is increasingly carried out by artists themselves, is how art can promote the understanding of androgenic environmental crises, such as climate emergency and the decline of biodiversity, and provide sensory-driven insights into the co-dependence of humans and the rest of nature (see, e.g. Arlander et al. 2017; Arlander and Elo 2017; Kokkonen 2014; MacDonald 2018; for ecomusicology see e.g. Torvinen 2012).

SENSOTRA's sensobiographic walks and the related ethnographic material provide new opportunities for exploring both artists and their environmental relationships. A central aspect of our research is to reject such narrow and elitist definitions of 'artist', which dictate that only those who represent traditional fields of high culture or have formal training in art can be considered artists. Rather, in SENSOTRA's material, all participants who identify as or call themselves artists fully qualify as artists. Artistic identity is not a predefined phenomenon but a feature or a position with which individuals associate in diverse and varying ways. Additionally, we do not claim that having an artistic identity itself gives better qualifications to sense changes in the environment compared to non-artists. It is not only artists who form an aesthetic, sensory relationship with their surroundings, evaluate public works of art, and engage with urban space creatively in ways that can be considered artistic. In general, artistic identity is a concept that is understood in many different ways. For example, Sari Karttunen, who has studied the changing definitions of being an artist, has suggested that, in recent decades, 'artistic identity' has transformed, become increasingly multidisciplinary, and divided itself across new types of artists (Karttunen 2017; cf. Lepistö 1992).

Due to the aforementioned reasons, the starting point of our analysis is not an assumed static definition of an artist. Instead, we look at artistic identity as a process. We ask how artistic identity and multisensory environmental connections intra-act during sensobiographic walks. Underlying this question is the ontological and epistemological assumption that 'an artist' and 'the environment' are not distinct, completed, clearly defined entities that only secondarily interact with each other. Here, we follow philosopher of science Karen Barad's onto-epistemological way of thinking, which has greatly impacted cultural studies and the humanities in general during the past decade, and thus we inspect the urban environment and its people as intra-actively emerging and unfolding entities. Intra-action (see, e.g. Irni, Meskus, and Oikkonen 2014), a concept coined by Barad, refers to how both the material world and the discursive and social reality (e.g. scientific knowledge and individual identities) develop and become meaningful in a constitutive relation to other material, discursive, and social processes and entities. For example, all kinds of materiality, from human bodies to natural environments, exist or happen in specific ways by virtue of particular intra-actions. Human beings do not stand in the world or take their place in it as separate and fully formed psychophysical entities. Instead, 'environments' and 'individuals' develop as material and symbolic beings based on their co-constitutive, intra-active relationships with each other. Even space cannot be thought of as a neutral 'vessel' for matter and beings. Rather, the qualities and effects of spaces co-develop together with the living beings, objects, technologies, etc., that are moving and acting in or with these spaces (Barad 2007, 170).

In artistic practices and research on the arts, Barad's theory of intra-actions has been recently applied, for example, in the study of the ways performing arts can impact their recipients and the social world (Arlander et al. 2017) and more broadly in the development of new artistic practice-as-research methods in relation to new materialism, represented by Barad among other thinkers (e.g. Kontturi et al. 2018). Our analysis examines the sensobiographic data created together with artists with the aim of answering the following questions: What special skills or methods do artists employ when sensing urban environments? Does an artistic profession or identity as a process enable special relations to – intra-actions with – urban environments? Our research participants are artists from a number of different fields whose ways of sensing and relationships to observing their habitats arguably reflect their specific background in and practice of the arts.

Next, we will further explain the method used in this article and the construction of the research data. Then, in the two analytical subsections, we will discuss how sensory habits and particular ways of observing one's environment become refined and the mutual impacts or intra-active relationship between the city and the participants' artistic work. Lastly, we will draw conclusions from the analysis.

Sensobiographic method and material

Figure 4.1: The routes of the sensobiographic walks conducted in Turku, based on GPS traces and video recordings saved in the central area. Map generator: https://erik.github.io/derive/. Map base: Stamen Design (http://maps.stamen.com/toner-lite/).

The anthropology of the senses has contested prevailing understandings of the senses in Western psychology by showing how the nature and construction of sensing and sense perception differ greatly from one culture and time period to another (Howes 2005; Classen 1993). The sensobiographic walking method adds the dimension of movement to the research methodologies of sensory studies. Cooperation of the senses while walking within an urban landscape and collective sharing of the atmosphere in relation to the surroundings can result in multifaceted data in which the environment and one's biography dynamically intertwine. In our study, we observe how experiencing the urban environment takes shape in a multisensory way and how cultural-historical changes both entangle with and differ from personal histories. We analyse these contextual sensobiographies as hybrid formations of cultural, political, and material-sensory encounters. We also touch upon whether the experiences of different generations are interlinked or to what extent they might be incompatible. The sensobiographic method thus offers new ways to see, smell, hear, and feel the city and the changes in its artists' environmental relationships.

This method has many origins, but its deepest roots are in Finnish and European soundscape research. Helmi Järviluoma, researcher of soundscapes and cultural studies, and her colleagues analysed the soundscapes of six different European villages in the *Acoustic Environments in Change* (AEC) project in the early 2000s. During the fieldwork for that project, Järviluoma realised that it was nearly impossible to study sound separately from the other senses. The participants' experiences of the sonic environments they walked in were always connected to other senses, too. When a participant was taken to a place where they could hear interesting sounds or remember forgotten smells, this encounter produced much more interesting data compared to more static research settings, for instance, if the conversation had been conducted at a kitchen table (Järviluoma 2019; 2021; see also Murray and Järviluoma 2020). Inspired by the insights of the AEC project, researchers started to develop listening walks and soundwalks into sensobiographic walks (cf. Järviluoma 2017, 191).

The material for this article was collected during the sensobiographic walks made in Turku and Brighton in 2017–2019. The method has been refined into a new form in the SENSOTRA project. This new form, the result of years of elaboration, is substantially influenced by the city walks (Tixier 2004; Thibaud 2013) developed by sociologist Jean-Paul Thibaud and the idea of topobiography mentioned earlier (Karjalainen 2009). To summarize it succinctly, the sensobiographic walk is an ethnographic research method that offers numerous opportunities to study sensory experiences and memories related to specific places or space-times (Järviluoma 2021).

SENSOTRA uses sensobiographic walks to study the environmental relationships of people from different generations in three medium-sized European cities (Ljubljana, Turku, and Brighton). In each city, around thirty pairs of walkers were formed, comprising an older participant born before the 1950s and a younger participant born between the years 1990–2005. In this way, the environmental experiences and related conversations unfolded across generations (Murray and Järviluoma 2020; Tiainen, Aula and Järviluoma 2019). Both participants chose a walking route that they considered or have previously considered as particularly meaningful from the perspective of their life in the city. One-third of the participants later participated in an in-depth interview. A video camera was attached to the waist of the participant who had chosen the route. The camera filmed the walk from their point of view and recorded the route through GPS tracking (see map 1). In addition, a Zoom H2n or H4n recorder was used, which enabled the high-quality audio recording of the conversations and environmental sounds. In addition to the route, the weather, season, and time of day influenced the nature of the walks. Most of the walks were made during the daytime, although one of the walks referred to in this article took place early on a summer's night after 10 pm.

In this article, we engage with six walks from Turku and two from Brighton (see material). While working on the article, we went through all of the sensobiographic walking material produced by artists, paying attention to situations and passages that involve discussion about the relationship between artistic work and the urban environment. In the analytical subsections, we approach this challenging research topic from three perspectives: (1) how sensory habits and ways of observing one's environment are constituted together; (2) the co-formation of urban relationships and artistic work; and (3) approaching the city as a field for artistic work – or as a work of art in itself.

Sensobiographic walks aim to evoke memories and sensations in a shared dialogue. The research participants act as co-researchers when questions of sensing, remembering, and urban relationships are discussed during the walks and in the subsequent interviews. This kind of ethnographic approach could be thought of in terms of conviviality (e.g. Brandel 2016). The interviewees were also encouraged to express their own points of view concerning our research design and questions. For example, during his walk, an older artist, Markku, questions the very possibility of having memories of one's environment:

> There's always an updating of some kind, or a little of something new, but you can't know what's made up and what's based on the present mode of experience, on the current mood. If I'm in a really good mood and I can, say, through smell or taste take myself back, I can massively distort the original experience. Because I'm feeling good right now. You start to compare, it was like this then, it's like that now, how they intertwine, that is, which one is kind of being distorted, the present or the past.

As Markku notes, one's present state inevitably affects one's access to the so-called original experience. Thus, the sensobiographic walking method produces new information and experiences contingent on the walks shared by the participants involved. An open interview enables shared reflection on feelings, thoughts, and topics that familiar places bring to one's body and mind as past and place-specific memories give rise to a unique description. Discussions while walking create new layers of remembrance. Every layer is significant, whether it is the original occurrence, one's present point of view, or a story that one will share about it in the future.

New humanistic research approaches and methodologies have lately foregrounded cities as places in which people live, experience, and remember (e.g. Lento and Olsson 2013; see also Aula 2018). However, it is not easy to study the sensory experiences and their changes across the decades in which a research participant has lived in a particular environment. Multisensory ethnography and studies using walking methods help to shed light on the relationship between city residents and their environment in ways that quantitative approaches cannot capture. Sensobiography connects these methodological approaches to explore and expose sensations and sensory memories as integral elements of environmental experience. Art is one important way to engage with what sensing is and how it transforms over time.

Developing ways of sensing and perceiving the urban environment

The research participants we engage with in this article include a wide range of artists from different fields; their ways of sensing and relationships to observing their daily environments have thus developed in mutually divergent ways. Experiencing the urban environment takes shape in multisensory ways and in connection to one's personal history. Via the sensobiographic walks with the artists, we examine if making art and having an artistic profession generate special ways to live in and observe the urban environment and its multisensory changes.

Different professionally practised skills, as well as all kinds of everyday practices and habits, affect how the environment is perceived. The way senses are constructed varies not only culturally and historically (Howes 2005; Virtanen and Saunaluoma 2017) but also on an individual level because the sensory orders and routines of observation differ from one person to the next. For example, synesthesia, blending of the senses, is more common in some people than others (Ådahl 2017). It can thus be presumed that practising and learning the arts also affords and shapes particular modes of perception. Markku,[1] a sculptor born in the 1940s, describes his studies of sculpting as disciplined work that resembles the way musicians work:

> It's like I'd been playing the piano the whole time. A lot of repetitions, yes. The way you learn to see the model, then you learn to make it with your hands, to translate it, like you had to develop it – when a person usually looks at something, the look in their eyes is so numb that they

---

[1] All interviewee names are pseudonyms.

only see what they are accustomed to seeing. With that in mind, if you try to mould something, nothing is going to come out of it [laughs], or it will become what it will become, so nothing much at all. So you have to learn to see in a different way. And when you learn to see in a new way, then you must learn it with your hands, the way that you transfer it into the clay. And that took a lot of repetition.

Thus, training or honing one's senses through repetition is a way out of this numbed glance. During an interview held in a café the day after the walk, Markku said that he later remembered the exact moment when he had started seeing differently. When he was looking at a portrait, its shapes combined in a new way, and afterwards, his whole process of working changed. The technique must first be learned, but later it is no longer needed on a conscious level.

During the walks and the following interviews, Markku talked of his mixed feelings about Turku, which he considers to be a fine cultural city full of historical layers, but simultaneously a parochial and insular place. Furthermore, he has had to actively assess his own outlook on Turku, because it is now also the hometown of his daughter. In addition to these reflections and images, Markku's special relationship with Turku becomes evident during the walk along the route he had chosen. When an urban environment is interpreted as lived and experienced space-time, it becomes formed at the different boundaries between the personal and the shared. In Turku, the Aura River is one of the central elements that shape sensescapes and people's relations with the city.

> Markku: Mostly this river. Of course. I found it very fascinating. Usually all cities with a river have this really good sound of their own. What I've been thinking afterwards is, that one thing, that constant movement of the water.
> Researcher: Mhm.
> Markku: It brings a kind of feeling that something is going on. Even though nothing is going on here [laughs].

The sensations conveyed during this walk are connected to Markku's experiences of ever-flowing water, a sense of movement while nothing concrete might actually be happening, and the endless repetitions of his sculpting lessons. The route Markku chose stretches between his home and the art school, a route Markku says he always walked "with blinkers on" to get quickly from one place to another. On his walks along Turku's riverside and in the parks, Markku reportedly focuses on his own thoughts. He gives a similar description of how he walked the route during the sensobiographic walk, thus reiterating the story he has spun of his life so far. Seemingly nothing is going on, but all of the minute changes, the everyday life of the city, and the passing of time fit into the circle of repetitions experienced by Markku.

The other older interviewees also ponder themes of recurrence and temporality. Mikko, a library worker and a freelance photographer also born in the 1940s like Markku, reminisced during his walk about how his interest in depicting the city had gradually shifted from the scenery to the people. Mikko's father was an amateur photographer who took photos on his travels around Europe. They also developed photographs at home. In the 1970s, Mikko focused on photographing sceneries, but gradually landscape photos started to feel "boring" and "meaningless," because they arguably lack the ability to "tell something." Mikko studied photography in different workshops, becoming, in his own words, a "street photographer." He describes:

> [t]he picture itself should tell something, the picture doesn't have to have any text in it, but it must tell something. But [landscape] photos didn't really tell anything, they were like ordinary tourist photos. Most of the photos, there's so many of them, people take an awful lot of photos, but most of those photos are unnecessary, you don't do anything with them. And that's what I felt myself, that there's really nothing in this picture and nothing happens in it. It doesn't give me anything and it won't give anyone else anything either.

The difference between how Mikko photographs a city's sceneries and people boils down to a perceived dichotomy between a *static* and a *dynamic* city. The sceneries that have been photographed countless times represent a stagnant, predictable, and well-known city, whereas photographing people provides Mikko with a chance to capture changes and what is "happening" in the urban environment. When we walked on the south side of the Aura River and through an old port area, this static and dynamic dichotomy resurfaced or was echoed in the division Mikko made between the *real* and the *manufactured*.

The dichotomies invoked by Mikko present noteworthy contradictions. On the one hand, the riverside that, as Mikko claims, is built for the rich and no longer belongs to everyone represents an artificially created environment, but on the other hand, a scenery with no people in it frozen in a photograph does not tell anything to the viewer either. The flow of time in a city is full of asynchronous changes, where repetition and boredom are also part of the rhythms of life. Many of the older artists, such as the interviewees discussed above, pointed to changes in bohemian or artists' lifestyles and the possibilities to discuss art within the urban spaces of Turku. According to these interviewees, face-to-face meetings in restaurants have become rarer, and theatre shows are no longer followed by colourful masses flocking into culture-oriented bars to debate the performance afterwards.

The intra-active relationship of artistic work and the city

During the sensobiographic walks in both Turku and Brighton, the artist-participants highlighted how meaningful places in the city are intertwined with the processes of making and experiencing art. These participants' unique and especially attuned ways of sensing the urban environment do not result only from their carefully developed professional skills in the arts or personal routines. Their art-making methods also produce ongoing reciprocal, intra-active effects within the relationship between the city and themselves. The perceptible changes in the city are thereby tied to people's life histories.

Anna-Sofia, a visual artist born in the 1980s, said that she chose her special sensobiographic walking route with photography in mind. She had previously photographed the same places in Turku where she was now walking with the researcher. Simon, a visual artist born in the 1930s, had also chosen his route in Brighton based on the intersections, or intra-actions, of his artistic work and urban space. During the walk, he systematically mentioned places and things that were connected to his long-term experiences of making art.

> Simon: The reason why I'm bringing you up here is because of this gallery, 35 North. It's shut at the moment, I know, so we'll just have a quick look at it. But the guy who started the artists' open houses is now showing, has got a one-man show in here. Just for this month, 'cause it's the open houses month. And it's just a celebration really of him starting this thing thirty-odd years ago. Right, so, you can't see much of his work, but that's where he is. I've had one exhibition here myself, about three or four years ago, which was alright. I thought I'd show that, visually, visually exciting thing. – See this bit of not-so-good graffiti.
> Researcher: Perhaps practising there …
> Simon: And a lot more, now a lot more shops sell pictures and things as well. Which is obviously part of my interest in everything.

Making art is clearly an existential part of these individuals' environmental relationships, and thus, it significantly defines how they inhabit and perceive their urban environs. The way Simon perceives the city of Brighton and what he wants to foreground in it is revealed in the way he points out things related to visual arts – such as art galleries, graffiti, and art shops – and also in his way of bringing up bygone things that visually express the city's bohemian atmosphere. It is inevitable that we pay attention to details in our environment that we deem interesting and meaningful in our personal lives. We do not perceive reality as such, so to say, but rather *our perception of reality is in constant intra-action with how we act in and how we have become in relation to our environment.* This means that one's professional identity and lived experience are conveyed in what one's attention is drawn to during the sensobiographic walks. Towards the end of the walk-in Turku, with the older participant Markku, everyone's hands began to grow numb because of the cold. This led to a discussion about the sculptor's hands and his worries about injuring his hands throughout his years of work.

> Markku: Casting bronze is, in a way, quite difficult itself.
> Researcher: Yeah.
> Markku: A difficult thing, so um.
> Researcher: Was your work somehow different regarding health and safety back then than what it is now?
> Markku: Nobody even talked about health and safety back then, so no, we didn't think about anything like that at all. It was very unhealthy; for example, if you think about the studios, they had very bad ventilation, and the work space was not properly separated from the living space either.
> Researcher: What is casting bronze-like? It's completely alien to me. Does it like emit some sort of toxic fumes?
> Markku: Yeah, it does. You see, the like molten metal releases all kinds of poisons into the air, and even though people usually try to have some sort of ventilation, no, it doesn't really work like that.

The urban environment can therefore be considered to appear differently to each and everyone: the web of personal life experiences shapes both how a person is a part of the city and how the city is a part of the person.

Architect and theorist Juhani Pallasmaa has noted that – in addition to very specific and focused observations – experiencing one's environment happens more holistically at the level of subconscious and non-targeted feelings. This holistic mode of experiencing is often integral to perceiving the environment (Pallasmaa 2011). This type of experiencing can be difficult to analyse, as sensing the environment is a continuous, everyday process. Learning from the practices of creative, artistic work can serve as a method of finding new experiential layers when observing a city's sensescape. On her walk, Anna-Sofia said that she had attained new ways of perceiving the urban environment of Turku through photographs and that she has learned to appreciate aspects of this environment that are commonly thought of as unattractive. These include the city's "concrete jungle" and the "sleazy" Brahe Center, a commercial space which has "always been a bit of a weird place."

Figure 4.2: A screenshot of a video taken on Anna-Sofia's walk at the spot where she talks about the concrete jungle of the city.

Anna-Sofia: I heard, now this might be total rubbish, but I heard this claim that architects from all over the world come to look at Turku's cityscape, because we have these weird contrasts here, that, that there is some historic building, and then there are these wonderful, like, box houses. Yeah, I, I somehow like this kind of concrete jungle. This is it; I'm comfortable here.

Researcher: Can you specify if, if, what, what makes it comfortable?

Anna-Sofia: I've kind of learned, kind of grown to like it, like, well, I don't know how to put it, it's kind of the scenery I grew up in, and I know that it hides a lot of interesting things. Then, somehow, well, I've gone to Berlin for work and stuff – so I've also realised the kind of potential that this kind of asphalt jungle can have, the way everything can be organised and that it, it can like be made interesting and – Like for example right here, I've shot a lot of photos here. I think this is absolutely wonderful.

The impact of creative work on one's relationship with a city space can also materialise as new ways of sensing and feeling. Eerika, born in the 1990s and pursuing a career in theatre-making, spoke of her experience of two Finnish cities, Turku and Lahti, using the vocabulary of her chosen artistic field. Theatrical practices and the ways of perceiving they afford have thus become part of how she makes sense of urban spaces.

> Eerika: And well, hmm, Lahti is, to me, like, feels more like an industrial city; it has quite a lot of industrial areas of sorts. Mm. What else?
> Researcher: What about the shape of the city or?
> Eerika: It's a bit vaguer, or it's like a concentration of sorts like it's so clear here, like, there is a clear dramaturgy here like there is a beginning and an end, it's like a journey, that you always go through, but in Lahti, it's more of a cluster, where anything can happen. It's not as clear.

Observing a city's constituent elements, analysing one's own observations, and ultimately incorporating them into art-making create a multi-layered experience of urban environments. When an artist parses what they experience through a camera lens, on a canvas, or as part of performance art, the cityscape and the art take form through their mutual intra-action; the cityscape affects the art, and the produced art, in turn, affects the way its maker can perceive, and experience the urban milieu. Just as the processes of creative work combine with the environment to build a connection to that environment, these processes also create a personal and multisensory connection to how one remembers a location.

The sensory memories of Ruth, a visual artist born in the 1930s, are strongly linked with drawing. For her, seeing buildings through her drawings and through the artistic process, in general, brought changes in the cityscape also into focus.

> Ruth: I did a lot of drawings of streets and buildings. I wasn't interested in doing rural landscapes. I only liked doing townscapes. And there were some old buildings which I drew, which of course have now been demolished.
> Researcher: Do you still have those drawings?
> Ruth: Yes, I do. Or photographs of them. For example, there was a painting I did of a building on the seafront. What they did in the regency time was they had things called mathematical tiles, and so, it would be a wooden building, and then they'd stick these tiles on the outside to look like bricks. So I've got a painting of that, which was on the seafront.

Ruth still remembered the buildings of Brighton that she had drawn when she was younger, although they no longer existed – some of them she remembered in great detail. Her way of talking about the city through her drawings shows that the rigorous observation required for creating art, as well as the resulting art itself, can work as efficient vehicles for remembering one's sensed environment.

Professional identity and its effects on our actions and thinking affect how we sense, perceive, and experience a city and its changes. Just as the techniques learned through creating art affect how an artist observes their environment, extracting a work of art from a cityscape is a process that requires analysing one's observations and materialising them in a new form that is characteristic of a specific art form and creative process. When an art-maker's observations translate into art, they also become a part of their site-specific life history. One's relationship with a cityscape thus emerges through intra-actions of creative work, personal identity, and urban sensory environments.

A city as art

On sensobiographic walks, the artist-participants recalled times when they had looked at the city in question as a deliberately crafted artwork, performance, or game. For example, Petri, an artist born in the 1950s, reminisced about how he and his friends, following the artistic and political movements of 1968, used to remove "keep off the grass" signs in the Turku cityscape. They would then replace the signs with new pictures and texts during the night. Petri mentions situationists as a direct source of inspiration here: he and his friends had a "Situationist programme," the sign-switching being one of its projects.

Seeing everyday phenomena as art-like has been referred to in the field of aesthetics as 'artification' (Korolainen 2012; Naukkarinen 2000; 2012) and 'aestheticization' (Lipovetsky and Serroy 2013; Welsch 1996). "The neologism 'artification' refers to situations and processes in which something that is not regarded as art in the traditional sense of the word is changed into something art-like or into something that takes influences from artistic ways of thinking and acting" (Naukkarinen 2012).

The art of everyday life is not in itself a new idea. For example, in his lectures in 1980, Michel Foucault traces the concept of the art of life (*techne*) to Greco-Roman philosophy (Foucalt 2005). In his late essay "What is Enlightenment?" Foucault revisits his thoughts on the modern "culture of the self" via Baudelaire's understanding of modernism. He summarises that the modern human being is not predominantly concerned with the nature of their being ("who am I") but with "inventing" and "producing" themselves (Tanke 2009; see also McCall 2010; Seppä 2004). Crossing or even destroying the barrier between the mundane and the artistic was also strongly present in the goals and manifestos of (Western) artistic avant-garde movements of the twentieth century, and the situationists were particularly known for this impulse in the 1960s (e.g. Spiteri 2015).

Taking over the urban space through art and as art was addressed during the sensobiographic walks also in connection with discussions of the "Turku Capital of Counter-Culture" (*Turku Euroopan alakulttuuripääkaupungiksi*) campaign, which was a counter-campaign to the "European Capital of Culture" year for Turku in 2011 (cf. Lähdesmäki 2013; Uimonen 2020). The counter-campaign's projects included, for instance, an "Art slum" – a combination between squatting, street reclaiming, and grassroots art festival curation that was built in a prominent location in the city annually. The participants who talked of the art slums saw that their value resided in challenging the prevailing aesthetic hierarchy, although they also noted that, at least at some point, the slums involved conspicuous use of intoxicants and other adverse effects. Ernesti, who took part in organising the slums, describes their aesthetic as "the total opposite of middle-class art culture," and comments on how a certain kind of "grunginess" was the exact point of the slums:

> In the eyes of the elite culture, it looked like an awful abomination, but that was probably the point, and I kind of saw it as good [laughs], somehow as a good thing, that it was kind of a, kind of like a grungy wart in the middle of the city's Cathedral Square, right in the middle there. And it's supposed to look like that, it was something, it was something completely different from the commercial and organised, the artificial or pretentious commercial art that you had to pay for and where everyone, everyone is dressed fine, and everything is clinical and, people buying experiences from everything … it was completely like different, the complete opposite, in 2011 it was the complete opposite to that kind of middle-class art culture.

Marita, a pensioner active in local politics and grassroots civic activity in Turku who had walked with Ernesti before, shares the same highly polarised impression of the "elite culture" and the local grassroots art culture. To Ernesti, the art slum is a "grungy wart" on the face of mainstream culture that betrays its commercial and artificial nature. According to Marita, the culture capital venues in Turku constituted a "kind of a tourist place and travel spot" that "was a bit far-flung for normal people." Instead of imported culture, Marita would have wished for a "consumer culture for the normal person." Ernesti, who does not "totally reject" the culture capital project, saying he "would give it about two out of five" stars, nonetheless stresses the importance of locality and criticises the project for not activating or sufficiently funding "specifically local or even Finnish, or like even artists who come from the Nordic countries."

The "Turku Capital of Counter-Culture" campaign, with its various activities, represents a public, political, consciously resistant and rebellious form of counterculture. However, many other alternative uses of the urban space – from skateboarding to graffiti – have already become a normalised part of urban life across the globe. However, they still can challenge and subvert urban rhythms and create or evoke alternative space-times and historical lineages.

Raisa, a visual artist born in the 1940s, told a SENSOTRA researcher during her walk how skateboarders had discovered the stairs to her home as their favourite spot to practise and film new stunts. Instead of disapproving of the skateboarders' actions – as the generation gap might imply – she has let the skateboarders know that they can be there as much as they like. Even a broken flowerpot or disapproval from others has not bothered Raisa. She has rather witnessed skateboarding as an important part of urban life and the "city as art."

> Raisa: And they, they're filming it, so they'll try it for however long it takes to do the trick properly, and they get it on video. And people have said like, "there they are again, terrible!" They've got my permission.
> Researcher: You have a kind of natural relationship, then.
> Raisa: It's art.

By using the situationists' concepts, one could speculate whether skateboarding or mural paintings, which have become more common in recent years (and were often discussed during the walks), have become "recuperated." That is to say, whether their counteractive potential has been completely subsumed into the idea of a "creative city" that can be easily exploited as part of a city's branding efforts. Media researcher Matteo Pasquinelli maintains that even squatting can be integrated as part of the creative economy discourse (Pasquinelli 2008, 145; cf. Venäläinen 2011). Likewise, a scholarly gaze can, at worst, be a way to recuperate and domesticate the very real struggles concerning the use of urban spaces into mere supposed aesthetic differences of opinion.

What forms of urban artification, then, might elude the tendency to include all alternative action, sensory experiences, and ways of thinking into the same urban, marketing-driven "buzz"? To adopt a term by philosophers Gilles Deleuze and Félix Guattari, one could talk about "minor" or minority-like forms of artification, which do not come in the form of manifestos or campaigns, but rather take place as coincidental and hidden or selectively shared aesthetic experiences. One example of this form of artification is a message hidden in the grass that was pointed out during a walk in Turku by an art student and live-action role-player, Kuura, who had lived in Turku for two years. Kuura knew about the existence of the paper slip, which they looked for in the grass for a while before finding it and showing it to the researcher.

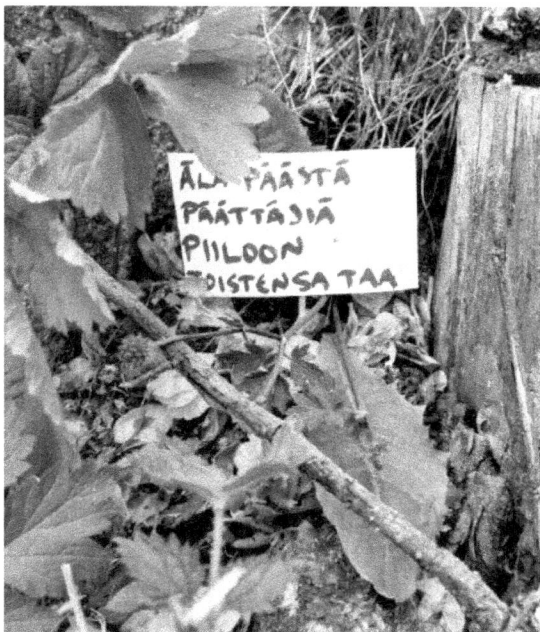

Figure 4.3: Message found by Kuura by the Aura River, hidden in the grass. It reads: "Do not allow decision-makers to hide behind each other's backs."

Although some of the sensobiographic walks during the SENSOTRA project resembled a well-rehearsed historical tour, some of the walkers took a very different approach and shared various transient moments and observations that had little to do with conventional narratives about the city.

Kuura's narration, for example, was punctuated by peculiar findings and events as they described their personal city experience. There is also a certain aesthetic of retreat associated with appreciating obscure details; the walking route chosen by Kuura is not headed towards the city proper but a riverside route towards Halistenkoski that resembles a nature trail. When the researcher asked whether Kuura frequently visits the city centre, they replied that they do not see a reason to go unless "I have to take a train or something like that," revealing that Kuura's visits to the city centre are more pragmatic (leaving the city) than for leisure.

Just like Petri's account described earlier, Kuura's descriptions invoke "detournement," the situationists' idea of challenging the prevailing order of the urban space through experimental and playful means. Kuura's interests, live-action roleplaying and associated activities are certainly sufficient to cause confusion among some of the city's inhabitants when they are practised in public spaces. For instance, they recount having prepared for a live-action roleplaying game by practising swordplay in the urban space with boffers – padded swords.

> Well, we've boffed there on that beach and during the previous [name of live-action roleplaying game], we had to do weekly training exercises, had to go boffing, so then we came here to smack each other around a bit with our silver baguettes.

After this account, Kuura continues with another memory about their friend who "does craft-making stuff." The friend had rotted elk bones in a kettle to remove all the "organic matter" from them. Kuura associated the memory with a specific place passed by during the sensobiographic walk; the kettle had to be opened underwater due to the smell, and this had happened at a particular spot by the Aura River.

> One time my friend had had some elk bones and rotted them in oxygen-free conditions in a kettle, they'd been there for six months, and then we had to open it. It was complete biohazard material by then. We opened it there underwater in that river, scrubbed all the gunk out of it. But good grief, the smell, seriously, that was not [good], we were stood there for hours in the scorching heat. We scraped the rotten bones with rubber gloves on and swished them about in the river.

In Kuura's narration, the urban space obtains an artified form in the sense that the city is "read" and narrated continuously, seemingly peripherally or outside of its more established representations. Aesthetic experiences are emphasised in this kind of narration, some of which are very subtle, personal, and perhaps only shared in close company. On the other hand, these experiences are implicitly associated with a communal dimension, as the canvas for these moments is the "shared urban space" (Pasquinelli 2008, 145) that offers opportunities for spontaneous events and encounters.

Conclusion

In this article, we have sought to outline a fresh sensobiographic approach to urban research from the perspective of cultural and sensory studies. The starting point was that cities and the artists living in them impact each other via mutually constitutive processes of intra-action. From this perspective, we focused on artists – and citizens who engaged with the urban space in artistic ways – representing different generations from Turku and Brighton and analysed their sensory experiences in their changing urban living environments. Our article is also part of recent developments in research on artists that have introduced novel perspectives on the relationship between artists and their environment. Sensobiographic walks bring the aspect of spatiotemporal and sensory movement to these new perspectives. In our research material, urban space is experienced in a variety of multisensory ways while, at the same time, changes in cultural history as well as cultural and political spheres and practices intra-act with personal histories.

The sensobiographic walks of the SENSOTRA project enable the dynamic emergence of biographical information and experiences: events, sensations, and memories are spoken into existence while moving through the cityscape. In this article, we have examined sensobiographical instances and narrations as hybrid formations of past recollections and present experiences which interlink and intra-act, sharing family resemblances. As historian Christina Florin (2014, 9) puts it, individuals are always shaped by wider surrounding processes and structures, both social and material. As researchers, we have also become entangled in the production of the SENSOTRA project's sensobiographic materials. To employ Barad's concept, this material is a result of complex intra-actions that have continued to take shape as we have listened to the audio and video recordings from the walks and written analytical texts on the biographical excerpts captured by the recordings and their transcriptions.

When analysing the changes in people's sensory environmental relations, we are aware of the highly situational and mediated, multi-layered nature of the accounts arising during the sensobiographic walks. Nevertheless, the sensobiographic method can still provide a helpful tool for urban research and also urban development. This method allows one to delve into sensory experiences as the outcome of the situational, intra-active intertwining of past and present. In this way, sensobiographic walks and interviews illustrate how socio-cultural changes are lived and interpreted by different generations, social groups, and institutions formed by people living in cities – with artists as a special case in point. During the sensobiographic walks in both Turku and Brighton, the participants brought up how places that they find meaningful in the city are intertwined with their processes and experiences of making art. Thus, artistic activities give rise to mutual effects and influences within the relationship between people and the city, where the sensed changes in the cityscape both shape and are shaped by people's own life histories. Moreover, and importantly, artistic activities continue to offer ways of escaping urban artification that attempt to hijack all alternative practices and experiences as part of the commercially motivated "buzz."

References

Sensobiographic walks in Turku

"Anna-Sofia." Interview by Heikki Uimonen. Turku, May 11, 2018. Audio, 71 min. (Featuring "Raisa.")

"Kuura." Interview by Sonja Pöllänen. Turku, May 17, 2018. Audio, 67 min. (Featuring "Liisa.")

"Marita." Interview by Juhana Venäläinen (post-walk interview). Turku, June 2, 2018. Audio, 17 min. (Featuring "Ernesti.")

"Markku." Interview by Inkeri Aula and Sonja Pöllänen. Turku, March 3, 2018. Audio, 56 min. (Featuring "Sanni.")

"Mikko." Interview by Helmi Järviluoma-Mäkelä and Juhana Venäläinen. Turku, April 26, 2018. Audio, 76 min. (Featuring "Marianne.")

"Raisa." Interview by Heikki Uimonen. Turku, May 7, 2018. Audio, 61 min. (Featuring "Anna-Sofia.")

Sensobiographic walks in Brighton

"Ruth." Interview by Eeva Pärjälä. Brighton, February 13, 2019. Audio, 55 min. (Featuring "Anissa.")

"Simon." Interview by Heikki Uimonen. Brighton, May 7, 2019. Audio, 99 min. (Featuring "Alex.")

Bibliography

Arlander, Annette. 2017. "Maisema, materia ja muutos. Harakan saaren luontokulttuuria dokumentoimassa." In: Mari Mäkiranta, Ulla Piela, and Eija Timonen, eds. *Näkyväksi sepitetty maa.* Helsinki: SKS. Pp. 23–39.

Arlander, Annette, and Mika Elo. 2017. "Ekologinen näkökulma taidetutkimukseen." *Tiede ja Edistys* 4: 335–346.

Arlander, Annette, Hanna Järvinen, Tero Nauha, and Pilvi Porkola. 2017. "Miten tehdä asioita esityksellä – annetuissa (työpaja)olosuhteissa?" *Tahiti* 3: 71–86.

Aula, Inkeri. 2018. "Aistikävely kaupunkimaisemaan: yhteisen tilan kokemus ja joutomaiden polut." *Elore* 25 (1): 74–95.

Barad, Karen. 2007. *Meeting the Universe Halfway: Quantum Physics and the Entanglement of Matter and Meaning*. Durham: Duke University Press.

Battersby, Christine. 1990. *Gender and Genius: Towards a Feminist Aesthetics*. Bloomington: Indiana University Press.

Benjamin, Walter. 1989. "Taideteos teknisen uusinnettavuutensa aikakaudella." In: Markku Koski, Keijo Rahkonen, and Esa Sirone, eds. *Messiaanisen sirpaleita: kirjoituksia kielestä, historiasta ja pelastuksesta*. Translated by Raija Sironen. Helsinki: Kansan Sivistystyön Liitto and Tutkijaliitto.

Brandel, Andrew. 2016. "The Art of Conviviality." *HAU: Journal of Ethnographic Theory* 6 (2): 323–343.

Caine, Barbara. 2010. *Biography and History*. New York: Palgrave Macmillan.

Classen, Constance. 1993. *Worlds of Sense: Exploring the Senses in History and across Cultures*. London and New York: Routledge.

Deleuze, Gilles, and Félix Guattari. 1987. *A Thousand Plateaus: Capitalism and Schizophrenia*. Minneapolis: University of Minnesota Press.

Foucault, Michel. 2005. *The Hermeneutics of the Subject: Lectures at the Collège de France 1981-1982*, edited by Fréderic Gros. New York: Picador.

Florin, Christina. 2014. "Biografia rajoja rikkomassa. Kolme esimerkkiä ruotsalaisesta elämäkertatutkimuksesta." In: Heini Hakosalo, Seija Jalagin, Marianne Junila, and Heidi Kurvinen, eds. *Historiallinen elämä: biografia ja historiantutkimus*. [Historiallinen arkisto 141.] Helsinki: Suomalaisen Kirjallisuuden Seura. Pp. 27–44.

Hakosalo, Heini, Seija Jalagin, Marianne Junila, and Heidi Kurvinen. 2014. "Johdanto: elämää suurempaa." In: Heini Hakosalo, Seija Jalagin, Marianne Junila, and Heidi Kurvinen, eds. *Historiallinen elämä: biografia ja historiantutkimus*. [Historiallinen arkisto 141.] Helsinki: Suomalaisen Kirjallisuuden Seura. Pp. 7–26.

Howes, David. 2005. *Empire of the Senses: The Sensual Culture Reader*. Oxford: Berg.

Irni, Kuura, Mianna Meskus, and Venla Oikkonen (eds). 2014. *Muokattu elämä: teknotiede, sukupuolisuus ja materiaalisuus*. Tampere: Vastapaino.

Jennings, Michael William. 2008. "The Production, Reproduction, and Reception of the Work of Art." In: Michael William Jennings, Brigid Doherty, and Thomas Y. Levin, eds. *The Work of Art in the Age of Its Technological Reproducibility, and Other Writings on Media*. Cambridge, Massachusetts: The Belknap Press of Harvard University Press. Pp. 9–17.

Järviluoma, Helmi. 2017. "The Art and Science of Sensory Memory Walking." In: Marcel Cobussen, Vincent Meelberg, and Barry Truax, eds. *The Routledge Companion to Sounding Art*. New York: Taylor and Francis. Pp. 191–204.

Järviluoma, Helmi. 2019. "'Kaikki elämän makeus ja riemu.' Aistielämäkerrallisen kävelyn taide ja tiede." In: Juha Torvinen, and Susanna Välimäki, eds. *Musiikki ja luonto: soiva kulttuuri ympäristökriisin aikakaudella*. Turku: Utukirjat. Pp. 221–245.

Järviluoma, Helmi. 2021. "Sensobiographic Walking and Ethnographic Approach of the Finnish School of Soundscape Studies." In: Geoff Stahl, and Mark Percival, eds. *Popular Music and Place*. London: Bloomsbury.

Järviluoma, Helmi, Pirkko Moisala, and Anni Vilkko. 2003. *Gender and Qualitative Methods*. London: Sage Publications.

Järviluoma, Helmi, and Noora Vikman. 2013. "On Soundscape Methods and Audiovisual Sensibility." In: John Richardson, Claudia Gorbman, and Carol Vernallis, eds. *The Oxford Handbook of New Audiovisual Aesthetics*. New York: Oxford University Press. Pp. 645–658.

Karjalainen, Pauli Tapani. 2009. "Topobiography: Remembrance of Places Past." *Nordia Geographical Publications* 38 (5): 31–34.

Karttunen, Sari. 2017. "Laajentuva taiteilijuus – yhteisötaiteilijoiden toiminta ja identiteetti hybridisaatio-käsitteen valossa." *Tahiti* 7 (1). Available at https://tahiti.journal.fi/article/view/85656, accessed August 29, 2019.

Kokkonen, Tuija. 2014. "Kun emme tiedä. Keskustelemassa 'meitä' uusiksi: lajienväliset esitykset ja esitystaiteen rooli ekokriisien aikakaudella." In: Karoliina Lummaa, and Lea Rojola, eds. *Posthumanismi*. Turku: Eetos. Pp. 179–210.

Kontturi, Katve-Kaisa. 2018. *Ways of Following: Art, Materiality, Collaboration*. London: Open Humanities Press.

Kontturi, Katve-Kaisa, Tero Nauha, Milla Tiainen, and Marie-Luise Angerer, eds. 2018. "Aesthetic Intra-Actions: Practising New Materialisms in the Arts." *Ruukku* 9. Available at https://ruukku-journal.fi/fi/issues/9, accessed August 29, 2019.

Korolainen, Kari. 2012. "Artification and the Drawing of Distinctions: An Analysis of Categories and Their Uses." *Contemporary Aesthetics* Special Volume 4.

Lento, Katri, and Pia Olsson, eds. 2013. *Muistin kaupunki: tulkintoja kaupungista muistin ja muistamisen paikkana*. Helsinki: Suomalaisen Kirjallisuuden Seura.

Lepistö, Vappu. 1992. *Kuvataiteilija taidemaailmassa: tapaustutkimus kuvataiteellisen toiminnan sosiaalipsykologisista merkityksistä*. Helsinki: Tutkijaliitto.

Leskelä-Kärki, Maarit. 2012. "Samastumisia ja etääntymisiä. Elämäkerta historiantutkimuksen kysymyksenä." In: Asko Nivala, and Rami Mähkä, eds. *Tulkinnan polkuja: kulttuurihistorian tutkimusmenetelmiä*. Turku: k&h.

Lipovetsky, Gilles, and Jean Serroy. 2013. *L'esthétisation du monde: vivre á l âge du capitalism artiste*. Paris: Gallimard.

Logrén, Anna. 2015. *Taiteilijapuheen moniäänisyys: tutkimus mediavälitteisen ja (kuva)taiteilijalähtöisen taiteilijapuheen muotoutumisesta*. Joensuu: University of Eastern Finland.

Lähdesmäki, Tuuli. 2013. "Cultural Activism as a Counter-Discourse to the European Capital of Culture Programme: The Case of Turku 2011." *European Journal of Cultural Studies* 16(5): 598–619.

McCall, Corey. 2010. "The Art of Life: Foucault's Reading of Baudelaire's 'The Painter of Modern Life.'" *The Journal of Speculative Philosophy* 24(2): 138–157.

MacDonald, Fiona. 2018. "Ant-ic Intra-Actions – an Experiential Exploration of Artistic Co-production with Wood Ants." *Ruukku* Special Issue 9. Available at https://www.researchcatalogue.net/view/371152/371153, accessed August 29, 2019.

Murray, Lesley and Järviluoma, Helmi. 2020. "Walking as transgenerational methodology." *Qualitative Research*, 20 (2): 229–238.

Naukkarinen, Ossi. 2000. "Joutomaalta keskikaupungille – miten esteettisyys sopeutuu arkeen?" In: Arto Haapala, and Jyrki Nummi, eds. *Aiesthesis ja poiesis. Kirjoituksia estetiikasta ja kirjallisuudesta*. Helsinki: University of Helsinki. Pp. 129–143.

Naukkarinen, Ossi. 2012. "Variations in Artification." *Contemporary Aesthetics* Special Volume 4.

Pallasmaa, Juhani. 2011. "Tila paikka atmosfääri: perifeerinen havainto arkkitehtuurissa." *Arkkitehti*, 5.

Pasquinelli, Matteo. 2008. *Animal Spirits: A Bestiary of the Commons*. Rotterdam: NAi Publishers/Institute of Network Cultures.

Renders, Hans, Binne de Haan, and Jonne Harmsma, eds. 2016. *The Biographical Turn: Lives in History*. New York: Routledge.

Rossi, Leena-Maija. 1999. *Taide vallassa: politiikkakäsityksen muutoksia 1980-luvun suomalaisessa taidekeskustelussa*. Helsinki: Kustannusosakeyhtiö Taide.

Seppä, Anita. 2004. "Foucault, Enlightenment and the Aesthetics of the Self." *Contemporary Aesthetics* 2.

Spiteri, Raymond. 2015. "From Unitary Urbanism to the Society of the Spectacle. The Situationist Aesthetic Revolution." In: Aleš Erjavec, ed. *Aesthetic Revolutions and Twentieth-Century Avant-Garde Movements*. Durham, NC: Duke University Press.

Stanley, Liz. 1992. *The Auto/biographical I: The Theory and Practice of Feminist Auto/biography*. Manchester: Manchester University Press.

Tanke, Joseph J. 2009. *Foucault's Philosophy of Art: A Genealogy of Modernity*. London/New York: Continuum.

Thibaud, Jean-Paul. 2013. "Commented City Walks." *Wi: Journal of Mobile Culture* 7(1): 1–32.

Tiainen, Milla. 2005. *Säveltäjän sijainnit: taiteilija, musiikki ja historiallinen kesto Paavo Heinisen ja Einojuhani Rautavaaran teksteissä*. [Nykykulttuurin tutkimuskeskuksen julkaisuja 82.] Jyväskylä: University of Jyväskylä.

Tiainen, Milla. 2017. "Sonic Technoecology: Voice and Non-Anthropocentric Survival in The Algae Opera." *Australian Feminist Studies* 32(94): 359–376.

Tiainen, Milla, Inkeri Aula, and Helmi Järviluoma. 2019. "Transformations in Mediations of Lived Sonic Experience: A Sensobiographic Approach." In: Riedel Friedlind, and Juha Torvinen, eds. *Music as Atmosphere: Collective Feelings and Affective Sounds*. London and New York: Routledge. Pp. 238–254.

Tixier, Nicolas. 2004. "La dynamique des cheminements." In: Pascal Amphoux, Jean-Paul Thibaud, and Grégoire Chelkoff, eds. *Ambiances en débats*. Bernin: À la Croisée. Pp. 115–127.

Torvinen, Juha. 2012. "Johdatus ekomusikologiaan: musiikintutkimuksen vastuu ympäristökriisien aikakaudella." *Etnomusikologian vuosikirja* 24: 8–34.

Uimonen, Heikki. 2020. "Kertojien kaupungit: aistielämäkerrallinen kävely ympäristön ja muistamisen tutkimusmenetelmänä." *Alue ja ympäristö* 49(1): 26–42.

Venäläinen, Juhana. 2011. "Oikeus urbaaniin tilaan. Huomioita poliittisen talonvaltausliikkeen uusvanhasta oikeuttamisperustasta." *Oikeus* 3.

Virtanen, Pirjo Kristiina, and Sanna Saunaluoma. 2017. "Visualization and Movement as Configurations of Human-Nonhuman Engagements: Precolonial Geometric Earthwork Landscapes of the Upper Purus, Brazil." *American Anthropologist* 119(4): 614–630.

Welsch, Wolfgang. 1996. "Aestheticization Processes: Phenomena, Distinctions and Prospects." *Theory, Culture & Society* 13(1): 1–24.

Ådahl, Susanne. 2017. "Kummat tuntemukset: aistikokemukset todellisuuden rajalla." In: Kaarina Koski, and Marja-Liisa Honkasalo, eds. *Mielen rajoilla: arjen kummat kokemukset*. Helsinki: SKS. Pp. 124–160.

Chapter 5

Modernisation of the Senses: Sensory Transformations of Ljubljana in the Early Twentieth Century

Sandi Abram

University of Ljubljana, Slovenia

Abstract

The chapter deals with the modernization of Ljubljana at the beginning of the twentieth century through the prism of sensory transformations. It shows how the flourishing of the industrial plants, the introduction of new means of transportation, and the renewal of public infrastructure transformed tastes, smells, movement, and sounds in urban space. The analysis of sensory changes in the cases of housing culture, deodourization of the city centre, hygienization and aestheticization of public space is based on ethnographic material obtained through the method of sensobiographic walks and is complemented by secondary archival material.

Keywords: modernization of the senses, Ljubljana, ethnography, sensobiographic walking, sensory transformation

* * *

The senses of Ljubljana

In the article,[1] I present a participant's sensobiographical narrative about Ljubljana in the 1920s and 1930s in the context of broader processes of the urban environment and, above all, in what I call the modernisation of the senses, i.e. in the context of experiencing the modernisation of the urban space. Her anecdotes about the glint of metal of an automobile whizzing by, her first

---

[1] This article is part of the research project SENSOTRA funded by the European Research Council under the European Union's Horizon 2020 Research and Innovation Program (grant agreement No 694893).

sight of a metal bird whirring overhead – an aeroplane, and the sweetness of slick candy are not just curious flashbacks but indicators of a profound change in the city's everyday sensory world that is worth to explore.

I had the honour of meeting Frančiška for the first time at a public event where she was a guest speaker. She was invited to share with the audience her teenage memories, refined and humble, from when she was a partisan activist who participated in guerrilla actions on the streets of Ljubljana in wartime turmoil. "*We always placed our own life in peril,*" she commented.[2] On the day we met, she was in a rush, yet she agreed to be part of the research project without further thought. Reconstructing Frančiška's sensory memories against the backdrop of historical contextualisation can serve as an indicative example that reveals previously unknown smells, textures, rhythms, tastes, and ways of moving around Ljubljana. These past sensory experiences can only be excavated, and a productive way to tap into them is through sensobiographic meanderings. The sensobiographic walking (see Bajič in Abram 2019) with Frančiška in 2017 represented a window into the transformations in the urban sensorium before the Second World War, or as she called it, "*the monstrous development*" of Ljubljana. Precisely such walks were the central methodological tool I used to explore sensory perceptions and sensory memories in the Slovenian capital.

I begin with a contextualisation of the production of new urban sensory space (see Abram 2021) from a historical perspective, and then I frame it in the embodied remembering of the oldest research participant, or "sensewitnesses" (Järviluoma 2016). I commence with an outline of sensory transformations at the end of the nineteenth century, when industrialisation, territorial expansion, population growth, and the modernisation of public infrastructure (including the beginnings of hygiene and the aestheticization of public space) arrived in the city and altered the perception of urban space.

Before turning to Frančiška's testimony, let's take a closer look at how the sensory landscape of the changing Ljubljana was described in newspapers of the time and how the modernisation of the city was understood by cultural historians.

---

[2] All verbatim quotations in italics were transcribed from the sensobiographic walks and in-depth interviews. They were corrected for grammar to improve readability. All personal data potentially suggestive of the research participants' personal identities were pseudo-anonymised.

"A sense, whose instrument is the nose": modernisation of public infrastructure and the first contours of the hygienization of urban space

The city introduced modern public services as early as the mid-nineteenth century, yet the intensive development of municipal infrastructure in Ljubljana only began after the devastating earthquake of 1895. This included the expansion of water and energy supply, public lighting, sewage, the cleaning of public areas, the maintenance of streets, roads, and squares, public transport, public gardens, and professional fire brigades (Kos 1981, 159). In place of the demolished earthquake-damaged houses, new and modern buildings with improved sanitary conditions were constructed according to the principles of modern hygiene. Likewise, the city expanded outwards, as the residential buildings were to have sufficient light and air (Studen 1991, 242-3; see also Kremenšek 1980). Other changes included the replacement of cesspools, which were usually located near houses, and of faecal barrels inside households (emptying of which caused an immense malodour) with flush toilets of the English model (Kos 1981, 160; Studen 1991, 243).

New technological approaches to hygiene were a harbinger of the coming changes in the regulation of the urban smellscape. By the beginning of the First World War, however, the improved sewage system had not eliminated the unbearable odours that plagued the city centre, especially in summer, nor the debris or faeces in the shallow Ljubljanica River. The deepening and concreting of the riverbed to regulate the Ljubljanica took three decades. It should not be surprising if the renovation of Ljubljanica between 1908-1938 was temporarily interrupted by the First World War, resulting in an (in)tolerance of stench in the Old Town. We can read about "sensory thresholds" (Corbin 2019, 48) in a witty, somewhat cynical newspaper article entitled *Ljubljanica and its Curiosities*. The chronicler first offers some factual information about the concreting of the riverbed, followed by comments about sights along the riverbank:

> After all the difficulties, this year's construction work in Ljubljanica is nearing its desired end. We are already experiencing autumnal weather, and soon winter will be pressing so that the smell will not be so bad, but we are all rejoicing in this event. [...] Of course, there are many jesters on both banks of the river who grumble that they would rather release the water flow so that the people of Ljubljana can be spared from unpleasant smells for at least one day. Well, the workers pay little attention to these sometimes desperate complaints. They calmly roam the water, chase wood and, to the great delight of the spectators, are

unusually polite. Sometimes a half-metre-long, storm-grey rat wanders across the beautifully green or beautifully grey surface of the Ljubljanica. [...] Such a walk along the Ljubljanica is a welcome pastime, despite all the congresses, guests, fairs and carousing. A person holding handkerchief to his nose asks our dyke dwellers if they smell anything. And how surprised he is when he learns that they smell nothing. Who knows, maybe this habit and insensitivity will lead to an atavism of the descendants towards this sense whose instrument is the nose. These people have been suffering for 25 years, who could blame them then! (Unknown 1933, 5)

Written in 1933, the reportage also captures the sensory atmosphere of early-industrial Ljubljana at the Cukrarna sugar refinery, which was the first factory in what is now Slovenia to install a steam engine in 1835 (Prelovšek 1972, 22). The author suggested that future generations would never experience the stench of Ljubljanica as the end of construction work was approaching:

We're near Cukrarna. We have to stop. The riverbed looks like a rainbow got lost in it, or as if a painter had thrown in a modern, smeared, palette-like painting. Here lies the true realm of all the goods thrown away by a luxurious and miserable city. It is a veritable paradise for all those who seriously intend to write lyrical poetry, for the fragrances of this bacilli field must be immortalised in such a way that the late historian would not criticise us for being bad chroniclers. (Unknown 1933, 5)

The article takes us to the suburbs in the process of transformation and, at the same time, gives us an impression of the writer's historiographical sensitivity to sensory transformations. The modernisation of the sensory virtually swam across the water and was reflected in the Ljubljanica. After all, according to the writer, the watercourse was coloured in a rainbow that may not have been caused by flotsam goods alone but can be understood as fuel or possibly even oil pollution reflected on the water's surface. There are several possible sources that could transport the oil across Ljubljanica to the described micro-location. In the interwar period, for example, many nearby industrial enterprises, including a leather factory and a foundry, were run on oil (see Lorenčič and Prinčič 2018, 159-60). Similarly, road oil was occasionally poured onto the gravel surface of the nearby squares to prevent dust formation (Židov 1994, 67).

In this perspective, we find another interesting text on the perception of the developing urban sensorium signed by Karl Petrič, a physician and the director of the Institute of Hygiene in Slovenia between 1933-1935 (Zupanič Slavec and

Slavec 2011). His article from 1934 deals with the hygienic conditions in Ljubljana and discusses, among other things, the hazardous emissions from combustion plants, the air emissions from a growing industry, and the impact of rail and road traffic on the environment and the health of the inhabitants of Ljubljana. He was not interested in "questions of hygiene of an individual, but those that affect the entire population of the city" (Petrič 1934, 128). In addition to a list of hygiene measures, Petrič recommended regular cleaning of the macadam roadways and construction of pavements with asphalt or wooden tiles because dust from these was blown into the air by "wind and driven into the dwellings" (Petrič 1934, 128). Petrič substantiated his claim about appropriate living conditions with two photos. The first photo represented an example of an unhealthy suburban housing unit and showed the Meksika apartment building, a dense social housing block for the working class that lacked sunlight and fresh air, as it was located near a dusty and noisy street. The second photo, contrarily, represents the exact opposite of Meksika, a suburban modernist villa with a garden was better "because fresh air and sun penetrate much more easily, children have a place to play, and there is no noise near such houses" (Petrič 1934, 128).

Petrič's report was a characteristic way of articulating the concern of city authorities for public morality and hygiene in public spaces. It sets the bourgeois standard as the general standard of living, regardless of class origin. In this respect, it gives a rather symptomatic narrative of how mechanisms of urban governance and renewal adopted scientific discourse on the hygienization of urban space. The doctor's scientific and medical view of Ljubljana was paired with the process of modernisation.

Figure 5.1: Petrič's display of an unhealthy apartment building (left) and demonstration of a healthy suburban villa in Vrtača (right) (Petrič 1934).

Sensory (micro)histories and urban transformations

Towards the end of the nineteenth century, among the mechanisms of urban governance and renewal, there appear also those based on a scientific treatment, starting with the question of hygiene. The miasma theory, according to which the causes of endemic diseases such as malaria and cholera are to be found in toxic fumes (e.g. from soil or from industrial plants), is gradually replaced by microbiology (Kenny 2014, 88). The scientific approach became the criterion of "urbanism" as a specific profession that determines new, global approaches to regulating cities (Benevolo 2004, 227-32). The first two decades of the twentieth century were thus marked by a new arrangement of the city, and human habitation was considered the most important element (Benevolo 2004, 227-32). In other words, a scientifically based way of designing and managing the city was flourishing, a trend that affected both housing and the quality of life in the city.

In this respect, Petrič's contribution discussed above is a typical scientific, medical view of modernisation in Ljubljana, establishing a link between medicine and space. In the name of general concern for human health, he proposes preventive measures to limit the negative consequences of modernisation. The social hygienist thus assumed a clear class position and political role, through which he justified an intermingling of medical space with social space (Foucault 2003). In this discourse, suburbs are not only seen as a simple contact with nature but also dominated by a beneficent atmosphere (fresh air, greenery, gardens) without anything to disturb comfort (dusty and noisy motorised traffic and industry). From this perspective, healthy ways of living had been established in new suburbs, in new buildings in the form of villas or multi-storey buildings, which had been connected almost immediately to the pipelines of modernity. They were equipped with a built-in sewerage system, had access to electricity and running drinking water, and, generally speaking, were built according to the new building standards and stringent safety regulations.

Another example that can help illustrate the above was the construction of a villa by a wealthy family erected in the emerging Vrtača district at the beginning of the twentieth century. After the earthquake of 1895 jeopardized the safety of households (Studen 1993), the Vellentschang family (Studen 1990) decided to move out from their dilapidated home in the Old Town and invest in the construction of a new one-storey villa connected to pipelines of modernity. During construction in the 1900s, however, the owners encountered an interesting obstacle, as the building commission advised that the fence be made "a little neater" (quoted in Studen 1990, 145). This case study indicates how strict the implementation of the new urban regulations of the building order came into force after the earthquake. The new measures required the construction of airy, light, spacious and hygienic dwellings. The example also shows how the process of aestheticizing the urban space had developed as a way of regulating the external appearance of this particular villa and, by analogy, of the entire residential milieu (see also Studen 1990, 146).

Social historian Andrej Studen (2010, 182; cf. Corbin 2019) describes these hygienic regulations, policies, and interventions in the urban environment related to the regulation of smellscapes in nineteenth-century Ljubljana, as a societal education process that involved modernised norms of behaviour, conduct, and mentality required by the urban way of living. Elsewhere, the civilisation of the senses (see Elias 2000), closely linked to the bourgeois definition of cleanliness and morality, was directed at the entire population, including the working class. To be clean meant to be morally pure (Le Breton 2017, 176). Cleanliness, however, was not just the in-domain of the sense of sight but encompassed a multisensory perception in which the olfactory sense reigned. "The lower classes smell" was how Orwell (2021, 87) summed up class differences in the West in a "sense-wise" way.

Next, we will learn first-hand how an inhabitant of Ljubljana felt the effects of the modernisation in the 1920s and 1930s.

"The collection of the immortal Ljubljana nosy parker": remembering modernisation through a sensobiographic approach

Frančiška experienced first-hand the modernisation of the senses in Ljubljana in the 1920s and 1930s as a child and young adult. In the interwar years, she moved with her family to Ljubljana, where a "*terrible hardship*" awaited them. During the interwar housing crisis, the family of five eventually found accommodation in a poor flat on Križevniška Street. During the sensobiographic walk that stopped at Križevniška Street, Frančiška vividly described the atmosphere of the street and the impoverished housing conditions of the time:

> The windows were dilapidated, everything was stuffy. There was a stench of damp and mould. Rats wandered through the courtyard and down the street. The street was in a very bad state. [...] In the upper part [of the street] a seamstress had her own sewing workshop for rich *Ljubljančanke* [women from Ljubljana]. Since there was no electricity, she [the seamstress] had a row of coal irons in the corridor. And because I went out all morning and blew on the charcoal [to make fire], I was repeatedly punished by my father because he was afraid I would poison

myself. [...] But the seamstresses were overjoyed. Sometimes, they gave me some candy or caressed me as the charcoal was always lit.

Shortly after the family moved to Križevniška Street, Frančiška's mother became very ill, after which she had to spend several months in the hospital. The father, therefore, looked for a maidservant to take care of the household of the family with five children. According to Frančiška, the situation at home was too difficult for potential helpers: "*Everyone who arrived, who saw the flat, which was extremely modest, without electricity, with only one waterpipe, without a bathroom. That [one] spigot was used for cooking, for washing, for laundry, it served for everything. But with five small children, every [potential maidservant] turned on her heel and walked away.*" In consequence, the housework was left to Frančiška and her sister, who was barely thirteen at the time:

I had to look after my brother, who was two years old! He [her brother] kept running down the stairs. As soon as I pulled him up, the brat would escape again. This was very toilsome. Well, when he got sweets from the mistress at the inn Pod Skalco [Under the Little Rock], he, a two-year-old [boy], knocked on the doors and shouted: 'miss, open up' because he knew she would give him a candy. Of course, every hour, he went in search of these sweets. [...] Well, luckily, there was no traffic so no accident could happen.

Recalling Križevniška Street, Frančiška finally came to the state of the city's roads, vehicles and modernisation of traffic. "*When I started my career in Ljubljana,*" she began her monologue with a cheerful smile on her face, "*there was only one car,*" and continued:

Our father [...] woke us up once, we were five children altogether. I remember crying at five in the morning that I would like to sleep, but the sky was crystal clear and he showed us a shiny thing through the window... [it was] like a metal bird whirring. He said, 'Kids, that's an aeroplane. But it doesn't just fly like that. There is a human being inside who is piloting it. Remember that.' Well, I could not imagine that man would be on the moon in a few decades. What a monstrous development that was!

New forms of motorised transport on macadam roads not only transformed the smellscape and established a new ecological consciousness but also altered the "auditory economy" (Le Breton 2017, 73) of the city. In this context, the tramway represented another milestone in the changing perception of urban space (see Jerman 2003; Brate 1990), especially in the auditory and proprioceptive sense. Frančiška pointed out its significance in front of the Neo-Renaissance building on Slovenska Street: "*This street was called Šelenburgova back in my day. It was paved with wooden cubes. [...] Otherwise, the [streets] around the city were mostly [paved] with granite [pavement cubes], or there were simply still unpaved streets.*"

Unlike the usual types of road consolidation, the impregnated wooden cubes were installed as a preventive measure to better alleviate the vibrations caused by the new tramway line. Other technical innovations also played a decisive role in road reconstruction, especially for the workers who demolished "the old road with more modern technical aids, with large steel chisels cutting into the concrete foundation of the old paved road, using compressed air at a pressure of 6 atmospheres" (Unknown 1931a, 2). "The plowing of the concrete in Selenburgova Street," as the headline of the article just quoted reads, took place also at night time and drowned out other sensory nuisances, such as brawls: "It is certain that the screams of the guests who left the café around midnight were drowned straight out in the roar of the machines. Many people could test their throats here, but of course, there was no hero to quell the engine and the two chisels" (Unknown 1931b, 3).

Figure 5.2: The collection of the immortal Ljubljana nosy parker (Tedenske slike. Priloga Domovini, 23. 4. 1931).

One of the long-term purposes of both the renovation of the Ljubljanica riverbed and the regulation of roads was the regulation of certain perceptions.

These events represented a public fascination of their time. I learned about the curious observation of the construction of the Ljubljanica riverbed and the perception of the river's smells from Frančiška, who participated in the construction spectacle at the time. As Le Breton noted, "[v]ision, taste, touch and hearing are all purveyors of memory, but odor possesses a rare evocative power" (2017, 144). This was also true for Frančiška, who remembered the smellscape of the riverbed during reconstruction.

> We, the kids, were happy when they started to regulate the Ljubljanica River. [...] This [construction process] looked like a formicary. The riverbed was emptied. Rats ran along the riverbed. They surfaced from various cloaca holes and tributaries. The workers loaded the sludge onto small [waggon] carts that were driven ashore by a small train, a small locomotive. It was all very interesting for us children. Sometimes we would sacrifice a little piece of food to the rats and watch them fight for it, so time passed quickly.

According to Frančiška, one could even hear the now-obsolete sound of croaking frogs on the grassy embankment. She recalled another scene from the past that had to do with the river – swimming, which was popular at the Špica, a bathing spot on the riverbank before the Ljubljanica turns towards the Old Town. This was a safer alternative to swimming in the nearby Grubar Canal, whose waters were polluted after the city's main meat-processing factory was built on its banks in 1881:

> It was impossible to swim in the Grubar Canal, but some people risked it because it was a slaughterhouse and these things, intestines, were floating [in the water], so it was dangerous because of anthrax. Sometimes we ran away and took a bath, but then dad was very cranky. Because it was life-threatening.

The remembrance of past sensory experiences, however, often revealed everyday practises and structures that eventually disappeared from the urban environment through renovations or demolition. One such example was a trade and retail store of an entrepreneur and patron (Šorn 1971), where Frančiška indulged in gustatory enjoyment. The salesman "*gave us candy that looked silky. The candy glittered, they felt silky, and they were filled with either jam or chocolate. Well, I've never seen these candies anywhere else.*" As for the quality of the air in Ljubljana, Frančiška, who used to work as a medical specialist, vividly described her concern that air pollutants were a health risk in the 1930s: "*The air in Ljubljana was very bad, because only fireboxes were used.* [...] *There was smog. So, you couldn't really breathe fresh air.*" In a picturesque description of the low hygiene standards of the Old Town, she claimed that the streets were:

> All cockroached [*zaščurjen*; infested with cockroaches]. You couldn't see the cockroaches in the daytime, but when you came home at night, they were swarming. [...] There was no water, no electricity, no means for cleaning, disinfectants, and everything else, just like today.

The analysis of sensobiography, as a complementary approach to the historical contextualisation of sensory transformations, offered a point-of-entry into the intimate texture of experiences and memories.

Conclusion

By analysing Frančiška's testimony, I attempted to show how the sensobiographical method in ethnographic research could provide a novel and productive starting point for further investigating the relationship between urban environment and sensory perceptions. This peripatetic method in urban space is a situated encounter through which one can achieve research participants' horizontal, grounded, and collaborative engagement (see Irving 2017). In a sense, the method complements cultural historians' periodization of the senses by analysing illustrative case studies. The presented modernisation of the senses encompasses the somatic transformations in urban space at the beginning of the twentieth century that touched on the body, be it the question of housing, the deodorisation of the city centre, hygiene or the aestheticisation of public space.

In conclusion, however, I would like to return to the shaky buildings and ruins left behind by the earthquake shock of 1895. Following the concept of disaster capitalism that Naomi Klein (2007) uses to describe the capitalist instrumentalisation of natural disasters as exciting market opportunities for the plunder of the public sphere, we can look at post-earthquake Ljubljana through what one could call disaster urbanism. By disaster urbanism, I do not just mean the natural disasters that disaster capitalism prays for. We should look at natural disasters in terms of the proposition that surplus capital is always reinvested in profitable urban areas in order to re-accumulate capital (Harvey 2008). In contrast to the "Haussmannisation" of the mid-nineteenth century, which Harvey understands as a project to solve the problem of surplus capital and unemployment through the urbanisation and renovation of Paris

(Harvey 2008.; see Harvey 2006), the post-earthquake reconstruction of Ljubljana based on what only began to establish itself with the natural disaster (and, of course, on the solid foundation of earlier synergies of interests between capital and power). The planning, management and maintenance of the city as a comprehensive living space falls within the realm of emerging "urbanism." At the interface of urban planning, urban administration, and capital (cf. Vigarello 1999), the hygienisation of urban space and the ideology of health care emerged, both of which were anchored in the new ecological consciousness in the form of a modernisation of the senses.

To this extend, it would be interesting to show in more detail how the disaster "urbanism" of the time not only invested surplus capital in new buildings and empty and vacant urban areas, thus monopolising construction (Valenčič 1970) but also produced space for profitable investment in the urban environment. The latter became the basis for experiencing the modernisation of the senses. In this respect, the Carniolan Building Company (*Kranjska stavbna družba*, founded in 1873 by the merger of numerous capitalists from Ljubljana, although by far the largest part of the capital was of German origin [Valenčič 1961]) played a pioneering role in the realisation of monopoly rent. Monopoly rent, which coupled with profit and wages as a form of capital accumulation (see Harvey 1974), was the economic gain of the Carniolan Building Company as a protagonist at the intersection of the local economic and political power, a company that had a decisive influence on construction activities in up-and-coming neighbourhoods.

It was also one of the few local construction companies (if not the only one) that afforded speculative construction (Valenčič 1970, 136), especially when it was able to commodify the sensory space of the area designated for construction. Such was the already-mentioned Vrtača district, a building land owned by the Carniolan Building Company that turned into a prestigious urban area in *fin-de-siècle* Ljubljana, built up with villas and residential houses intended primarily for rent. As we learn from an article published in 1882, the new infrastructure build by the company on the "Vrtača meadows" would connect the villas with the park and its surroundings, reduce noise in the city, multiply promenades as well as increase greenery in the form of rows of trees (Unknown 1882, 3).

We should also look at this precedent with an eye to the current situation, as an upgraded form of modernisation and commodification of the sensory arguably accompanies us in urban space (see Abram 2023; Abram and Bajič 2023). In other words, if the example described represents the beginning of the destruction of the relationship between the production of abstract and sensory space (see Lefebvre 1991), then the production of contemporary urban space – or, to use another popular term, atmosphere – probably manifests itself precisely as the production of abstract-sensory space. The production of contemporary space and atmospheres turns out to be a concrete ideological neutralisation of Lefebvre's (1991) dialectics between sensory space as a form of space emancipated from capitalism and abstract space as produced by capitalism. He understood abstract space as a space that is "read" through representations and is associated with the state, technocracy, and patriarchy, among others. In contrast, sensory space (also sensory-sensual space, *l'espace sensoriel-sensuel*) is a form of perceived space that escapes ocularcentrism because it concentrates on the body and bodily perception (Lefebvre 1991; 2004). Finally, based on this historical and theoretical perspective, one might be baffled by another question that will require further examination. How is the commodification of (sensory) space to be understood in today's times of health and social crisis? Is urban space experiencing another form of disaster urbanism in the Covid-19 pandemic?

References

Abram, Sandi. 2021. "Sensory Capital: Sensing Transformations in Ljubljana, 1850s-2020." PhD dissertation. Joensuu: University of Eastern Finland.

Abram, Sandi. 2023. "Sensoryfication of Place: A Sensobiographic Approach to Sensing Transformations of Urban Atmospheres." In: Iñigo Sánchez-Fuarros, Daniel Paiva, and Daniel Malet Calvo, eds. *Ambiance, Tourism and the City*. London and New York: Routledge. Pp. 137–48.

Abram, Sandi, and Blaž Bajič. 2023. "Perception Against: Reflecting Ethnographically on the Sensory, Walking, and Atmospheric Turns." *Etnološka tribina* 52(45): 112–26.

Bajič, Blaž, and Sandi Abram. 2019. "Čutnobiografski sprehodi: med antropologijo čutov in antropologijo digitalnih tehnologij." *Glasnik SED* 59(1): 27-38.

Benevolo, Leonardo. 2004. *Mesto v zgodovini Evrope*. Ljubljana: Založba *cf.

Brate, Tadej. *Ljubljanski tramvaj: 1901-1958*. Ljubljana: Državna založba Slovenije, 1990.

Corbin, Alain. 2019. "Urban Sensations: The Shifting Sensescape of the City." In: Constance Classen, ed. *A Cultural History of the Senses in the Age of Empire, 1800-1920*. London, New Delhi, New York, and Sydney: Bloomsbury Academic. Pp. 47–68.

Elias, Norbert. 2000. *The Civilizing Process. Sociogenetic and Psychogenetic Investigations*. Revised Edition. Oxford: Blackwell.

Foucault, Michel. 2003. *The Birth of the Clinic. An Archaeology of Medical Perception*. London: Routledge.

Harvey, David. 1974. "Class-Monopoly Rent, Finance Capital and the Urban Revolution." *Regional Studies* 8(3–4): 239-255.

Harvey, David. 2006. "The Political Economy of Public Space." In: Setha Low, and Neil Smith, eds. *The Politics of Public Space*. London and New York: Routledge. Pp. 17-34.

Harvey, David. 2008. "The Right to the City." *New Left Review* 53: 23-40.

Irving, Andrew. 2017. *The Art of Life and Death: Radical Aesthetics and Ethnographic Practice*. Chicago: Hau Books.

Järviluoma, Helmi. 2016. "Art and Science of Sensory Memory Walking." In: Marcel Cobussen, Vincent Meelberg, and Barry Truax, eds. *The Routledge Companion to Sounding Art*. New York: Routledge. Pp. 191-204.

Jerman, Katja. 2003. *Promenada v Ljubljani*. Ljubljana: Viharnik.

Kenny, Nicolas. 2014. *The Feel of the City: Experiences of Urban Transformation*. Toronto, Buffalo, and London: University of Toronto Press.

Klein, Naomi. 2007. *The Shock Doctrine: The Rise of Disaster Capitalism*. New York: Metropolitan Books.

Kos, Janez. 1981. "Oris poglavitnih točk razvoja nekaterih komunalnih dejavnosti v Ljubljani 1850-1941." *Kronika* 29(2): 159-166.

Kremenšek, Slavko. 1980. *Uvod v etnološko preučevanje Ljubljane novejše dobe*. Ljubljana: PZE za etnologijo Filozofske fakultete Univerze Edvarda Kardelja.

Le Breton, David. 2017. *Sensing the World: An Anthropology of the Senses*. London: Bloomsbury.

Lefebvre, Henri. 1991. *The Production of Space*. Translated by Donald Nicholson-Smith. Oxford and Cambridge: Blackwell.

Lefebvre, Henri. 2004. *Rhythmanalysis. Space, Time and Everyday Life*. London and New York: Continuum.

Lorenčič, Aleksander, and Jože Prinčič. *Slovenska industrija od nastanka do danes*. 2018. Ljubljana: Inštitut za novejšo zgodovino.

Orwell, George. 2021. *The Road to Wigan Pier*. Oxford: Oxford University Press.

Prelovšek, Damjan. 1972. "Ljubljanska cukrarna." *Kronika* 20(1): 17-26.

Petrič, Karel. 1934. "Higiena mesta Ljubljane." *Kronika slovenskih mest* 1(2): 128-132.

Studen, Andrej. 1990. "Nekaj drobtinic o vili v Šubičevi ulici 10 (o njenem nastanku, strukturi in prvih lastnikih)." *Borec: revija za zgodovino, literaturo in antropologijo* 42(1): 144-151.

Studen, Andrej. 1991. "Stanovanjska kultura nekaterih ljubljanskih ulic 1910." *Zgodovinski časopis* 45(2): 239-257.

Studen, Andrej. 1993. *Pedenarca, ksel, kelnerca, žnidar. Socialnozgodovinska analiza izvora in poklicne strukture stanovalcev izbranih ljubljanskih ulic iz let 1869-1910*. Ljubljana: Zgodovinski arhiv.

Studen, Andrej. 2010. "Ko zabolijo nosnice: razmišljanje o straniščih in smradu v dolgem 19. stoletju." *Ekonomska i ekohistorija: časopis za gospodarsku povijest i povijest okoliša* 6(6): 173-186.

Šorn, Jože. 1971. "Šarabon, Andrej (1860-1941)." Available at http://www.slovenska-biografija.si/oseba/sbi639499/#slovenski-biografski-leksikon, accessed on April 7, 2021.

Valenčič, Vlado. 1961. "Gradbeni razvoj Ljubljane od dograditve južne železnice do potresa l. 1895." *Kronika* 9(3): 135–144.

Valenčič, Vlado. 1970. "Ljubljansko stavbeništvo od srede 19. do začetka 20. stoletja." *Kronika* 18(3): 135–146.

Vigarello, Georges. 1999. *Čisto in umazano: telesna higiena od srednjega veka naprej.* Ljubljana: Založba *cf.

Židov, Nena. 1994. *Ljubljanski živilski trg: odsev prostora in časa (1920-1940).* Ljubljana: Viharnik.

Zupanič Slavec, Zvonka, and Ksenija Slavec. 2011. "Dr. Karel Petrič (1900-1944), eden pionirjev slovenskega javnega zdravstva: ob 110-letnici rojstva." *Isis: glasilo Zdravniške zbornice Slovenije* 20(2): 70–75.

Newspaper

Unknown. 1882. "O preložitvi tržaške državne ceste." *Slovenski narod*, April 27, 1882. http://www.dlib.si/?URN=URN:NBN:SI:DOC-QXEQ3F7R.

Unknown. 1931a. "Ljubljana." *Slovenec: političen list za slovenski narod*, May 22, 1931. http://www.dlib.si/?URN=URN:NBN:SI:DOC-VTSK1AGX.

Unknown. 1931b. "Oranje betona v Selenburgovi ulici." *Tedenske slike: priloga Domovini*, April 30, 1931. http://www.dlib.si/?URN=URN:NBN:SI:DOC-8ZZDIRI5.

Unknown. 1933. "Ljubljanica in njene zanimivosti." *Jutro: dnevnik za gospodarstvo, prosveto in politiko*, September 21, 1933. http://www.dlib.si/?URN=URN:NBN:SI:DOC-LTD4EITH.

Chapter 6

Temporalities of the Mythical Park: Reassessing the Past for the Future

Saša Poljak Istenič and Katja Hrobat Virloget

ZRC SAZU and University of Primorska, Slovenia

Abstract

Mythical Park was established in 2021 in the village of Rodik, Slovenia, as a project advocated by the local community. It serves as a case study to analyse how sensory environmental relationships affect pasts, presents, and futures; and how different temporalities influence people to rethink their relationship with the ever-changing environment. The paper is based on the ethnographic study of local narrative tradition and the Park's conceiving, establishing, and functioning. Deriving from the anthropological understanding of the landscape as a cultural phenomenon, the analysis is inspired by Halbwach's notion of the collective memory as a result of communities and the place they inhabit, Okely's notion of visualism as a dominant perception of landscape, which can be linked to all the senses, and the anthropology of the futures which oriented the authors to reflect on what the perception of the landscape communicates about the common future(s).

Keywords: mythology, place-lore, collective memory, visualism, heritage future

* * *

By visiting the exhibition [set up as an introduction to the mythical Park], everyone can answer the questions: Who are we? Where are we? Where are we going?

Valerija Pučko, head of the Mythical Park Rodik, for RTV Slovenia (Rolih Maglica 2021)

Introduction

In 2021, after several years of preparations, a Mythical Park in Rodik, a small village in the Karst Region of Slovenia, was established as a tourist destination. The idea originated over a decade ago during the research of one of the article's authors on the mythical Karst landscape (Hrobat Virloget 2011). Starting point for the Park's establishment was developed in the Living Landscape Interreg project between Slovenia and Italy (2012–2015), while the Mythical Park Interreg project between Slovenia and Croatia (2018–2021) brought the re-evaluation of the initial ideas and the Park's establishment. Besides the Park in Rodik, the latter project also resulted in renovating an already existing mythical path in Trebišća village on the slopes of Učka mountain in Croatia.

"The inhabitants of Rodik know every inch of their land, and a story can be told anywhere in the surrounding nature that has been touched by human hands. The Mythical Park and its 12 mythological/folklore points take you back into the world of our ancestors [...]," begins the introduction on Rodik Mythical Park's website (Mitski park n. d.). The Park's aim has been to present these stories, i.e., different folklore narratives embedded in the local landscape from which they originate, *in situ* (Hrobat 2007, 2010). Despite relying on the place's past, the Park was advocated by the local community wishing to use it as a medium to realize its vision of the future; it has been perceived as a vessel for new economic opportunities arising from the development of heritage-based sustainable tourism.

The Park offers two walking routes, one of which can also be used for cycling: the first is called Lintver (dragon) loop, leading visitors through the forest on the flysch Brkini ridge; the second, called Baba (hag) loop, is created on the limestone-based Karst part of the area. Usual information boards to guide visitors and interpret intangible heritage have been omitted; instead, the mythical landscape locations are presented via the GMS application or on the map and marked *in situ* by stone sculptures indicating a specific folklore narrative embedded in the landscape. The sculptures reflect the past experience or understanding of the world, the living environment, and folklore beings; explain the origins of oneself, one's community, and the world; and communicate the beliefs concerning the ancient perception of the world and the landscape. These twelve mythical locations thus represent materialized narratives interpreting and marking the natural environment: the mythical giant predecessors Ajdi; the archaic mythological being Baba, embedded in the stone monolith; the serpent-dragon Lintver from the Lake, a pre-Christian cult site; the devil on a burning cart called Šembilja; stories about entering the afterlife through caves; narratives of "supernatural" or liminal beings from the cadastral border, marking the liminal space between the world of the living and the dead; and the Christian legends about the creation of the landscape (Hrobat 2007, 2010). Young visitors can engage in interactive games, the solutions of which are used to activate interactive exhibits in the visitors' centre at Rodik and Trebišće. They were created to enable additional interpretation of the mythical landscape.

The experience is enhanced by the exhibition *Mythical and other world-makings* in the info-centre Rodik, which presents different perceptions of the world through today's dominant scientific as well as marginal mythical and artistic discourses (Hrobat Virloget 2021, 2023). The artistic interpretation of the "world-makings" (van der Port and Meyer 2018, 2), created by Unesco's peace artist Marko Pogačnik, is complemented by the geomancy perspective (Pogačnik 2020), which can enhance the sensory experience of the Park, at least for particular, "new-age-oriented" visitors; however, it also affects place-sensing by some (although rare) inhabitants.

The article uses the Mythical Park Rodik as a case study to analyse how sensory – primarily visual – environmental relationships affect pasts, presents, and futures and vice-versa – how different temporalities influence people to rethink their relationship with the ever-changing environment. The article is based on the long-term ethnographic study of local narrative tradition marking a syncretic mythical landscape of Christian and pre-Christian origins and of the Park's conceiving, establishing, and functioning. Deriving from the anthropological understanding of the landscape as a cultural phenomenon, the analysis is particularly inspired by Maurice Halbwach's (1971) notion of the collective memory as a result of communities and the place they inhabit, Judith Okely's (2001) notion of visualism as a dominant perception of landscape, which can be linked to all the senses, and the anthropology of the futures which oriented us to reflect on what the perception of the landscape communicates about the common future(s). We first present our theoretical framework, then discuss the sensoriality of the mythical landscape, and at the end, reflect on the heritage future(s).

Perception of landscape between memory studies and the future or heritage

The article attempts to analyse the described case study by combining the different expertise of the authors, both anthropologists. It joins the perspectives of memory studies and the anthropology of the future to understand sensory environmental relationships imbued by our pasts, presents, and futures.

Despite embeddedness in the landscape, Rodik Mythical Park is based on intangible cultural heritage. Formerly often labelled "folklore" in ethnology and related disciplines as well as Unesco, it became important for the shift from considering cultural expressions as objects to regarding them as processes and conceived not only as "consecrated masterpieces of the past to be venerated and preserved but also as a symbolic and living space appropriated by local communities who are the bearers of a collective and active memory" (Bortolotto 2007, 21). In contrast to anthropology, which long treated space only as the background of research – it was only in the 1990s that it was reflected as a co-creator of social practice and socio-cultural meanings (cf. Feld and Basso 1996; Gupta and Ferguson 1997; Hirsch and O'Hanlon 1995; Low and Lawrence-Zúñiga 2003) – memory studies have early recognized the connection between collective memory, tradition, and an environment. Works of Maurice Halbwachs from the pre-Second-World War on collective memory established its spatial framing by environmental reference points and its role in structuring our living space. He underlined that landscape embodies the tradition of the ancestors, which supports the community identity, and provides a "stable" material basis for collective memory; memories of things past survive only if they adhere to the material milieu from which they originate, and places have no meaning if they are not linked to the communities who inhabit them (Halbwachs 1971, 2001). Collective identities were recognized as structured on time-space references, strengthening the memory of a shared past (Halbwachs 1971; cf. Fabietti and Matera 1999; Jonker 1995).

In the 1990s, the belief in an "absolute" landscape was replaced by the perception of it as a cultural process based on the relationship between place and space, inside and outside, and image and representation, which depends on the cultural and historical context (Hirsch 1995). It became a phenomenon emerging from certain perspectives and conceptual schemes (Lenclud 1995). It was recognized that the meanings are not fixed in space but activated by social practice and invoked by actors who bring their own discursive knowledge and intentions to the interpretation of spatial meanings; advocated by Pierre Bourdieu (1977), space has been perceived as having no meaning apart from practice or habitus, which constitutes and is constituted by actors' movement through space. The idea of movement has lately become particularly influential in anthropological theory (cf. Gregorič Bon and Repič 2016) as well as in ethnographic practice, e.g., of walking as a "multi-sensory experience" (cf. Ingold 2004; Pink 2008); Tim Ingold (2000), among others, thus defined landscape not as "space" or "land," but by its experiencing through movement, action, and participation.

Ingold also linked movement with memory and compared the act of remembering to the movement through the landscape; remembering was found to be embedded in the perception of the environment (Ingold 2000, 148). Other research on the "non-Western traditional societies" confirmed that the knowledge of their mythical ancestors and moral principles is gained through the perception and movement through the landscape (Basso 2002, 105-149; Casey 1996, 24-26). Keith H. Basso called this cultural activity the "sensing of place" to focus the attention on "an ordinary way of engaging one's surroundings and finding them significant" (Basso 2002, 143). However, despite clear links of "folklore" preserved by collective memory and landscape, "place" as a concept entered European folklore studies relatively late, only in the last decade.

Folklorists started to refer to the spatial dimension of folklore by introducing the concept of *place-lore*. It combines a place and lore connected with the place, and despite the equal importance of both elements, the relationship between them can be relatively loose – a place narrative can survive the disappearance of the object or can "migrate" to other sites with similar characteristics (Kama 2016, 3; cf. Šrimpf Verdramin 2021; Valk and Sävborg 2018). Narrative tradition, linked to its natural environment, provides the history, personality, and mysticism as well as advice on how to behave in the natural environment (Gunnell 2018, 27; cf. Hrobat 2010; Šrimpf Verdramin 2021). Analyses of place-lore generally relate to the past and discuss the age of the place-lore elements; as assessed by Kama (2016, 3), "folklore has been used to interpret and to illustrate very distant temporal times and events." Estonian researchers believe comparing place-lore with archaeological information can link certain narrations to the first millennium A. D. while older projections have been highly doubtful. Such debates about the age of heritage underline its main feature, i.e., "belonging to the culture of a particular society [...] that were created in the past and still have historical importance" (Cambridge Academic Content Dictionary). On the other hand, researchers increasingly underline that heritage "has very little to do with the past but actually involves practices which are fundamentally concerned with assembling and designing the future" (Harrison 2015, 35).

Anthropology, established as a diachronic/synchronic discipline, has recently started to reflect the future(s) explicitly (Bryant and Knight 2019; Gulin Zrnić and Poljak Istenič 2022; Salazar et al. 2017), including in the field of heritage studies (Harrison et al. 2020a). As noted by Harrison et al. (2020b, 4) – and confirmed by the analyses of the national ethnologies' formation as "rescue actions" for descendants – scholars have generally failed to reflect "on the role of preservation practices of different kinds in assembling and making futures, despite ubiquitous claims that the aim of such procedures is the preservation of objects, places, and practices for future generations." In this article, we thus follow the call "for a renewed, open and future-focused approach" (Pink and Salazar 2017, 3) and understand "heritage as a series of activities that are intimately concerned with assembling, building and designing future worlds" (Harrison et al. 2020b, 4). Following Rodney Harrison (2015, 35), we focus on "the tangible and intangible traces of the past [...] in anticipation of an outcome that will help constitute a specific (social, economic, or ecological) resource in and for the future."

Sensory mythical landscape

Much has been said about the prevalence of sight among the senses and its crucial role in science (cf. Ihde 2002); among anthropologist, Johannes Fabian (1983, 106) points out that "the ability to 'visualize' a culture or society almost becomes synonymous for understanding it." 'Visualism,' as he calls it, "connote[s] a cultural ideological bias toward vision as the 'noblest sense.'" However, Judith Okely (2001) underlines a difference between 'looking' and 'seeing' a landscape based on whether one observes it or participates in it; she argues that in Western cultures, non-labouring spectators, i.e., the tourists (observers), 'look' at a landscape, while cultivators, i.e., the locals (participants), 'see' the landscape. In contrast to looking, seeing is linked to all the senses and subjective engagement, which can provide new insights, as reflected when comparing "the gaze" (Urry 1990) of the locals and the tourists visiting the Mythical Park in Rodik.

The idea of the Park was to set up the sculptures indicating locations of narrative tradition, as not only the narratives but also their locations in the environment were mainly forgotten by the locals when one of the article's authors started the research in the area. However, local legends were preserved in a book by a local collector of the narrative tradition (Peršolja 2000). Since she was handicapped since childhood and could not get familiar with the local environment physically, the spatial contexts of the stories were only described in the words of her interlocutors. For relevant research of the mythical landscape, i.e., embedded folklore narratives, it was thus necessary to identify locations in the environment from which they derive. One of the older Rodik inhabitants guided the researchers through the landscape and identified most of the places connected to local legends, but he died at the start of establishing the Park, and the spatial knowledge of the narratives was lost. However, despite being an experienced connoisseur of local landscape and tradition, even he could not identify all the locations because the landscape had changed drastically since his childhood when narratives were transmitted to him from his parents and other Rodik inhabitants. Afforestation of the former pastures and overgrowing of traditional paths, accompanied by the declining of agricultural lands, changed all the physical – but also symbolic – landmarks as well as everyday interactions with the environment, which caused him – in some places – to become "lost in space," to fail "seeing" the environment in the way he was used to. Despite walking through the landscape and trying to find the locations according to visual landmarks, he could not identify where certain narratives could be embedded in the landscape.

After his death, the researchers encouraged other connoisseurs of the local environment to find the connection between their childhood memories of certain symbolic places and today's locations; however, numerous discussions and many walks through the landscape were needed to agree on the most probable – but not necessarily authentic – locations of the narratives. Most of the interlocutors were relying on the specific visual image of the places, the sense of the distance from particular sites, or the unique "feeling" of a place as the anchors for their orientation, but were uncertain of their senses because of drastic landscape changes since their childhood and vanishing interactions with the environment. For example, one of the current mythical points, the monolithic stone symbolizing the archaic mythical figure of Baba (hag), was visually changed not only because of the overgrowing vegetation but also by the physical destruction of the place due to the construction of the aqueduct. The locals intensively discussed where the original Baba stone, remembered from their childhood, was located – if what remained of it was a pile of stones or another rock nearby. People tried to orient by walking around and "feeling" the "right" place marked by the remnants; however, vision remained their primary sense spatial memories relied on. Visual orientation in space proved to be the most crucial link between the collective memory and the environment, which endows spatial memories with meaning.

The case illustrates that the stories about a site may persist even if the object they relate to does not exist anymore (Remmel in Kama 2016, 3). The villagers got aware of the importance of this symbolic place – the Baba stone – only decades after its dereliction when the research showed its importance as the physical remnants of the belief in the pre-Slavic and Slavic mythical being. When realising the loss of an "authentic" intangible heritage place, people started to value narrative tradition, which was fairly unimportant to them until that moment (Hrobat 2010, 185-186; Hrobat Virloget 2019, 33-34). After the Second World War, with the growing faith in modernity and progress, local traditions and traditional architecture – today's main objects of local pride –

were neglected and even destroyed as a sign of backwardness; local heritage started to be revived or renewed only after Slovenia's independence from Yugoslavia, which called for the re-nationalization of culture to create symbols of national identity (Fakin Bajec 2011; Poljak Istenič 2013). In the case of Rodik, one of the authors of this paper defined local folklore as heritage and – having an authority and a mandate to evaluate local culture (Muršič 2005, 35) – "returned" it into the hands of people. The official heritage discourse (Smith 2006), i.e., the evaluation of heritage "from above," was accepted enthusiastically by the locals, who made it a basis for the establishment of a tourist destination (Hrobat Virloget 2019). After joint research for the Rodik Mythical Park, the community was able to reconstruct its mythological landscape and marked it with sculptures and other markers that took on the role of new landmarks in the space.

The previously forgotten landscape, rich with local narrative tradition, has become newly valorised with the establishment of the Park. It positively influenced the transfer of narrative tradition and spatial knowledge to younger generations with no agriculture- and traditions-based engagement with the landscape practised by their ancestors. It also enabled new participatory engagement with the landscape, at least for the touristic purpose; the development of "specific skills and knowledge grounded in labour" (Okely 2001, 107) – e.g., when they work as tourist guides – may result in "seeing" the landscape replacing mere "looking" at it.

The shifting attention from material to intangible cultural heritage increased reflexive consideration of the entire sensorium not only by the experts but also by the locals and tourists (Bendix 2021). The "alternative" sensing of the place was also embraced by the Rodik Mythical Park's creators when Slovenian artist Marko Pogačnik, Unesco artist for peace, offered his geomantic-art interpretation of the landscape to complement expert and mythical presentations in the Park's visitor centre. He saw this as an opportunity to challenge established notions of landscape presentations and to start a (long-expected) "equal" dialogue between science and art based on geomancy. He approached the research without knowing the oral tradition linked to specific places he studied. He walked through the landscape, guided by the principal researcher, and narrated the "energies" he "sensed." Despite the sceptical attitude of most people involved, geomantic sensing and local narrative traditions showed many congruencies. At the toponym Kobilja glava, where local folklore marked the place with legends about liminal beings, deaths, and killings (Hrobat 2010), the geomancy revealed a link to the energy of death (Pogačnik 2020). Pogačnik then artistically interpreted findings; the paintings are exhibited at the visitor's centre in the village. Introduced geomantic interpretations of landscape sites increased the popularity of the Rodik Mythical Park for certain groups of tourists – the artist is well-known among people interested in "sensing" the landscape – however, the locals generally regard it as a "new age" practice and continue to engage with the local environment "in the old way."

On the other hand, in intimate settings, some people do admit to believing in bio-energies. An older inhabitant of Rodik told the researcher, "*it is good to embrace older beech trees,*" as she believed in the geomantic interpretation of their positive energies. This raises a question of the influence of such interpretations on the locals' "seeing" of the landscape (i.e., "sensing" these kinds of "energies" of the landscape), but also of the trust between them and the Mythical Park creators; the local opened up only after the researcher shared his thoughts on the topic during the coincidental meeting in the forest.

Re-evaluation of the past: heritage futures and the heritage for the future

"*For me, Mythical Park is by no means a finished story, even though it is a finished project. [...] It must continue to develop into a comprehensive tourist destination that will involve the locals even more,*" explained a local tour guide when asked what the Mythical Park brought to the local community. The gained visibility of the Park on the regional, national, and international level and its recognition – also by the locals – as a "unique" and "magnificent" place "*where there is something more than paths and sculptures*" has opened up new ways for the community's future which, however, still very much relies on the land the locals live on and off. It has been perceived as crucial for the local way of life, pride, and identity. Small-scale agriculture, gathering forest fruits, traditional architecture, and festivities (often connected with the land and its produce) have shaped their everyday practices and, at least for some, still provide the economic base.

Rodik has been especially well-known for the hospitality of its inhabitants, as they not only operate several restaurants or inns in the village – one of them is awarded by Michelin Bib Gourmand and Green Star for gastronomy and sustainability – but also organize some of the most popular festivals in the municipality. Both forms of hospitality rely on local features deriving from the land(scape) – traditional houses or (ceremonial) sites, local crops, herbs, forest fruits (e.g., chestnuts), and local traditions. Indeed, better conditions for hospitality and the opportunities the Park brought to enhance it was the most stressed characteristic the locals mentioned when they thought about the future. The chef of the local Michelin restaurant stressed that "*our work is much more than just food. It represents different cultures, history, customs, and feelings of a community of people*" and that the park enriched connections among the local stakeholders that tourists appreciate the most: "*Together we can brag about what we have and promote each other.*" The locals active in tourism also plan different tourist offers, travel packages, and infrastructure (e.g., parking spaces, a museum, renovation of heritage, setting up other attractions) to welcome, entertain and keep tourists in the village for more than a couple of hours. Hospitality in the future, however, does not concern only tourism workers but also the local community, preserving the participatory approach used for the creation of the Park: "*Locals must be attracted to the so-called hospitable community, which will be able to present something else to guests and visitors, such as everyday life then and now, to inform them, to tell them some story ...*"

As already noted, afforestation, overgrowing of agricultural lands, other visual changes of the landscape, and the loss of place-lore crucially affected inhabitants' relationship with the land. They no longer "saw" it despite "looking" at it. The participatory creation of Rodik Mythical Park managed to revive the collective memory of the mythical narratives, now firmly – i.e., visually – embedded in the landscape. However, can they still be perceived as 'local tradition' since they are no longer used in their historical context and everyday life outside tourism (cf. Kockel 2008) neither are they transferred to younger generations in (extended) families, but at storytelling events? By "freezing" them in time and space, i.e., giving certain narratives a contemporary audio-visual form, the inhabitants – strongly influenced by expert and bureaucratic understanding of heritage deriving from funding conditions – turned it into their future heritage and laid the ground for the reflection on its future and the heritage for the(ir) future.

The key question the researchers of heritage futures ask is what to preserve and why. In the case of Rodik, it was not folklore narratives inhabitants wanted to preserve *per se*, but rather the landscape. They felt its value diminished as the narrative tradition embedding it was practically extinct. They aimed to revive – or find new – ways to engage with, use, participate in its conservation, and "see" it. In this way, they wanted to boost local identity built on hospitality and openness to the visitors, which is a decisive factor for tourism, a desired (current and future) economic activity for many villagers. Other activities aim to maintain or enhance the link between folklore and landscape. For example, storytelling events – perceived as a method to creatively transform the past into the future (Glassie in Frlic 2020, 28) – were organized for the larger public to revive the narrative tradition and for children to transmit it to them while also for establishing and practising storytelling as a method for tourism promotion

(Korez-Vide 2017, Potočnik Topler 2022). Many inhabitants were also educated as tourist guides, and especially women now work to satisfy visitors' curiosity and tend to their needs, citing "proudness" and "joy" to present to them "special traditions of the village" arising from the landscape. The practices through which they realized what they perceived as a heritage worthy of preservation now form "templates" (Harrison et al. 2020b, 6) for their future worlds.

However, it is to be noted that heritage practices could also negatively affect future possibilities "by choosing what pasts to push into the future and, indeed, in other choices with political, social and economic ramifications" (Holtorf and May 2020, 338). Indeed, concerns emerge about the commodification of the landscape for sole tourism purposes, in which case the value of the landscape would be reduced to twelve mythical points connected by recreational routes. "*The future is not as straightforward as most people think. Just look at the old civilizations [...], how they destroyed themselves in the future,*" the artist who filmed a movie in the Park articulated a possible pessimistic scenario. On the other hand, the locals have felt that the Park provided some of the anchors already lost in the landscape otherwise characterized by a very rich place-lore but needed for the community's identity and even more for their pride for being "distinctive" – and thus allowed a desired future to happen. Many restaurants and the villagers selling their local products in the visitor's centre already profit from these new forms of local heritage and heritage practices, as the Park and new events attract many visitors. While the concerns about the effects of "mass tourism" (in terms of the village capacity) are valid (cf. Boissevain 1996), the inhabitants of today attempted to make a decision from which also future generations might benefit and still occasionally debate on "what futures individuals and organisations are planning for, how they are addressing the ways in which the future will differ from the present, and how exactly they think their work in the present will benefit people in the future" (Holtorf and May 2020, 338). The established encounter of folklore, landscape, and tourism laid a new foundation for collective identity, opened new opportunities for the local people, and gave rise to the self-reflection of their (different) future(s).

Conclusion

Holtorf and Högberg (2015, 519) asses that the past "provides the conditions for how we live in today and how we create our futures." They used the concept of historical consciousness to describe "symbiotic relations that prevail between interpretations and perceptions of the past, an understanding of one's own or everyone's present, and perspectives and expectations concerning the future" (Holtorf and Högberg 2015, 517 518). They pointed out the importance of understanding how people activate the remains of the past in the present, ascribe them with meaning, and use the past to create the future. As argued, historical consciousness can thus be understood as future consciousness manifested in the use of the future.

Following the idea of "preserving the past (or the heritage) for the future," the preserved place-lore (i.e., something identified with the "past") was used as a "strategic resource" for a better living in the future. Even though experts and the municipality were the main project initiators and leaders, they included the locals in the Park's creation and thus succeeded in "democratizing" the future (Sande 1972), i.e., gave the inhabitants the power to influence its shaping. Relying on hospitality as a critical feature of their identity, the locals re-evaluated the landscape to provide the means not only to welcome the visitors but also to redefine their sensory relationship with the environment, which, through everyday engagement, forms the basis of their collective identity.

Although most people experience their every day as unplanned and undesigned, the maintenance or a change of a particular routine requires an effort of imagining, aspiring, and anticipating, as Arjun Appadurai (2013) defines the cultural resources for the future. They are collective practices that consider opportunities, act on shared values, and speculate about the risk to create a difference. Future is thus "a space for democratic design" (Appadurai 2013, 299), but also one which can be authorized – or seized – by the elites, leaving the people "deprived" of their capacity to envision. It seems that the project, which enabled the Rodik Mythical Park's establishment, avoided the autocratic tensions embedded in the very nature of the funding mechanisms – e.g., expert proposal, local authorities' participation, bureaucratic control – still, the risk remains in the functioning of the local community and its ability to give a voice to the marginalized. If people living off tourism overpowered other inhabitants, the heritage future might be differently assessed, and the heritage for the future redefined (if not simply commodified). However, as the village's cultural associations and businesses nurture not only the festivities for the tourists but also the social life of its inhabitants, one can hope for further democratization of imagining, aspiring to, and anticipating the possible future worlds.

Acknowledgement

The bilateral research project Urban Futures: Imagining and Activating Possibilities in Unsettled Times, which this article derives from, was financed by the Slovenian Research Agency (J6-2578) and the Croatian Science Foundation (IPS-2020-01-7010). More information on the project, research team, and activities is available at www.citymaking.eu.

The first author also acknowledges the financial support from the Slovenian Research Agency for the research programme Ethnological, Anthropological, and Folklore Studies Research on Everyday Life (P6-0088).

References

Appadurai, Arjun. 2013. *The Future as Cultural Fact: Essays on the Global Condition*. London: Verso.

Basso, Keith H. 2002. *Wisdom Sits in Places: Landscape and Language among the Western Apache*. Albuquerque: University of New Mexico Press.

Bendix, Regina. 2021. "Life Itself: An Essay on the Sensory and the (Potential) End of Heritage Making." *Traditiones* 50 (1): 43–51.

Boissevain, Jeremy, ed. 1996. *Coping with Tourists: European Reactions to Mass Tourism*. Providence and Oxford: Berghahn Books.

Bortolotto, Chiara. 2007. "From Objects to Processes: UNESCO'S 'Intangible Cultural Heritage.'" *Journal of Museum Ethnography* 19: 21–33.

Bourdieu, Pierre. 1977 [1972]. *Outline of a Theory of Practice*. Cambridge, New York, Port Chester, Melbourne, and Sydney: Cambridge University Press.

Bryant, Rebecca, and Daniel M. Knight. 2019. *The Anthropology of the Future*. Cambridge: Cambridge University Press.

Cambridge Academic Content Dictionary, n. d. Heritage. Available at https://dictionary.cambridge.org/dictionary/english/heritage, accessed February 9, 2022.

Casey, Edward S. 1996. "How to Get from Space to Place in a Fairly Short Stretch of Time; Phenomenological Prolegomena." In: Steven Feld and Keith H. Basso, eds. *Senses of Place*. Santa Fe: School of American Research. Pp. 13–52.

Fabian, Johannes. 1983. *The Time and the Other: How Anthropology Makes its Object*. New York: Columbia University Press.

Fabietti, Ugo and Vincenzo Matera. 1999. *Memorie e identità: Simboli e strategie del ricordo*. Rome: Meltemi.

Fakin Bajec, Jasna. 2011. *Procesi ustvarjanja kulturne dediščine: Kraševci med tradicijo in izzivi sodobne družbe*. Ljubljana: Založba ZRC, ZRC SAZU.

Feld, Steven and Keith H. Basso, eds. 1996. *Senses of Place*. Santa Fe: School of American Research.

Frlic, Špela. 2020. *"Zgodbe si jemljemo za svoje!" Za 2 groša fantazije in sodobno pripovedovanje na Slovenskem*. Ljubljana: Slovensko etnološko društvo.

Gregorič Bon, Nataša and Jaka Repič, eds. 2016. *Moving Places: Relations, Return, and Belonging*, New York and Oxford: Berghahn.

Gulin Zrnić, Valentina and Saša Poljak Istenič. 2022. "Etnologija i kulturna antropologija budućnosti: koncepti za istraživanje nečega što (još) ne postoji." *Narodna umjetnost* 59 (1): 137–162.

Gunnell, Terry. 2018. "The Power in the Place: Icelandic Álagablettir Legends in a Comparative Context." In: Ü. Valk and D. Sävborg, eds. *Storied and supernatural places: Studies in spatial and social dimensions of folklore and sagas.* Helsinki: Finnish Literature Society. Pp. 27–41.

Gupta, Akhil and James Ferguson, eds. 1997. *Anthropological Locations: Boundaries and Grounds of a Field Science.* Berkeley and London: University of California Press.

Halbwachs, Maurice. 1971. *La topographie légendaire des évangelis en terre sainte: Etude de mémoire collective.* Paris: Presses Universitaires de France.

Halbwachs, Maurice. 2001. *Kolektivni spomin.* Ljubljana: Studia Humanitatis.

Harrison, Rodney. 2015. "Beyond 'Natural' and 'Cultural' Heritage: Toward an Ontological Politics of Heritage in the Age of Anthropocene." *Heritage & Society* 8 (1): 24–42.

Harrison, Rodney, Caitlin DeSilvey, Cornelius Holtorf, Sharon Macdonald, Nadia Bartolini, Esther Breithoff, Harald Fredheim, Antony Lyons, Sarah May, Jennie Morgan and Sefryn Penrose, eds. 2020a. *Heritage Futures: Comparative Approaches to Natural and Cultural Heritage Practices.* London: UCL Press.

Harrison, Rodney, Caitlin DeSilvey, Cornelius Holtorf and Sharon Macdonald. 2020b. "'For ever, for everyone ...'" In: Rodney Harrison et al., eds. *Heritage Futures: Comparative Approaches to Natural and Cultural Heritage Practices.* London: UCL Press. Pp. 3–19.

Hirsch, Eric and Michael O'Hanlon, Michael, eds. 1995. *The Anthropology of Landscape. Perspectives on Place and Space.* Oxford: Clarendon Press.

Hirsch, Eric. 1995. "Introduction. Landscape: Between Place and Space." In: Eric Hirsch and Michael O'Hanlon, eds. *The Anthropology of Landscape: Perspectives on Place and Space.* Oxford: Clarendon Press. Pp. 1–30.

Holtorf, Cornelius and Anders Högberg. 2015. "Contemporary Heritage and the Future." In: E. Waterton and S. Watson, eds. *The Palgrave Handbook of Contemporary Heritage Research.* Basingstoke: Palgrave Macmillian. Pp. 509–523.

Holtorf, Cornelius and Sarah May. 2020. "Uncertainty, Collaboration and Emerging Issues." In: Rodney Harrison et al. eds. *Heritage Futures: Comparative Approaches to Natural and Cultural Heritage Practices.* London: UCL Press. Pp. 336–343.

Hrobat, Katja. 2007. "Use of Oral Tradition in Archaeology: The case of Ajdovščina above Rodik, Slovenia." *European Journal of Archaeology* 10 (1): 31–56.

Hrobat, Katja. 2010. *Ko Baba dvigne krilo. Prostor in čas v folklori Krasa.* Ljubljana: Filozofska fakulteta Univerze v Ljubljani.

Hrobat Virloget, Katja. 2011. "Mitično-arheološki parki: predlog kakovostnega dediščinskega turizma." In: Simona Klaus and Ambrož Kvartič, eds. *Uporaba prostorov: Strokovni zbornik.* Ljubljana: Znanstvena založba Filozofske fakultete. Pp. 7–12.

Hrobat Virloget, Katja. 2019. "O aktivni in pasivni vlogi stroke ter javnosti pri ustvarjanju nesnovne dediščine: primer Mitskega parka in starovercev." In: Ana Svetel and Tihana Petrović Leš, eds. *Nesnovna dediščina med prakso in registry.* Ljubljana and Zagreb: Slovensko etnološko društvo and Hrvaško etnološko društvo. Pp 26–45.

Hrobat Virloget, K. 2021. "Mitska krajina: razmisleki in smernice za Mitski park." In: Katja Hrobat Virloget, ed. *Mitska krajina: Iz različnih perspektiv.* Koper: Založba Univerze na Primorskem. Pp. 17–55.

Hrobat Virloget, Katja. 2023. "Mythical Park. Reflections on folklore, its natural environment and tourism." In: J. Hunter and R. Ironside, eds. *Folklore, People and Place. International Perspectives on tourism and tradition in storied places.* Abingdon and New York: Routledge. Pp. 199–213.

Ihde, Don. 2002. *Bodies in technology.* Minneapolis: University of Minnesota Press.

Ingold, Tim. 2000. *The Perception of the Environment: Essays on Livelihood, Dwelling and Skill.* London and New York: Routledge.

Ingold, Tim. 2004. "Culture on the ground: The world perceived through the feet." *Journal of material culture* 9 (3): 315–340.

Jonker, Gerdien. 1995. *The Topography of Remembrance: The Dead, Tradition and Collective Memory in Mesopotamia.* Leiden, New York, and Köln: E. J. Brill.

Kama, Pikne. 2016. "Place-lore concerning bog bodies and a bog body concerning place-lore." *Journal of Wetland Archaeology* 16 (1): 1–16.

Kockel, Ullrich. 2008. "Putting the Folk in Their Place. Tradition, Ecology, and the Public Role of Ethnology." *Anthropological Journal of European Cultures* 17: 5–23.

Korez-Vide, Romana. 2017. "Storytelling in sustainable tourism management: Challenges and opportunities for Slovenia." *Journal of Advanced Management Science* 5 (5): 380–386.

Lenclud, Gérard. 1995. "L'ethnologie et le paysage." In: C. Voisenat, ed. *Paysage au pluriel. Pour une approche ethnologique des paysages.* Paris: Éditions de la Maison des sciences de l'homme. Pp. 3–18.

Low, Setha M. and Denise Lawrence-Zuniga, eds. 2003. *The Anthropology of Space and Place: Locating Culture.* Malden, Oxford, Carlton, and Berlin: Blackwell Publishers.

Mitski park, n. d. Mythic Park: Rodik. Available at https://mitski-park.eu/rodik-3/, accessed February 1, 2022.

Muršič, Rajko. 2005. "Uvod: H kritiki ideologije dediščinstva ter slepega enačenja znanosti in stroke." In: Jože Hudales and Nataša Visočnik, eds. *Dediščina v očeh znanosti.* Ljubljana: Filozofska fakulteta, Oddelek za etnologijo in kulturno antropologijo. Pp. 7–10.

Okely, Judith. 2001. "Visualism and landscape: Looking and seeing in Normandy." *Ethnos* 66 (1): 99–120.

Peršolja, Jasna Majda. 2000. *Rodiške pravce in zgodbe.* Ljubljana: Mladika.

Pink, Sarah. 2008. "An urban tour: The sensory sociality of ethnographic place-making." *Ethnography* 9 (2): 175–196.

Pink, Sarah and Juan Francisco Salazar. 2017. "Anthropologies and Futures: Setting the Agenda." In: J. F. Salazar, S. Pink, A. Irving and J. Sjöberg, eds. *Anthropologies and Futures: Researching Emerging and Uncertain Worlds.* London: Bloomsbury Academic. Pp. 3–22.

Pogačnik, Marko. 2020. *Elementarne sile in bitja Rodika.* Ljubljana: Društvo za sožitje človeka, narave in prostora Vitaa.

Poljak Istenič, Saša. 2013. *Tradicija v sodobnosti.* Ljubljana: Založba ZRC, ZRC SAZU.

Potočnik Topler, Jasna. 2022. "Preserving and Presenting Heritage through Sustainable Energy Tourism: The Case of Kobarid in Slovenia." *Sustainability* 14 (2): 659.

Rolih Maglica, Mateja. 2021. Kjer Kras poljubi Brkine, je doma Mitski park Rodik. *Radio Koper, MMC RTV SLO*, April 26, 2021. Available at https://www.rtvslo.si/radio-koper/prispevki/zgodbe/kjer-kras-poljubi-brkine-je-doma-mitski-park-rodik/578061, accessed February 1, 2022.

Salazar, Juan Francisco, Sarah Pink, Andrew Irwing and Johannes Sjöberg, eds. 2017. *Anthropologies and Futures. Researching Emerging and Uncertain Worlds.* London: Bloomsbury Academic.

Sande, Öystein. 1972. "Future consciousness." *Journal of Peace Research* 9 (3): 271–278.

Smith, Laurajane. 2006. *Uses of Heritage.* London and New York: Routledge.

Šrimpf Vendramin, Katarina. 2021. *Zgodbe in prostor.* Ljubljana: Založba ZRC.

Urry, John. 1990. *The Tourist Gaze: Leisure and Travel in Contemporary Societies.* London: Sage.

Valk, Ülo and Daniel Sävborg, eds. 2018. *Storied and supernatural places: Studies in spatial and social dimensions of folklore and sagas.* Helsinki: Finnish Literature Society.

Van de Port, Mattijs and Birgit Meyer. 2018. "Introduction. Heritage Dynamics: Politics of Authentication, Aesthetics of Persuasion and the Cultural Production of the Real." In: B. Meyer and M. van de Port, eds. *Sense and Essence. Heritage and the Cultural Production of the Real.* New York and Oxford: Berghahn. 1–39.

Chapter 7

Environmental Relationships in Transhumant Pastoralism in Bohinj, North-Western Slovenian Alps

Jaka Repič

University of Ljubljan, Slovenia

Abstract

The chapter addresses how people involved in transhumant pastoralism and related livelihood practices in Alpine Slovenia make, remake, and unmake environmental relationships. Specifically, it examines how the environment is perceived, experienced, conceptualised, and shaped through practices of dwelling and moving in the context of agriculture and pastoralism in Bohinj in the North-Western Slovenian Alps. The chapter argues that environmental relationships, which involve relationships between humans, animals, plants, forests, mountains, pastures, weather, and other environmental attributes are continuously in the making. It interweaves the economic, political, and structural levels that account for historically situated and habituated practices with the experiential and sensory levels that pertain to the perception of the environment and the making of environmental relations and knowledge. The chapter shows that environmental knowledge, skills, or habituated practices serve to constitute affordances for the development of new practices, thus providing possibilities for imagining futures and coping with the changing world.

Keywords: Alps, environmental relations, pastoralism, cheese making, tending, breeding, movement, walking

* * *

Introduction:
Environmental relations in transhumant pastoralism in the Slovenian Alps

This chapter addresses how people involved in transhumant and other forms of pastoralism, as well as related livelihood practices in the Bohinj region of the Julian Alps in Slovenia, perceive, conceptualise, shape, and appropriate the environment and, by means of dwelling, moving, tending the environment, breeding animals and other livelihood practices, make, remake, and unmake environmental relationships. It also addresses how people of Bohinj experience, anticipate, imagine, and cope with environmental, social, and other forms of change, including phenomena such as (de)forestation, droughts, and other local manifestations of climate change, changes in the makeup of wildlife, changes due to the pressures of tourism or other economic endeavours. I argue that environmental knowledge in its innumerable forms and habituated practices provides for affordances potentially leading to the development of new practices and adaptations in a changing world and a changing environment.

The chapter also aims to demonstrate that environmental relationships, that is to say, relationships between humans, animals, plants, mountains, weather, and other constituents of the environment, are continuously in the making. I address two different but ultimately interwoven and overlapping aspects of environmental relationships. The first aspect accounts for historically situated practices and includes various structural factors, among them economic and political factors, relating mainly to pastoralism as part of the agricultural economy. The second experiential and sensory perspective pertains to the perception of the environment. Both aspects are interwoven in the making of environmental relations and adaptation in habituated practices as people live and move along their daily lives, tending the environment but also perceiving and conceptualising environmental changes. The first part of the chapter describes the political ecology of mountain transhumant pastoralism and its economic, political, and historical characteristics. The second part describes examples of how people involved in pastoralism perceive and make sense of the environment through practices of dwelling and moving, breeding animals, tending the environment, and making environmental relations, and how they 'use' their environmental knowledge in anticipating, imagining, and doing new practices. By bringing together historically constituted structural aspects of environmental relations with their experiential aspects, I argue, by way of conclusion, that practical knowledge of pastoralists enables creative new ways of coping with social, economic, political, or environmental changes.

Brief history of political ecology of Alpine transhumant pastoralism

Transhumant pastoralism refers to the seasonal migration of people and domesticated herd animals between different ecological zones. The Alpine transhumant pastoralism practised in Bohinj of north-western Slovenia consists of the summer migration of shepherds and animals from valleys to high-altitude communal pastures. There are several types of pastoralism in Alpine Slovenia, that range from seasonal communal pastoralism on communal pasturelands as evident in Bohinj (Cevc 1992; Ledinek Lozej 2002; 2013; 2016, Novak 1989; 1995; Repič 2014; Simonič 2014; Valečič 1990), individual pastoralism on communal pasturelands, for example, on Velika Planina[1] (see Cevc 2004), and grazing on private pasturelands, as, for example, practised in Solčavsko in Kamnik-Savinja Alps (see Vršnik 2022).

As mentioned, this chapter focuses on the ecology of transhumant pastoralism developed in Bohinj in the North-Western Alpine region of Slovenia.[2] I use the term ecology to denote a set of changing environmental relations, or more precisely, relations between human and non-human inhabitants and their immediate environment. Ecology is a vaguely defined concept with different focuses, such as historical analysis of human-environment interaction (see Crumley 1994; Dodaro and Reuther 2017), analysis of political and economic factors in these relationships (see Karlsson 2015; Wolf 1972) or an "ecology of life" (Ingold 2000, 20-21), stressing, among other characteristics, the relational and processual nature of the environment.[3]

Drawing on aspects of all these focuses, I will show that the environmental relationships of transhumant pastoralists are influenced by historical factors as

---

[1] The main difference between seasonal transhumant pastoralism on communal pastures in Bohinj and Velika planina in the Kamnik-Savinja Alps was in individual or communal organisation of herding and cheese making. On Velika planina each farm had a shepherd herding their animals and making cheese. In Bohinj, on contrary, a shepherd herded animals of the entire agrarian community. The cheese produced on the mountain pastureland was then distributed among the framers according to the number of cattle or sheep. Nowadays, they mostly herd their own animals on communal pastures and use communal cheese making facilities.

[2] I have conducted most of the fieldwork between 2011 and 2014, with occasional subsequent visits and interviews. The focus of the research was family farming, especially the recent development of family farm-based cheese making.

[3] Ingold stresses that environments are "forged" through activities of living beings that inhabit them: "so long as life goes on, [the environments] are continually under construction. So too, of course, are organisms themselves." (Ingold 2000, 20).

well as environmental experiences, knowledge, and skills. Furthermore, their relationships, environmental knowledge and practices are influenced by different institutions and policies such as conservation, agricultural, developmental, cultural and heritage institutions. The relationships are continuously in the making, in an "ecology of practice" in which environmental knowledge and skills bring relationships between humans and other beings and their environment (cf. Grasseni 2009, 10) into existence. These include, for instance, encounters with various actors, i.e., other local inhabitants, tourists, entrepreneurs, animals, both domesticated and wild, relationships of pastoralists with their immediate environment as the landscape in which they live, work, herd their animals, or tend the pasturelands.

Bohinj is an east-west oriented glacial basin in the Upper Carniola region of north-western Slovenia, bounded to the west by the high mountains of the Julian Alps and centred around a periglacial Lake Bohinj. Most of the local population is settled in small to mid-size villages in the two inhabited valleys, the Upper and Lower Bohinj Valleys, lying at an elevation of about 500 to 620 meters above sea level, with the mountains surrounding the basin well over 2.000 meters of elevation. The region was settled in the Iron Age. Until the middle of the twentieth century, the main economic activities were forestry, iron mining and agriculture, mainly based on dairy farming and, to a lesser extent, on producing meat and leather products. Since at least the Middle Ages, the locals practised some form of transhumant pastoralism.[4] These included grazing on the valley's meadows and pastures, as well as on several medium- and high-altitude pastures in the mountains (see Cevc 2006; Ledinek Lozej 2002; 2013; Novak 1989; Repič 2014). These are located between a few hours to a full day of walking from the villages.

As these mountain pastures were used for seasonal grazing, the locals built temporary settlements of wooden buildings and animal enclosures for summer cattle and sheep herding and dairy making and tended the pasturelands from overgrowth. Furthermore, they built the roads and cleared the paths leading to the pastures, forests, and hunting grounds. Tending the animals and pastures and moving along the paths was, then, a crucial part of the subsistence economy, daily practices, and the makeup of environmental relations.

In Bohinj, pastoralism developed on individually owned pastures in the valley and communal pasturelands in the mountains. In pre-feudal times, villages were

---

[4] For comparison of transhumant pastoralism with other parts of the Alps see e.g., Viazzo (1989: 126).

organized into 'srenje,' which were collective grazing beneficiaries in the forests and on mountain pastures. Village social organisation and local belonging were related to environmental subsistence practices, particularly agriculture and pastoralism. During feudalism (until the mid-nineteenth) century, these local village-based organisations were turned into feudal agrarian communities, which – regardless of the legal ownership of forests and pastures by the feudal lords – still considered these forests and pastures to be their communal lands. Even if the locals didn't legally own them, they considered the lands, forests, and pastures theirs to tend, shape, and live in. After the land reform in 1848, these local agrarian communities remained grazing beneficiaries. In Bohinj, the villages were organised into nine agrarian communities that were the beneficiaries of the communal pastures: Studor-Fužinar agrarian community (the villages of Studor and Stara Fužina), Srenj (the village of Srednja vas), Češnjica, Bukovje, Bitenjska, Rovte, Ravne, Bistrica, and Nomenj agrarian communities (Cevc 1992).

After 1945 and the agrarian reform of socialist Yugoslavia, the village-based agrarian communities were officially abolished, and the grazing rights and the management of mountains and pastures were transferred to municipal-based agrarian cooperatives (Vojvoda 1995, 18-19; cf. Ledinek Lozej 2002, 74; Novak 1995). During the socialist period, forestry and related industries became more important in the local economy, whereas pastoralism practically died out due to agricultural modernisation, favouring in-stable cattle farming and industrial cheese production.[5] Many farmers abandoned farming, especially cattle grazing on mountain pasturelands, thus remaking and even unmaking their pastoralist environmental relations. General abandonment of pastoralism, with only a few individual former grazing beneficiaries informally still practising mountain pastoralism, resulted in the overgrowth of many pasturelands, as well as the decay of the former shepherds' cottages or their transformation into holiday homes for private leisure or tourist purposes. In the 1970s and early 1980s, policies on the protection of nature and cultural heritage were introduced. The cooperatives and the Triglav National Park (established in 1981) aimed to preserve at least some of the pasturelands in the mountains; hence grazing rights were again extended to previous grazing beneficiaries.

---

[5] In 1971 a modern cheese factory Bohinjska sirarna was established in Srednja vas.

A more substantial revival, however, occurred with the end of socialism in 1991 and the subsequent "denationalisation"[6] process, as the land and land rights were returned to their previous owners. This was not a straightforward process; it often took several years as individual farms had to prove past ownership and land confiscation during the Yugoslav agrarian reform.[7] In 1993, grazing rights of the agrarian communities and their members were re-established (Ledinek Lozej 2002, 75). Transhumant pastoralism was revitalised, even if not to the pre-1945 degree. The reasons for revitalisation, one should note, had in part to do with the increasing importance of conservation and heritage politics. In other words, new forms of transhumant pastoralism in Bohinj are influenced by nature conservation politics, production of cultural heritage, the revaluation of traditional local agricultural subsistence practices, and the development of tourism (see Bajuk Senčar 2005). This revival also relied on new forms of transport and modernized production in the mountain environment (cf. Novak 1989). Several new roads were built, or paths widened so that the mountain pastures became accessible by tractors. One of my interlocutors, a shepherd and cheese maker Gregor Gartner, who established a family farm-based cheese company in 2000, revived regular grazing and cheese-making on the Laz mountain pastureland. During our conversation on the mountain pasture told me:

> "...it was nice to keep the mountain pastures calm and accessible only on foot. But on the other hand, we need tools for cheese making, such as a milking machine and fuel. It is difficult to deliver all of this only with horses."

---

[6] Denationalisation signifies the process of returning the lands that were confiscated by the Yugoslav socialist state after 1945.

[7] The agrarian reform in the socialist Yugoslavia between 1945 and 1948 included confiscation of the privately-owned lands and establishing land funds for large agrarian cooperatives, a process called 'nationalisation' (see Čepić 1995). Most family farms remained privately owned but usually only kept small part of the land. After 1991 the reverse process was called 'denationalisation.'

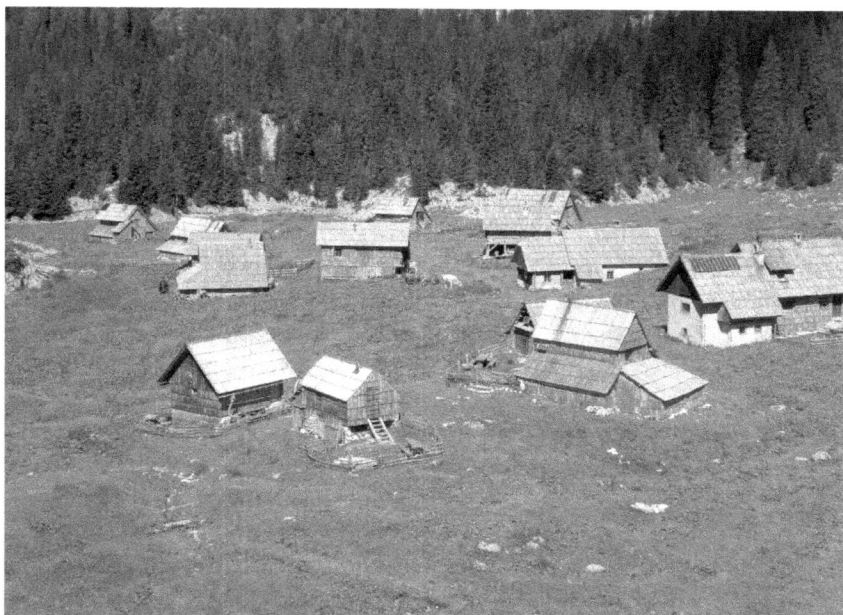

Figure 7.1: Laz pastureland. Photo by Jaka Repič, 22 July 2013.

This very brief historical background of the contemporary agricultural and pastoralist practices aims to provide for an understanding of the economic and political conditions that influenced the continuous remaking of environmental relationships; in fact, they engendered the specific shaping of the environment, its experiences, and multisensory perceptions, not to mention the multiplicity of encounters between human and non-human inhabitants – it is these encounters to which I now turn.

Moving, tending, breeding

Drawing on my ethnographic fieldwork in Bohinj between 2011 and 2014 among the farmers, pastoralists and especially cheese makers, I elucidate some of the pastoralist practices that are in themselves specific environmental relationships: moving in the environment, tending it, for example, as pastures, paths, buildings, and breeding animals. These practices are interwoven with one another and are specific to pastoralism. In themselves, they not only *make* environmental relations but *are* relations in the sense that any relation is in a continuous process of becoming in mutual correspondence of human and non-human inhabitants. Thus, breeding and herding animals, walking to the pastures, tending the roads, paths, and pastures, and cooperating with other farmers, constitute an ecology of practices that require pastoral knowledge and skills, as well as enable the development of new practices in changing social, political, environmental contexts.

For example, since 2000, when Gregor Gartner took over the management of the family farm in Studor, Upper Bohinj valley, he broadened its main activity to include tourism and cheese making. It was a decision based on several factors: as an educated cheese maker, he was employed at the Bohinj cheese company. Owning a farm, having grazing rights, and being experienced in mountain pastoralism, the family decided to stop selling milk and rather start a small cheese company, selling all the products at their farm and at marketplaces. Pastoralist knowledge and skills, involvement in the agrarian community, grazing rights, and the possibility to use communal pastures afforded the decisions for future practices, such as reviving and remaking transhumant pastoralism and cheese making. After the establishment of this small cheese company, several other similar small family farm-based cheese producers emerged and continued to develop practices linked to tradition or heritage of pastoralism, e.g., traditional *Mohant* cheese with a designation of origin (cf. Grasseni 2011), tastings and demonstrations of cheese making for tourists – which, in turn, opened the door to a plethora of new challenges.

Figure 7.2: Cheese making on Laz. Photo by Jaka Repič, 22 July 2013.

As mentioned, environmental relations are always enacted, in the making, a set of bodily and sensory practices, influenced by structural factors, as well as by experiences of dwelling and moving along. I use the term dwelling in the sense of inhabiting and being in active engagement with an environment. Dwelling, writes Ingold, is "a way [in which] inhabitants, singly and together, produce their own lives" (2011: 10). In daily pastoral life, the structural (historical and political) factors merge with everyday practices and experiences. Environmental relations are, therefore, a set of bodily, sensory and subsistence practices always enacted and potentially adapted to new contexts. The making of environmental relations in transhumant pastoralism depends upon the political framework of land ownership and grazing rights or national and EU agricultural subventions, modes of social organisation (agrarian community and collective pastures), economic possibilities of dairy and cheese production, marketing, and selling/consumption, as much as on dwelling and moving.

The environmental and economic history of Bohinj was, as mentioned, for a long time, based mainly on iron mining, forestry, and agriculture. The more organized forms of transhumant pastoralism were established with the end of feudalism and agricultural development of the late nineteenth century. In the 1870s, under the influence of Austrian agricultural politics and the technological development of dairy and cheese making, the agrarian communities started to establish cheese and dairy associations based on a cooperative economic model and communal transhumant pastoralism. In 1871, the pastor Janez Krstnik Mesar established the first cheese company and invited Tomas Hitz, a cheese maker from Switzerland, to teach local farmers how to make better quality cheese using the 'Swiss method' (for Emmental cheese), but also how to efficiently organise their herding and tending the pastures. Transhumant pastoralism included in-stable livestock breeding during the winter months, animal grazing on private pastures of the farms close to the villages in the spring and autumn, and grazing in the collectively owned mid- and high-altitude pastures in the mountains during the summer. The farmers practised seasonal multi-level migration, with shepherds and animals leaving farms and valley pastures in late spring or early summer. They firstly moved to mid-altitude mountain pastures for a few weeks and then to high-altitude mountain pastures for two to three months in the summer. There they built cottages, animal shelters and communal buildings with cheese-making facilities. When shepherds and animals migrated to the high mountain pastures for the summer, the farmers collected the hay on their pastures in the valley and on communal lower mountain pastures (*senožeti*) for animal fodder during the winter, with technological development, dairy farming and cheese making changed from predominantly self-sufficient agricultural subsistence to cooperative pastoralism, cheese making, and marketing of their agricultural products (not only cheese, but also butter, and meat products).

Technological development not only changed the production of cheese but also affected modes of social, human-animals and other environmental relations: cattle breeding increased, whereas goat and sheep breeding, otherwise important for preventing overgrowth of pastures, decreased. Settlements in high-altitude pastures were also transformed: agrarian communities set up collective cheese-making facilities on mountain pasturelands and increased the scope of already existing transhumant pastoralism, taking greater care of the mid-and high-altitude pasturelands and paths and roads leading up to them.

In the late nineteenth century, Tomas Hitz (1878) criticized the "very poor conditions of pastures in the Bohinj mountains." He described the paths as arduous and lengthy for the cattle and noted that the pastures were often overgrown and hence provided the cattle with little quality grass:

> Instead of getting good and plentiful pastures here, the poor cattle must be content with the meagre fodder, which they get on distant and desolate pastures after having crossed long and rocky paths; with such grazing, they can barely survive, let alone graze decently and give more milk. (Hitz 1878, 327)

He also pointed out the overgrowth of mountain pastures, which occurs because of limited grazing or abandonment of transhuman pastoralism:

> Livestock farming and a good mountain economy are crucial for the prosperity of the locality; therefore, they constantly need special care. (Hitz 1878, 327)

Later, the geographer Anton Melik, too, noted that tending paths and pastures is an essential task of the pastoralists:

> Great care had to be taken of the paths to the mountains, the trails for livestock and shepherds, water supply, watering places, etc. (Melik 1950, 134)

Even during the socialist modernisation of in-stable livestock breeding, the recognition of the importance of tending pastures and paths remained widespread. Since traditional agrarian communities were abolished, agrarian cooperatives took over the management of mountain pastures.

The cooperatives only remained interested in promising pastures and abandoned poor and unpromising ones. There was a selective improvement, clearing, and intensification of grazing areas in the pastures, management of water supply systems, cheese factories, and stables, which led to the preservation of good and abandonment of unprofitable pasturelands. (Vojvoda 1995, 19)

Tending the pastures by the municipal cooperatives was poor and selective. Some of the pasturelands, especially those accessible with motorized vehicles, changed into places for tourism. Regular grazing on the pastures is the main way of preserving them and holds various connotations of the importance of landscape preservation (see Vranješ 2005; Vršnik 2022). The shepherd and cheese-maker Gregor, who had cows on the Laz mountain pastureland during the summer, explained that overgrowth could be a real problem on pastures. When we were walking from his shepherd cottage towards the building with the cheese-making facilities, he pointed to patches of weed that spread because there was less grazing practised than in the past: "*The cattle will not touch this weed; it is not good for their health. We must clear it ourselves or we use pigs to eat it, or break and dig up the soil…*"

The cattle bred in Bohinj is called the Cika cattle and is attributed with specific characteristics that make it very suitable for inhabiting the mountain environment. Cika cattle came to be highly regarded and started to serve as an aid in imagining peoples' practices and relationships. For example, in September 2022, at the Cow Ball,[8] a local celebration of cattle driving from the mountain pasturelands back to the valley at the end of the summer grazing period, there was a "cow fashion show" with the prize awarded for the finest cow. Many local farmers participated: dressed in traditional local costumes; they herded some of their best-looking cows onto a meadow, where the celebration took place. The cows were then examined, evaluated, and the most beautiful one was selected. Cristina Grasseni notes how at animal fairs, "disciplining of the breeders' vision into a certain way of seeing, a certain way of looking at the animal body, is instrumental in steering their skilled practice toward the industrialization of organisms" (Grasseni 2005, 35). Appreciation of the breed's properties was shared with farmers and visitors at the Cow Ball. The representative of the Association of Breeders of the indigenous Cika cattle explained her virtues. He described the Cika cow as suitable for pasturing in

---

[8] The Cow Ball is one of the largest local celebrations and a huge tourist event, attracting thousands of visitors each year (see Habinc 2013).

mountainous environments and suitable for ecologically sustainable breeding. She has, it was said, good footing and is skilful in walking along the steep and narrow mountain paths and is also adaptable to the harsh mountain environment. *"Much like the Bohinj people,"* the representative added. He added that due to her good constitution, adaptability to harsh environments, endurance, and skilful movement, *"the Cika cow is a suitable breed for coping with climate changes such as this year's drought... Even in places with little vegetation, she will find and eat even the smallest plants."*

Figure 7.3: Display of cows at Cow Ball. Photo by Jaka Repič, Bohinj, 18 September 2022.

When talking to Gregor on a mountain pasture, he also mentioned how skilful the cows are:

> They know which plants are good for them or good for their health. If they are sick, they themselves know which flowers they need to eat to get well... They can also be picky, not eating some plants or firstly eating the best-tasting mountain flowers... Their milk and the cheese we make here [on the pastureland] also taste better because of the different vegetation.

His daughter Lucija said that when they take the cows to the mountain pasture at the beginning of the summer, they soon realize they are going to the mountains, not their daily pastures. *"Sometimes they run away with excitement, when they find out we are going to the mountain pasture... and they know very well which way to go."*

The pastures are places constantly tended by people and by their domestic animals, cattle, or sheep (not to mention that they are places inhabited by wild animals). Preserving grazing and related pastoral practices means preserving mountain pastures. Gregor also stressed the importance of regular tending of the cottages and enclosure fences, as well as clearing of the weeds and other overgrowth. If the pastures are overgrown, they become inappropriate for grazing and they also lose their aesthetic value and become less attractive for visitors. He pointed out that some other pasturelands around Bohinj were overgrown because they had not been used for decades. Tending the pastures is not merely an economic necessity of cattle breeding; at the same time, it is also a way of tending and preserving the aesthetics of the landscape.[9] An overgrowth of the pastures due to the abandonment of grazing is one of the concerns for the pastoralists who strive to maintain the pastures as part of their local landscape.

Figure 7.4: Repairing the cottages and regular chores around the pastures. Photo by Jaka Repič, Laz pastureland, 6 July 2013.

[9] Matej Vranješ argues that in the neighbouring Trenta region, overgrowth is conceptually related to the experiences of deagrarisation, industrialisation, emigration from Alpine regions, social changes after the Second World War (Vranješ 2005, 287).

We have seen that tending the environment and grazing and breeding the animals are essential to pastoralist daily life, especially for those who are professionally involved with dairy and cheese production. Breeding of animals involves repetitive daily habits, such as morning milking, feeding the animals or taking them to the pastures, cleaning, and making cheese from the milk, as well as seasonal migration to mountain pastures. These tasks are essentially practices of movement, especially walking. In the following part, I want to address movement or wayfaring as the way of inhabiting the environment (Ingold 2011).

Walking as a practice of making environmental relations and knowledge

Roads and mountain paths leading to the pastures and high mountains are amongst the lines along which pastoralists move. It is along these paths and in the places related by them (the farms, villages, pastures, mountains, fairs, markets, etc.) that the lives of farmers, pastoralists, and cheese makers take place. Paths and places of movement, dwelling, and work form a meshwork of lines along which their lives unfold (cf. Ingold 2007, 80-81). It is by moving along these lines that environmental relations are constantly made and woven into the landscape.

To describe the processes of movement, Tim Ingold introduced the concept of meshwork. The idea, however, was originally proposed by the philosopher Henri Lefebvre. Lefebvre described meshwork as

> the reticular patterns left by animals, both wild and domestic, and by people (in and around the houses of village or small town, as in the town's immediate environs),' whose movements weave an environment that is more 'archi-textural' than architectural. (Lefebvre 1991, 117-118 in Ingold 2007, 80)

Ingold also relied on the notion of the meshwork to critique a sedentary and territorial understanding of place, claiming that human experiences of place, and consequently knowledge of the environment, stem from movement along the lines that we weave in life. Places, then, are not territorially bounded units located in Euclidian space but knots of ways, paths, and roads (Ingold 2007; 2009). He argues that "it is in the entanglement of lines, not in the connecting of points, that the mesh is constituted" (Ingold 2007, 81; cf. Ingold 2011, 10). To point to the differences in spatial experiences, he describes two modes of movement, namely wayfaring and transport (Ingold 2007, 75). Wayfaring, he writes, is "the most fundamental mode by which living beings, both human and non-human, inhabit the earth." It is in and through wayfaring that environmental relations and knowledges are made whilst more or less (im)permanently reshaping the landscape. It couples locomotion and perception. Transport, on the other hand, is a destination-oriented mode of movement that carries across, from point to point, in which the experience of movement is curtailed. "[T]he lines that link successive destinations, like those that join the dots, are not traces of movement but point-to-point connectors." (Ingold 2007, 79).

Wayfaring (of people and animals) is an important component of farming and pastoralism, for example, as daily grazing on the pastures in the vicinity of the village, seasonal migration of shepherds and livestock to and from the mountain (*basenga*), walking around the mountain pastures, herding animals, transporting material to the pastures, driving to markets etc. Walking around the village and taking the cattle to the pastures is a daily routine that contributes to and enacts a precise knowing of the ownership of the land and distribution of grazing areas. The farms often include several smaller pastures and other plots of arable land dispersed in the vicinity of the village. A seemingly trivial daily walk to a nearby pasture is, then, connected with profound knowledge of place, land divisions, boundaries, and ownership, as well as local land and social histories. This environmental knowledge is topographical in that it pertains to land plots inherited, divided, bought, sold, or leased. Moreover, it is not so much knowledge as it is a "practice of knowing" (Ingold 2011: 159), embodied in the stories told about land, people, animals, plants, cheese, etc. Telling stories amounts to attending to environmental relations and knowing as a practice of being-in-the-world.[10]

Taking the livestock to the mountain pasturelands in June and their return to the valley in September are particularly important events in the life of farmers. Their return from the mountains is, as mentioned above, in Bohinj celebrated

---

[10] I also talked about memories of pastoralist life with a former shepherd in Solčava in Kamnik-Savinja Alps, where transhumant pastoralism is also developed. She talked about her fond memories of idyllic summers she spent "*up there in the mountains*" on the Grohot pastureland as a young woman. "*It was so beautiful up there,*" she kept saying throughout the conversation. Her image of the beauties of the Grohot pastureland overlapped with the memories of being independent, spending summers surrounded by cattle, busy with daily chores, tending the surrounding and animals, making cheese, having close relationship with other young women on the pasture, and meeting hikers. Her spatial memory is both temporal (related to summer grazing and her youth), social (involving relationship on the pastureland) and bodily (milking, tending the animals, making dairy products etc.).

at Cow Ball. Cow Ball in Bohinj was established by the local tourist association already in 1954 but with similar local festivities dating back to at least 1925 (see Habinc 2013).[11] In relation to pastoralists' movement to the mountains, Tone Cevc (1992, 44-45), for example, wrote that "the (hard) Bohinj farmer's face brightens when he thinks of his mountains – of shepherd's settlements with pastures and mountains that surround them. The very thought of moving to the mountains overwhelms them."

On a warm summer day in early July 2013, I accompanied the Gartner family from Studor and their herds from the village to the Laz mountain pastureland (altitude of approx. 1560 metres). This was both a methodologically interesting ethnographic work while walking (cf. Ingold and Vergunst 2008; Solnit 2000) and, above all, an insight into the importance of the diverse practices of wayfaring as an inseparable part of life, work, and economy of the farmers.

The evening before leaving for the mountain, I stayed at the farm and watched the last frantic preparations for the early morning departure. The preparations consisted of a series of tasks, from checking the condition of the animals, organizing transport for some older cows and for the stuff needed on the mountain pastureland, to preparing provisions for the shepherd who would stay on the mountain pastures. While drinking tea and casually conversing with the farmers and with a few tourists who were also there to join the walk the next day, Gregor came into the kitchen every now and then to check if everything was ready. He repeatedly told us to get up early the next morning, as we would be leaving at five o'clock. We did get up early, but I noticed after breakfast and coffee that we were running a bit late. We quickly put our things in the backpacks, put them in the car, and each of us took a beautifully carved wooden stick used in herding cattle. We were given brief instructions on how to keep the cows from wandering off the path, and we left. The cows were already used to the first part of the route as it passed the nearby grassland pastures. The path then led to a neighbouring village of Stara Fužina and over the Devil's bridge towards the junction with the road and onto one of the mountain pasturelands of Planina Blato, which is also a popular starting point for mountaineers. Some of the cows were transported there to shorten their way as they only had to walk the last part to the Laz pastureland. A pregnant cow was taken all the way to that pastureland by a tractor. We took a path that avoided a nearby lake because, as the shepherd put it, "*if the cows*

---

[11] Similar festivities are very common in other places of transhumant pastoralism in the Slovenian Alps.

would see the lake, they would run towards the water and onto the pastures and it would be difficult to gather them together again."

The entire journey took about seven hours due to the hot day, and Gregor was visibly relieved when all the cows arrived at the mountain pasture safely. He emphasised that many things can happen along the way and began to tell stories about the mishaps in previous years. In one case, they failed to get one cow over the steepest part of the path:

> You know, where there are three steps, she just couldn't go over them. I would go back to check on her and feed her for three days, but then I could barely pull her over the steps with my horse.

Walking with animals takes on a different rhythm than without them, so the perception of the environment is also different. Gregor explained that when walking with the cows, the walk is usually slower and he has to be attentive to how they walk, not to stray from the path. His wife Anica also mentioned that sometimes they meet hikers on narrow mountain paths and have to make sure the animals (and people) do not get frightened: *"I know it is a mountain path, but it was first our path leading to the pastures."* When walking with animals, specific stories are told, usually referring to past experiences of herding cattle to the pastures. Sometimes an animal wanders astray, so the shepherd must go to find it. Being a shepherd requires knowing the landscape, especially the paths to the mountain pastures, springs and watering holes, flora and fauna, treatment of animals, and the different weather conditions throughout the year (cf. Ledinek Lozej 2013, 53). Memories and stories about herding are *placed* along the path (see Ingold 2010) and include weather events, problems, encounters with people, conditions of the previous years, and other sorts of occurrences. During the walk, there was a repeated comparison with the previous year, when they had hail during the walk up the mountain.

The present-day cattle grazing on mountain pastures during the summer months also overlaps with outdoor recreational tourism. Climbers, hikers, and other visitors walk along the mountain paths that also cross the mountain pasturelands. They stop there to rest, talk to shepherds, taste their locally produced food, or visit the cheese-making facilities, take pictures of the landscape, the animals, the shepherds themselves, and their cottages. The shepherd shares knowledge about possible hikes and climbs in the surrounding mountains, ski touring routes, even about dangers of avalanches in the winter, about wild animals, and the like. When walking around the Laz pastureland with Gregor, he pointed to tracks of wild animals and showed me where marmots often make their den.

Figure 7.5: Walk to the Laz mountain pasture. Photo by Jaka Repič, 6 July 2013.

Figure 7.6: Encounters on the mountain path. Photo by Jaka Repič, 6 July 2013.

The present-day cattle grazing on mountain pastures during the summer months also overlaps with outdoor recreational tourism. Climbers, hikers, and other visitors walk along the mountain paths that also cross the mountain pasturelands. They stop there to rest, talk to shepherds, taste their locally produced food, or visit the cheese-making facilities, take pictures of the landscape, the animals, the shepherds themselves, and their cottages. The shepherd shares knowledge about possible hikes and climbs in the surrounding mountains, ski touring routes, even about dangers of avalanches in the winter, about wild animals, and the like. When walking around the Laz pastureland with Gregor, he pointed to tracks of wild animals and showed me where marmots often make their den.

Pastoralist movement, especially walking through familiar places and along familiar paths in the mountain environment, tending the environment and animals, is a way of knowing the environment through practice. The shepherds or cattle breeders, Grasseni would say, have "skilled visions" of the environment. "[S]killed visions are embedded in multi-sensory practices, where look is coordinated with skilled movement, with rapidly changing points of view, or with other senses" (Grasseni 2009, 4). The hikers also have skilled visions of the environment, which differ from that of the shepherds (cf. Kianicka et al. 2006). They learned to *see* and appreciate the "beauty" and "remoteness" of pasturelands in tourist imagery, brochures, advertisement, and numerous tourist or municipal web sites and social media.

Conclusion

This chapter addressed how people involved in transhumant or other forms of pastoralism and related livelihood practices in the Slovenian Alps make, remake, and unmake environmental relationships in the case of abandonment of pastoralism. These include social relationships among people and encounters and relationships between humans and animals, plants, forests, mountains, pasturelands, weather, and other environmental attributes. These relationships are mutually dependent and constitutive: it is by breeding animals, grazing on the pastures, building, and tending paths, pastures, cottages etc., that the environment is perceived, conceptualised, and made. But it is also the other way around: the pasturelands, forests, paths, and the animals present affordances of making and remaking life of transhumant pastoralism, adapting its forms to anticipated future economic, social, and environmental changes. Moreover, the environmental relationships are influenced by diverse political, economic, and structural factors that afford the making of historically situated and habituated pastoralist practices. However, environmental knowledge also depends on experiential and sensorial levels and the making of environmental relations, for example, intending the environment, breeding animals and doings of pastoralist life in a changing world.

The chapter first presented a history of Alpine pastoralism in Bohinj that depended upon the local agrarian community, its social organisation, and its relationship with nearby pastures, as well as forests and mountain pasturelands. In turn, the local agrarian communities and cooperative organizations that depended on transhumant pastoralism on collective lands were essential in shaping the mountain environment. Historically, transhumant pastoralism with grazing on high-altitude communal pastures developed, along with practices of breeding the animals, making and maintaining mountain paths, clearing forests and bushes for grazing, setting up cottages on mountain pastures and generally tending the environment. This practice was reinforced due to Austrian agricultural politics and the teaching of new ways of making cheese and other dairy products according to the "Swiss method." This teaching not only involved the cheese-making procedures but involved new tools, new ways of social and pastoralist organisation (collective grazing and cheese making) and ways of tending the environment so the pastures remain clear and livestock get proper food and care. Thus, the changes not only involved individual and collective practices but also changed relationships with animals and the environment.

The second part of the chapter focused on movement, breeding, and tending. It elucidated the social dimension of breeding the appropriate cattle breed that can adapt to harsh mountain environments and cope with the recent changes, such as droughts and high temperatures (often attributed to climate change). Local life must cope with the harsh environment and the pressures of modern life, tourism, conservation policies (nature and culture protection in nature or national parks), state management of wildlife (return of wolfs etc.), and the like. The chapter also presented practices of tending pastures and the importance of walking in the making the environmental relationships and knowledge. Here, the analysis of environmental knowledge-making follows Tim Ingold's argument that "[a]long the way (of life), events take place, observations are made, and life unfolds" (Ingold, 2010, S126). The encounters, observations, and reflections are involved in forming environmental knowledge, skills, and habituated practices that develop affordances for coping with the changing world and imagining future possibilities.

Acknowledgment

Project DigiFREN is supported by MIZŠ, Slovenia; NCN, Poland; AKA, Finland; HRZZ, Croatia and RCN, Norway under CHANSE ERA-NET Co-fund programme, which has received funding from the European Union's Horizon 2020 Research and Innovation Programme, under Grant Agreement no. 101004509.

The research for this chapter was also supported by the research program *Ethnological Research of Cultural Knowledge, Practices, and Forms of Socialities* (nr. P6-0187), cofinanced by the Slovenian Research Agency from the national budget.

References

Bajuk Senčar, Tatiana. 2005. *Kultura turizma: Antropološki pogled na razvoj Bohinja.* Ljubljana: Založba ZRC SAZU.

Cevc, Tone. 1992. *Bohinj in njegove planine: Srečanja s planšarsko kulturo,* Radovljica: Didakta.

Cevc, Tone. 2004. "Sirarjenje v planinah v Kamniško Savinjskih Alpah v luči arheoloških najdb in zgodovinskih virov." *Traditiones* 33(1): 57-82.

Cevc, Tone. 2006. "Kdaj so začeli v planinah sirariti? po sledeh arheoloških najdb in zgodovinskih virov do spoznanj o začetkih sirarjenja v planinah na slovenskem. In: Tone Cevc, ed. *Človek v Alpah: Desetletje (1996-2006) raziskav o navzočnosti človeka v slovenskih Alpah.* Ljubljana: ZRC SAZU. Pp. 242–258.

Crumley Carole L., ed. 1994. *Historical Ecology: Cultural Knowledge and Changing Landscapes.* Santa Fe, NM: School of American Research Press.

Čepič, Zdenko. 1995. *Agrarna reforma in kolonizacija v Sloveniji (1945-1948).* Maribor: Založba Obzorja Maribor.

Dodaro, Lauren and Dustin Reuther. 2017. "Historical ecology: Agency in human-environmental interaction." In: Helen Kopnina and Eleanor Shoreman-Ouimet, eds. *Routledge Handbook of Environmental Anthropology.* London and New York: Routledge. Pp. 81-89.

Grasseni, Cristina. 2005. "Designer Cows: The Practice of Cattle Breeding Between Skill and Standardization." *Society & Animals* 13(1): 33-49.

Grasseni, Cristina. 2009. "Introduction." In: Cristina Grasseni, ed. *Skilled Visions: Between Apprenticeship and Standard.* New York and Oxford: Berghahn Books. Pp. 1-19.

Grasseni, Cristina. 2011. "Re-inventing food: Alpine cheese in the age of global heritage." *Anthropology of Food* 8.

Habinc, Mateja. 2013. "Tradicionalnost prireditev Kravji bal, Vasovanje in Kmečka ohcet v Bohinju s perspektive njihovih organizatorjev." *Traditiones* 42(2): 85–104.

Hitz, Tomaž. 1876. "Napredek sirarstva v Bohinji na Gorenjskem." *Novice,* 23. avgust 1876, pp. 269–270.

Hitz, Tomaž. 1878. "Razmere pašnikov v Bohinju." *Kmetijske in rokodelske novice* 19. Oktober 1878, pp. 327–328.

Ingold, Tim. 2000. *The Perception of the Environment: Essays on Livelihood, Dwelling and Skill.* London and New York: Routledge.

Ingold, Tim. 2007. *Lines: A Brief History.* London and New York: Routledge.

Ingold, Tim. 2009. "Against Space: Place, Movement, Knowledge." In: Peter Wynn Kirby, ed. *Boundless Worlds: An Anthropological Approach to Movement.* New York and Oxford: Berghahn books. Pp. 29–43.

Ingold, Tim. 2010. "Footprints through the Weather-World: Walking, Breathing, Knowing." *Journal of the Royal Anthropological Institute* 16: S121–S139.

Ingold, Tim. 2011. *Being Alive: Essays on Movement, Knowledge and Description.* New York: Routledge.

Ingold, Tim and Jo Lee Vergunst, eds. 2008. *Ways of Walking: Ethnography and Practice on Foot.* Hampshire and Burlington: Routledge.

Karlsson, Bengt G. 2015. "Political ecology: Anthropological Approaches." *International Encyclopaedia of Social and Behavioral Sciences* 18 (2): 350–355.

Kianicka, Susanne, et al. 2006. "Locals' and Tourists' Sense of Place: A Case Study of a Swiss Alpine Village." *Mountain Research and Development* 26(1): 55–63.

Ledinek Lozej, Špela. 2002. "Pričevanja o nekdanji ureditvi in življenju v planini Krstenica." *Traditiones* 31(1): 69–90.

Ledinek Lozej, Špela. 2013. "Paša in predelava mleka v planinah Triglavskega narodnega parka: kulturna dediščina in aktualna vprašanja." *Traditiones* 42(2): 49–68.

Ledinek Lozej, Špela. 2016. "Dairying in the mountain pastures in the Julian Alps: Heritages, utopias, and realities." *Studia Ethnologica Croatica* 28(1): 91-111.

Melik, Anton. 1950. *Planine v Julijskih Alpah.* Ljubljana: Slovenska akademija znanosti in umetnosti.

Novak, Vilko. 1960. *Slovenska ljudska kultura: Oris.* Ljubljana: DZS.

Novak, Anka. 1989. "Življenje in delo planšarjev v bohinjskih gorah." *Glasnik SED* 29(3-4): 121–152.

Novak, Anka. 1995. "Življenje in delo planšarjev v Bohinju." In: Tone Cevc, ed. *Planšarske stavbe v vzhodnih Alpah: Stavbna tipologija in varovanje stavbne dediščine.* Ljubljana: ZRC SAZU. Pp. 25–39.

Simonič, Peter. 2014. "Pretekle in sodobne oblike skupnega v dolini Trenti." *Ars&Humanitas* 2014: 15-37.

Solnit, Rebecca. 2000. *Wanderlust: A History of Walking.* London: Penguin books.

Valenčič, Vlado. 1990. "Začetki organizacije našega mlekarstva" *Kronika* 38(1-2): 30–43.

Viazzo, Pier Paolo. 1989. *Upland Communities: Population and Social Structure in the Alps Since the Sixteenth Century.* Cambridge et al.: Cambridge University Press.

Vojvoda, Metod. 1995. "Geografska oznaka planinskega gospodarstva v Bohinju." In: Tone Cevc, ed. *Planšarske stavbe v vzhodnih Alpah: Stavbna tipologija in varovanje stavbne dediščine.* Ljubljana: ZRC SAZU. Pp. 12–24.

Vranješ, Matej. 2005. "Zelena puščava. Kulturna krajina iz 'domačinskega zornega kota.'" *Etnolog* 15(1): 281-301.

Vršnik, Elizabeta. 2022. "Local perception and knowledge of changing Alpine pastures." *Anthropological Notebooks* 28(3): 136-158.

Wolf, Eric. 1972. "Ownership and Political Ecology." *Anthropological Quarterly* 45(3): 201–205.

Chapter 8

Lockdown Listening:
Moving and Sensing the Urban Seaside
Environment through Pandemic Times

Bethan Mathias Prosser
University of Brighton, UK

Abstract

The English urban seaside is a distinct landscape that has undergone waves of re-imaginings from gentry resort to mass tourism through decline to nostalgic regeneration. Coastal liquidity (Burdsey 2016) helps us understand the contested pasts, unfinished presents, and uncertain futures of the seaside. For seaside residents, living through fluctuating covid-induced constraints heightened their sensory environmental relationships. This chapter draws on doctoral research carried out with urban seaside residents on the UK south coast during 2020 to explore how such disruptions affect temporal experiences of place. Using a socio-sonic-mobile methodology, residents undertook remotely-guided listening walks and listening-at-home activities, capturing their observations and reflections in a variety of media before exploring their changing sense of place in elicitation interviews. Participant-generated material is used to explore how listening practices within an embodied, emplaced and sensory approach can generate observations and reflections about past, present and imagined experiences of seaside neighbourhoods.

Keywords: listening, seaside, soundwalks, mobilities, place

* * *

Introduction

The English urban seaside is a distinct landscape that has undergone waves of re-imaginings from gentry resort to mass tourism through decline to nostalgic regeneration. It holds a conspicuous yet complex temporal and sensorial position in the national imagination. As described by Steele and Jarratt (2019, 1), the "shoreline has proven a blank canvas, onto which several meanings have been drawn over time." These meanings constitute seaside narratives that draw to varying degrees on ideas of nostalgia, restoration, wellness, pleasure, marginality and liminality. These narratives often make use of our senses, conjuring up the squawk of seagulls and hubbub of children playing on the beach, the taste of salty chips, the scrub of sand on our skin and intermingling smells of suntan lotion and seaweed. This 'seasideness', therefore, offers fertile ground for exploring the complex interplay between sense, place, and time.

Coastal liquidity (Burdsey 2016) helps us interrogate seaside temporalities with their contested pasts, messy and unfinished presents, and uncertain futures. This liquidity is ever salient as we grapple with the disruption of the pandemic. Competing media and policy narratives swing between fear-mongering images of 'irresponsible' masses on beaches to heralding a 'staycation' boom. For seaside residents living through fluctuating covid-induced constraints, sensory environmental relationships have been heightened by restrictions on mobility. How do these disruptions frame, mediate and affect residents' temporal experiences of place? How do resident-environment sensory relationships blur and challenge a sense of pre/during/post-pandemic times?

This chapter will explore these questions using doctoral research[1] carried out with urban seaside residents on the UK south coast as the nation moved out of spring lockdown and then back into autumnal restrictions in 2020 (for UK lockdowns summary, see Brown and Kirk-Wade 2021). Firstly, it will review existing literatures that contextualise the urban seaside environment. Secondly, it will briefly outline the 'lockdown listening' method that guided residents to undertake listening walks and listening-at-home activities in Worthing, Brighton and St-Leonards-on-Sea. Thirdly, it will share findings by focusing on the absent, imagined and returning sounds identified by seaside residents. These sounds spark reflections that entwine with existing seaside narratives as residents try to make sense of 'the pandemic times,' opening up interpretative possibilities for understanding sensory temporalities.

---

[1] I acknowledge my South Coast Doctoral Training Partnership scholarship grant no. ES/P000673/1, funded by the Economic & Social Research Council. Thank you to the residents who gave their time to this research, my supervisors for their ongoing guidance and support: Lesley Murray, Daniel Burdsey and Sarah Leaney. Thanks also to Paul Stapleton for seaside inspiration.

The urban seaside environment

The English seaside is frequently positioned "on the edge," physically, geographically and socio-politically (Burdsey 2016, 18; Millington 2005; Shields 1991). This is echoed academically, where the seaside does not constitute a recognised or coherent disciplinary area (Gray 2014). Literatures mainly herald from cultural history (Walton 2000), sociology and human geography (Burdsey 2016; Gilchrist et al. 2014; Shields 1991) and tourism studies (Agarwal et al. 2018; Beatty and Fothergill 2004; Jarratt and Gammon 2016). All refer to the physical and environmental characteristics of the seaside, namely the proximity of the sea and 'a beach with resort' as an urban feature that distinguishes the 'seaside' from 'coastal' (Burdsey 2016, 46-50).

Threaded through academic, policy and media literatures are seaside narratives commonly clustered around heritage, tourism and regeneration, which compete, borrow and overlap with each other. Whilst each has its own tempos and rhythms, these narratives often focus on a 'seasideness' of the past that needs to be either preserved, commodified, or revived for the present and future. For example, Ward's (2018, 129) study in Margate argues that its urban re-branding project codifies a particular representation of space, 'the original seaside.' The well-documented and rehearsed 'original seaside' storyline starts with a fishing village that was developed in the eighteenth century into a spa resort for the gentry (Walton 2000). Becoming increasingly fashionable, the built infrastructure was transformed with railway networks and industrialisation, bringing mass tourism (Walton 2000). But as the twentieth century progressed, international holidays became more accessible, domestic tastes changed, and the story shifted into one of decline (Walton 2000). Poverty, precarity and deprivation then marked the seaside as a cheap place with empty beds and breakfasts into which local authorities could relocate many under their care (Millington 2005; Smith 2012; Ward 2015). Coastal regeneration has since tried to herald its revival, accompanied by arts-led initiatives and gentrification (Lees and McKiernan 2012; Shah 2011; Ward 2018).

Within, through and alongside this historical timeline, seaside narratives differently configure themes, including nostalgia, restoration, wellness, pleasure, marginality and liminality. Steele and Jarratt (2019), for example, examine the distinctive place identity of nostalgia and wellness produced by the interaction between the seaside's natural and built environment. In contrast, Lees and McKiernan (2012) detail a tale of seaside decline, identifying tension between policymaker claims of successful arts-led regeneration and the sense of abandonment and social exclusion felt by residents. Brydon et al. (2019) argue that a sanitised historic seaside tale has been heavily curated, neglecting a plurality of meanings, especially residential experiences. Such tensions between top-down and everyday place-making are echoed by Järviluoma's (2017, 191) critique of the heritage industry's conservative need for one shared story over disparate narratives.

To make sense of these narratives, the plurality of meanings and temporalities encompassed by the urban seaside environment, I propose using Burdsey's (2016) concept of coastal liquidity:

> Coastal liquidity underscores the manner in which spaces, places, community formations identities, seasons, demographics, inter-cultural relations, political trends, landscapes, seascapes, the built and "natural" environment, tourist infrastructure, and regeneration processes are all themselves dynamic and indefinite. (Burdsey 2016, 19)

Burdsey (2016, 19) employs "the idea of coastal liquidity to challenge and write against static portrayals of the seaside" that risk fixing it to a particular time period or separating from other geographical environments. The concept is developed from seaside-based research investigating race, unpicking how static views, if left unchallenged, "'fix' particular types of racialised bodies within and outside it" (2016, 19). Crucially, it can help us to think temporally through "an acknowledgement of the contested pasts, the messy and unfinished presents, and the uncertain futures of seaside and coastal places" (2016, 20).

Allowing for seaside plurality and degrees of fluidity/fixity, coastal liquidity can also help us grapple with the reverberations and ruptures of the global pandemic. Phrases such as 'in pandemic times' or 'in the covid era' have become increasingly common, used to denote how we are living through a distinct epoch. Bryant and Knight (2019, 2) note that individual experiences of time can be scaled up to collective perception, creating a "sense of living within a period that has a particular temporality with a set of orientations." 'Pandemic times' can therefore be considered a "vernacular time-space," described as a time of uncertainty and crisis (2019, 2). Coastal liquidity keeps us open to the messy fluidity of this present and how uncertain futures might play out at the seaside:

> Some people, places, and processes can be more fluid, viscous and mobile than others. Those with less coastal liquidity are more likely to be "fixed" or "stuck" in space and/or time. (Burdsey 2016, 20)

By considering this potential messy fluidity, we are more adept at listening to how seaside narratives are fluctuating 'in pandemic times.'

Initial media coverage saw contrasting stories that re-configure existing narratives of pleasure and therapeutic escape. 'Pandemic tourism' in 2020 was portrayed as over-tourism, with masses crowding the beaches. Fearmongering raised the spectre of the beach as a 'super-spreader,' though this was later rebuffed (Bland 2021; Chapman 2021). Yet at the same time, media stories about people escaping dense cities to buy up coastal retreats abounded (Jenne 2021; Joyner 2021). Alongside, policy and some media stories focused on covid's uneven impacts on coastal communities, chiming with narratives of decline and marginality (Davenport et al. 2020). These have more recently started aligning, fixing the seaside into a more coherent story of hard-hit coastal communities rebounding through a 'staycation boom' that continues the revive and regenerate narrative (Chapman 2021; Elks 2021).

It is important to interrogate how these top-down narratives inform and frame collective and individual experiences of past, present and future seasides. However, exploring residents' sensory relationships opens up a different way of understanding their place identity and temporalities. The next section will therefore look at how listening practices within an embodied and emplaced multisensory approach stimulate reflections that draw on, challenge and blur seaside narratives.

Lockdown listening and sensory relationships

Although many seaside literatures draw on the senses to evoke 'seasideness,' few explicitly generate knowledge through the sensorium. Obrado Pons (2009) provides one example of haptic geographies using touch to explore sandcastles and sunbathing, thereby opening up the pleasure narrative from ocular-centric, romantic 'Edenic' accounts of the beach. The findings used in this chapter are taken from research that instead foregrounds listening as a method. This research project developed a socio-sonic-mobile methodology that could respond to the pandemic conditions to investigate residential experiences of urban seaside gentrification and displacement injustices (Prosser 2022). A brief overview of this methodology will be provided, followed by an explanation of how listening-generated material has been conceived for analysis and producing knowledge.

This tripartite methodology draws on a range of mobile (Fincham et al. 2010; Kinney 2017; Murray and Järviluoma 2019) and sound methods (Behrendt 2018; Drever 2013; Gallagher and Prior 2014; Westerkamp 1997). Making a covid-induced digital pivot, seaside residents were supported remotely to undertake individual listening walks or listening-at-home activities. As part of a participatory ethos, participants chose where to listen in their homes or their walking routes within the parameters of their neighbourhoods, located close to the seafront. Twenty-two residents participated, living along the Sussex coast in Brighton, Worthing and St Leonards-on-Sea. After their silent listening experience, participants re-traced their steps or re-sat to capture their observations and reflections. Roughly half chose to describe these to me over the phone whilst they walked, which I recorded; the other half chose to record these on their own, using a variety of media (audio/visual recordings, notes and drawings). This listening-generated material formed the basis for online or telephone follow-up interviews.

Positioned within an embodied and emplaced sensory approach, this method has similarities with sensobiographic walking (Järviluoma 2017) and urban ambience studies commented walks (Thibaud 2013). However, the researcher was positioned in an extreme and unintended 'ex-situ' positionality due to covid restrictions, which is different from more commonly situated ethnographic approaches. As a remote researcher, I used prompts to stimulate participants' observations about their listening experience and also other sensations, including emotions and memories. During more restrictive early lockdowns experienced in many parts of the world, some heralded "a sensory revolution" (McCann and Tullett 2021). There was increasing interest in 'lockdown listening' as people grappled with changing soundscapes alongside altered behaviours and perceptions (Lenzi et al. 2021; Mitchell et al. 2021). This project's particular form of 'lockdown listening' created a nuanced and in-depth opportunity to capture a slice of these changing sensory environmental relationships at the English seaside in 2020.

There was a treasure trove of material captured by this 'lockdown listening' method, amounting to 10 commented walk audio recordings, 17 participant-recorded audio recordings, 235 participant photos, 53 participant video recordings, 22 pages of drawings and 5 pages of notes. To analyse and interpret all of this, I build on Anderson and Rennie's (2016) idea of field recordings as "self-reflexive narratives." Anderson and Rennie (2016, 222) draw on the narrative turn in social sciences to critique and expand on sound art processes, which have traditionally viewed field recordings as "authentic, impartial and neutral documents":

Field recordings can be subjective, expressive, meaningful and personal to the recordist rather than purely objective documents of sound environments. (Anderson and Rennie 2016, 222)

Anderson and Rennie (2016) create narrated audio recordings as part of a conversation exchange to make sound art. By making explicit that field recordings are narratives, the audio becomes documents of their makers, which they argue is an alternative form of knowledge (Anderson and Rennie 2016, 224).

Several of the participants' audio recordings fit Anderson and Rennie's (2016) style of narrated audio. While other participants' multi-media may not exactly fit this format, it can still be framed as such. For example, one participant, Joan,[2] captured environmental sounds in audio recordings, but her commentary accompanies by drawings and written notes. Another resident, Mary-Jane, made notes every minute on sounds she could hear seated at her window with her commentary threading throughout. Furthermore, all commented phone recorded walks captured an exchange that mingles participants' listening commentary, my prompts and the background environmental sounds. The striking range of participant approaches to 'lockdown listening' in their neighbourhoods are part of their self-questioning and self-positioning within their changing neighbourhoods. Some listeners were surprised by what they could or could not hear, the tension between their visual and aural sensations, and their underlying sensory assumptions about their neighbourhoods. Some found listening transformative, whilst others found it difficult, struggling to engage with sounds over other stimuli or, conversely, finding it too intense.

The seaside narratives reviewed earlier are often told from the outside, usually from a tourist perspective (Brydon et al. 2019, 209). Exploring seaside residents' self-reflexive narratives produced by a sensory practice, therefore, offers a different perspective of the everyday and mundane. Their self-reflexive narratives represent processes of remembering/forgetting the past, experiencing the present and imagining possible futures. Findings from this research will be discussed in the next section, focused on three types of 'sound sparks' that help us attend to temporal dimensions: absent, imagined and returning sounds.

---

[2] All participants' names are pseudonyms.

Absent, imagined and returning sounds

As participants listened to their neighbourhoods, each attempted to make sense of the changing seaside, sensorially heightened by the early 'pandemic times.' One resonance across the listening material is the identifiable 'sound sparks' that prompted emotions, memories and stories. These form part of the self-reflexive narratives that can be analysed to understand sensory environment relationships. Absent, imagined and returning sounds particularly help us explore the temporal dimensions of 'lockdown listening.' I will discuss a range of these sound types before moving into a more in-depth discussion of temporal dimensions and seaside narratives in the next section.

Absent sounds

Absent sounds are sounds that participants either anticipated hearing but found not there or observed that they would normally hear at a particular location. Silent, attentive listening often brings about 'sound surprises,' celebrated by soundwalk practitioners as a virtue of the method (Drever 2013; Westerkamp 2017). The expectation of hearing specific sounds expressed by many participants denotes a degree of familiarity with being in and moving through the neighbourhood. But it also taps into residents' relationships with the seaside and how they think it should sound. Participants chose their walking routes as a way of showing me around their neighbourhood, sometimes taking on the role of a tour guide with a degree of anticipated listening.

One St Leonards resident, Logan, explained that he chose places that were "*local for local people, if you don't know where it goes, you wouldn't know it*" (Interview 17). As he moved to one listening spot on his mobility scooter, he recorded his surprise:

> Funny, it's only 70 yards from the sea, but because of Marine Court right in front of us, I can't hear it. It's quite displaced. (Listening Walk 17)

Later Logan photographed Marine Court from the promenade, considering it a significant visual and architectural landmark built to look like a cruise ship (Interview 17). However, aurally it acts as a barrier to the sea and creates a sense of sound displacement.

The absence of sea sounds is identifiable in other participants' listening experiences. Many expressed frustration at not hearing the sea on traffic-dominated seafront roads. Jane, a Brighton resident, observed how her enjoyment of the seafront changed depending on what senses she focused on:

But actually, sort of that day, when I was specifically listening, it made me realise that actually, the sea definitely isn't as enjoyable from a sound point of view as it is from a visual sense. (Interview 1)

Sea sounds, in these instances, are made absent by something else. In Logan's case, the building displaces the sea sounds, but for Jane, traffic instead masks it. These 'sound surprises' show how participants expect certain sounds as part of their sensory relationship with the seaside. When absent, it is noteworthy, often prompting an emotional response and unsettling their understanding of the seaside neighbourhood.

Other absent sounds identified by participants were attributed to the lockdown. One Worthing resident, Desdemona, noted the absence of music in her listening walk:

But normally, when we walk past the swimming pool, you can always hear music coming from the gym or exercise classes. And that's really noticeably not there because all of that's closed at the moment. And I've done quite a bit of noticing sounds that aren't there. (Listening Walk 10)

She goes onto laughingly describe how she would be "*usually walking past with my partner and we do some stupid dance, cos they're doing Zumba*" (Listening Walk 10). These are absent sounds that mark the place personally for Desdemona but also signify the rupture of lockdown restrictions on everyday neighbourhood usages and mobilities. She reflects that "*the whole sort of sounds landscape, sound condition, whatever, was really, been quite distinctive during lockdown.*"

Some residents observed how the 'usual' human sounds in public spaces were replaced by different ones during the lockdown. As Jordan, who grew up along the Sussex coast, expressed:

So it's an interesting time to do this experiment because there have been different sounds, and it has been quieter as if we've gone, it felt like, the very beginning of lockdown; it felt like the 1980s again, it felt really, it felt like we'd gone back in time. (Interview 12)

Jordan also described how a seafront park soundscape had changed due to homeless people congregating, "*bless them, they don't have anybody else, so they weren't socially distancing at all, because that's their bubble*" (Interview 12). Another Worthing resident Rafael also described how the park had changed because of people drinking and socialising outside: "*rather than being a lovely place to be, has now become a place where people, you know, are shouting and screaming"* (Interview 3).

These example absent sounds show how this sensory practice elicits in-depth residential reflections on seaside neighbourhoods in the messy present of the 'pandemic times.' In anticipating or missing particular sounds, participants expressed their expectations of what their seaside neighbourhoods should sound like, tapping into seaside narratives, which will be examined in the later discussion section.

Imagined sounds

Imagined sounds are sounds that residents conjured up in a specific location, often as part of wondering what it would have sounded like there at a different time. These are different from expected absent sounds because participants may not have ever heard those sounds or sound-sources at that location and may be completely fictional. They were often used by participants as a sensorial route to telling a story or memory, connecting vividly into personal and collective narratives. These sounds were much less commonly noted, but although few, they constitute a particularly interesting interplay between sensing, place, and time.

Two Worthing residents both discussed imaginary sounds that drew on historical narratives of the seaside. Dr X, a resident who had moved down from London in her fifties, expressed wonder in her audio recording:

> Ah, look at it, it's beautiful; imagine its hey-day, elegant ladies, can hear it now, carriages, genteel chatter, no swearing, of course. Fabulous, look at it. Ahh, don't like the look of this. What's over there? The monstrosity they put up there. (Listening Walk 11)

Dr X was listening at the Beach House park next to a Regency-style villa. Opened publicly in the 1920s, the park is described by the local authorities as "Worthing's Premier Park", replete with a bowling green and pavilion (Adur and Worthing Council 2022). Dr X contrasts this seaside attraction with a new luxury apartment tower being built nearby, "*the monstrosity.*" In the interview, she later describes the valiant efforts of the local preservation society to conserve the historic built environment and fight against this new-build. Dr X clearly values this Regency past, taking pleasure in imagining how the "*genteel*" classes would have sounded in the park.

Desdemona, a historian who also moved to Worthing in recent years but from Brighton, combines actual and imagined sounds whilst discussing a different working-class history. Whilst walking on the beach, she notes the sounds of a mechanised hauling system boat, which sparks a story about the local fishing community. Although she initially names this an "*enduring sound,*" she quickly qualifies this and starts imagining how this industry might have sounded different in the past without such mechanisation. Desdemona goes onto recount how she volunteered for a local history project called *The Last Fisherman Standing,* premised on the last full-time working fisherman retiring in 2015. She used her skills to meet new people and get involved in her new home when she had recently moved. These examples of imagined historic sounds show how both residents place value on seaside histories in their relationships with the seaside. They focus on different parts of the seaside timeline, but both evoke the sounds of the past. For Desdemona, it represents a significant experience of getting to know her new town; for Dr X, such sensorial imaginings bring joy.

Some other residents engaged in a degree of imaginary listening. But in these cases, participants intentionally invented a fantasy sound-source causing the sound they could hear. Rafael noted scaffolding on his walk but instead described the sounds of boats: "*as the wind rushes through it, it sounds a bit like a quay or a harbour, sounds like lots of sails*" (Listening Walk 3). In his interview, he later explains how he enjoys imagining that something else is causing the sounds:

> The sound of the scaffolding opposite is delightful. I really like it. It does sound like I live near a quay or regatta or something. (Listening Walk 3)

This form of imaginary listening does not necessarily draw from the past, but it signifies a particular imagining of living by the seaside. Quays and regattas have an upper- and middle-class association as opposed to the working-class livelihoods represented by Desdemona's fishing story. These imagined sounds also tap into what residents think the seaside ought to sound like, sharing a characteristic with absent sounds.

Returning sounds

Returning sounds are sounds that participants observed they were able to start hearing again after being absent during the strictest spring lockdown. These sounds are the most specific to 'lockdown listening' as residents tried to make sense of 'the pandemic times.' There are variations in what participants perceived had stopped sounding during the strict lockdown and which they chose to reflect on. 'Returning' gives the impression of the environment going back to 'the before times,' another pandemic "vernacular timescape" (Bryant and Knight 2019). However, participant reflections encompassed a temporal and affective range, from welcoming back sounds to sonic anticipation of uncertain futures.

The re-introduction of construction sounds, in particular scaffolding, was a striking and frequently discussed returning sound. As stated by Brighton resident Tim:

> What is very noticeable now is all the scaffolding, and the builders are back. For a while there was hardly any of that, which is very unusual... You know, it's a noisy business putting up scaffolding. The whole seafront is all, the buildings are about 200 years old so it's not surprising they need a lot of work. (Listening Walk 5)

Participant descriptions of scaffolding poles clanging, clamps being drilled and scaffolders calling out to each other commonly went hand-in-hand with observations about constant neighbourhood renovation. Several commented on how jarring these sounds appeared after a period of relative quietness. Llewellyn, a Brighton resident listening at home, found the sound frustrating but also commented:

> I suppose it's a sign that people are back to normal and work is continuing despite the coronavirus. (Listening-at-home activity 4)

Whilst there was a new awareness of building works post-lockdown, most residents observed this was a common part of their neighbourhood soundscape. Like Tim, they ascribed this to the salty wind conditions requiring extra up-keep of the Regency architecture. Others also attributed constant renovation to gentrification, both DIY pioneer homeowners and landlords upgrading to exploit a profitable rental market. The construction sounds of bigger redevelopment projects, such as "*the monstrosity*" noted by Dr X, were also observed to be returning. However, there was less certainty about how these would unfold during and post-pandemic.

All participants noted how the sound of traffic dominated the listening activities, which was another type of returning sound. As described earlier, participants were often surprised by how much the traffic masked other sounds. Jordan found it difficult to listen on the seafront road because traffic had "*been dubbed over everything else*" (Interview 12). Several participants recounted how the traffic had been stopped during the early lockdown. In Brighton, Jane explained how cars continued to be banned in the lower seafront promenade to allow for better social distancing, resulting in a battle to make this permanent (Interview 1). She welcomed this debate and felt the impact of cars strongly:

> You know from the walk I did with the sound, it's quite a heavy traffic area round here. And, you know, that's not always very pleasant when we live here, you know, cos of the car fumes, cos of the sound and everything. And, erm, obviously, the natural habitat. (Interview 1)

Many residents expressed anti-car rhetoric. The use of walking methods may have attracted participants with a pedestrian preference. However, the stark absence of traffic followed by its return also appears to have heightened these sentiments. As shown in Jane's reflections:

> But, if you think when people are told, only get in your car if you really, really have to, you have to work, you have to get some food. And it makes, and then suddenly the streets are really, really clear. It makes you think, then, are those journeys really necessary?

The pandemic rupture prompted residents to think about future neighbourhood mobilities, opening up different imaginings during the early pandemic times.

Returning sounds, therefore, let us hear the ways the pandemic heightened residents' sensory relationships to their neighbourhood environments in the present as well as re-think future possibilities. The next section will further interrogate such temporal dimensions, putting residents' self-reflexive narratives into dialogue with existing seaside narratives.

Self-reflexive narratives on pasts, presents and futures

Absent, imagined, and returning sounds offer a distinct way of examining residential sensory relationships. This last section will draw out the temporal dimensions identified in these 'sound sparks,' examining how participants were grappling with 'the pandemic times' from early summer into autumn 2020. All discussed the pandemic disruption in detail, some in more temporally explicit ways. For example, Desdemona commented, "*time under Covid is doing strange, stretchy and contracty things*" (Interview 10). This disruption frames, mediates and affects existing coastal liquidity at these urban seaside sites, with different degrees of stretchy fluidity and entanglement with existing seaside narratives (Burdsey 2016). Absent, imagined, and returning sounds can be mapped against the contested pasts, messy and unfinished presents, and uncertain futures to which coastal liquidity makes us attend. However, in doing so, linear temporal distinctions are challenged and blurred, making audible the complex ways in which the pandemic has affected residents' temporal and sensorial experiences of place.

Absent sounds: messy and unfinished presents?

Absent sounds are expected as part of everyday soundscapes; therefore, they most closely align with messy and unfinished presents. However, as already discussed, the sensory relationships that can be unravelled from such sounds look to the past and affect future imaginings. In the examples identified, the majority of absent sounds represent a challenge to something that participants would normally find enjoyable living by the seaside. For Jane, she enjoys the sea view, but by focusing on listening, her enjoyment is challenged, and she is made conscious of urban sounds. In her interview, Jane explains how important nature is to her, which taps into restorative and wellness themes of the seaside. However, the disconnect between the sea view and the sea road sounds reveals the tension between the natural and urban environment. This adds a different angle to understandings of the interaction between the natural and built environment producing 'seasideness.' The discussion usually draws on a tourist perspective and focuses on seaside buildings of the past (Steele and Jarratt 2019). The ship-like Marine Court, captured by Logan, fits the *Seaside Moderne* architecture more commonly discussed as restorative (Steele and Jarratt 2019). Yet, from a residential perspective, the built environment can be expanded to the mundanity of roads.

Jane also identifies as an activist, including involvement in climate change campaigns. Anti-car discussions permeate the interview, prompted by the absent sea sounds and also the returning sounds of traffic. She attributes increased and different types of car usage to more affluent people moving into the area, explaining, "*You notice it by the cars*" (Interview 1). When asked if the pandemic might affect future car mobilities, she answered uncertainly, "*I hope so, but I just don't see, I just don't really see that.*" This example details some of the messiness of present sensory experiences of the seaside that challenge more fixed narratives of the seaside, both personal and collective. But it also threads into uncertain futures, which for Jane, include concerns over ongoing gentrification at the neighbourhood level and climate change at the global.

The other absent sounds identified above are more specific to the pandemic disruption and messiness of the lockdown present. Desdemona's missing music appears to trigger a sense of nostalgia for a more joyful care-free way of navigating public space with her partner pre-pandemic. Jordan's reflection that the early lockdown *"felt like the 1980s again"* also evokes this emotional state (Interview 12). Nostalgia abounds in seaside narratives, often understood as a reconnection to the past or a different perception of time, reflecting a *"dissatisfaction with the present"* (Steele and Jarratt 2019, 4). Although this is nostalgia for a very recent past, it chimes with a pandemic vernacular timescape that creates a distinct 'before times.' Jordan and Rafael's discussions grapple with public space soundscapes by contrasting the current with the recent past. Although their observations of street drinkers and the homeless community chime with a less nostalgic seaside past, linking instead into seaside narratives of decline and marginality. Absent sounds, therefore, present a different way of understanding the seaside, which challenges and blurs existing narratives and reveal the messy way they might be experienced, sensed, and related to in the present.

Imagined sounds: contested pasts?

The two main imagined sounds discussed earlier draw on historic pasts: the first, an upper-class Regency resort, and the second, a lost working-class fishing industry. These contrasting class histories immediately indicate their contested nature, signifying how these types of sounds might map onto contested pasts. However, both utilise this history to heighten their current sensory relationships with their neighbourhoods. Shared seaside heritage helps them understand the present changing environment and anticipated futures.

Dr X's enjoyment of the Regency's history chimes again with the restorative and nostalgia themes. Desdemona's old fishing industry sounds and community efforts to document it pluralise this seaside historical narrative. However, both quickly bring these into the present. For Desdemona, it represents a significant part of her relationship with Worthing as a historian and a newcomer. Dr X also contrasts Regency sounds with present redevelopments of the seafront and the need for preserving this heritage. Dr X goes into a detailed discussion in her interview about how *"the monstrosity"* luxury new-build is out of place at the seaside. She associates *"shiny white towers"* instead with London, dramatically describing them as *"an ode to everything that's wrong with our current political system"* (Interview 11).

Prioritising historic buildings and viewing redevelopment as out of place fixes Worthing spatially and temporally. Dr X expresses future fears of seaside gentrification, desiring a different urban trajectory. However, the pandemic potentially gives a future reprieve to the spectre of new-build gentrification. She muses that:

> As we're about to go into a recession, I don't see how any of this building's going to... I think there'll just sit on the land for a long time. (Interview 11)

In contrast, Rafael's imaginings about the sounds of scaffolding represent a different way of relating to and narrating changes to the built environment. Rafael was the only participant who liked this new-build for being "*a practical and pragmatic solution to a difficult* [housing] *problem*" (Interview 3). He taps into the regenerate narrative, viewing the sound of construction as a defining aspect of urban living: "*part of living in a town is that it's never finished*" (Interview 3). As part of residents' relationships to the seaside, these imagined sounds, therefore, strongly relate to contested pasts but reveal the complex ways they entwine with unfinished presents and uncertain futures.

Returning sounds: uncertain futures?

Although returning sounds are those coming back from the past and entangled with the present, predominantly, these sounds sparked reflections on possible future trajectories of urban seaside neighbourhoods. For residents, construction sounds signified a return to constant renovation, a classic gentrification feature. The distinct coming together of Regency buildings requiring upkeep against salty winds shows another different built/nature environment interaction than usually noted in seaside literatures (Steele and Jarratt 2019). Tim and Llewellyn both explained the grade-listed regulations surrounding the constant upkeep of their own Regency flats. These policies are part of a heritage narrative that views historic buildings as tourist and place-branded commodities. However, the jarring nature of construction sounds commented on by residents show the heritage and tourism impacts on residents' everyday sensory experiences.

As already discussed, construction immediately brings up reflections on the future, whether fears over losing the seaside of the past and present (Dr X) or representing the seemingly natural trajectory of urban redevelopment (Rafael). Constant changes to the built environment and Rafael's description of town living strikingly embody the unfinished present. But for some, the pandemic disruption appears to have opened up the possibility of a different type of future. At the time of her interview, Dr X felt that a recession was inevitable, which would break the current wave of gentrification-related construction

(Interview 11). Other participants also wondered how public-private partnership redevelopments might progress post-pandemic. As commented by Mary-Jane:

> I mean, now, after all this situation, I imagine councils will have absolutely no money for them to do anything. We're going to have completely rethink all sorts of things, aren't we? (Interview 6).

This uncertainty expressed by participants mixes different future orientations, including speculation, potentiality and hope (Bryant and Knight 2019).

The anti-car rhetoric connected to the return of dominating traffic sounds also prompted future speculation. For example, Barney had turned back from his planned seafront walk due to the overwhelming sensory discomfort produced by traffic in Brighton (Listening Walk 18). This prompted him to imagine his neighbourhood differently:

> Do we really need so much private car ownership here? And, you know, I just think it would be great just to stop private cars just invading all these residential parts of the city. It would take a lot of change and a lot of effort, a lot of hard upset and shenanigans for that to be achieved. But I would be, I'd be so much happier living in a place where traffic, the noise, the pollution, were lowered. (Interview 18)

The returning traffic sounds, therefore, disturb the pleasure and wellness narratives of existing seaside narratives. But they also ignite a rethink of possible and desirable futures. These future rethinks bring in consideration of mobility, environmental, climate, housing, and urban justice. For Dr X, she hopes the new-build gentrification that she fears cascading down from London will be paused, even if only temporarily, whilst land banking takes place. For Barney, although acknowledging the "*upset and shenanigans,*" he dares to imagine a safer, less polluted, and quieter environment within which he could have a happier life.

Returning sounds, therefore, entangle past, present, and future as participants grapple with having experienced a shift in their sensory-environmental relationships. The "*strange, stretchy and contracty things*" that the pandemic has done to time (Desdemona, Interview 10) presents an opportunity for participants to reflect on and rethink the future of their seaside neighbourhoods. These are narrated with different degrees of hope and cynicism. Whether this change plays out or not, these temporal disruptions challenge dominant seaside narratives that do not commonly engage with residential concerns or issues of urban justice.

Conclusion

This chapter has brought together the urban seaside environment with an embodied and emplaced sensory practice to explore the complex interplay between sensing, time, and place. The English urban seaside environment entangles a plurality of meanings, including different policy and media narratives that have been challenged by the global pandemic disruption. Tourism, heritage and regeneration narratives often focus on the outsider viewpoint; therefore, this research project offers a different understanding through residents' aural perceptions. I argue that the concept of coastal liquidity can help us better attend to plural perceptions, tuning into differing degrees of fluidity/fixity (Burdsey 2016). 'Lockdown listening' has generated nuanced and in-depth material, which can be framed as "self-reflexive narratives" (Anderson and Tullis 2016). Using this framework, I have examined three types of sounds that participants identified in their listening activities. Absent, imagined, and returning sounds sparked emotional responses, memories and stories, which encompass complex temporalities. These temporalities have been mapped against the contested pasts, messy and unfinished presents, and uncertain futures offered by the coastal liquidity conceptualisation.

Through this mapping, it has become apparent that there is a high degree of fluidity in the ways participants engage with time in their sensory environmental relationships. Residents draw on different historic pasts as they grapple with the messiness of the present and imagine the future. Some conform with existing seaside narratives, whilst others blur and challenge more fixed notions of the seaside. But all continually move between different time states. Historical and more immediate pasts are used to relate and engage with the present seaside environment. The unfinished present sparks speculation of possible futures. Whilst the current environment also ignites sensory imaginings of the past. These findings, therefore, expand the notion of coastal liquidity by revealing the non-linear experience of time in residential seaside sensory relationships. 'The pandemic times' created a momentary shift in the way residents moved through, sensed, and related to the seaside, raising questions about how these relationships will continue to unfold during and eventually post-pandemic.

References

Adur and Worthing Council. *Beach House Park.* Available at https://www.adur-worthing.gov.uk/parks/find/worthing/beach-house-park/, accessed on February 13, 2023.

Agarwal, Sheela et al. 2018. "Disadvantage in English seaside resorts: A typology of deprived neighbourhoods." *Tourism Management* 69: 440-459.

Anderson, Isobel and Tullis Rennie. 2016. "Thoughts in the field: 'Self-reflexive narrative' in field recording." *Organised Sound: An International Journal of Music Technology* 21 (3): 222-232.

Beatty, Christina and Steve Fothergill. 2004. "Economic change and the labour market in Britain's seaside towns." *Regional Studies* 38 (5): 459-480.

Behrendt, Frauke. 2018. "Soundwalking." In: M. Bull, ed. *The Routledge Companion to Sound Studies*. London: Routledge.

Bland, Archie. 2021. "How the beach 'super-spreader' myth can inform UK's future covid response." The Guardian. Available at https://www.the guardian.com/world/2021/feb/19/how-the-beach-super-spreader-myth-can -inform-uks-future-covid-response, accessed on February 13, 2023.

Brown, Jennifer, and Esme Kirk-Wade. 2021. *Coronavirus: A history of 'lockdown laws' in England*, No. 9068, House of Commons Library [Online].

Bryant, Rebecca and Daniel Knight. 2019. "Orientations to the future: An introduction." In: Rebecca Bryant and Daniel Knight, ed. *Orientations to the Future. American Ethnologist*. Available at https://americanethnologist.org/ features/collections/orientations-to-the-future/orientations-to-the-future-an-introduction, accessed February 13, 2023.

Brydon, Lavinia, Olu Jenzen, and Nicholas Nourse. 2019. "'Our pier': Leisure activities and local communities at the British seaside." *Leisure/Loisir* 43 (2): 205-228.

Burdsey, Daniel. 2016. *Race, Place and the Seaside: Postcards from the Edge*. Basingstoke: Palgrave Macmillan.

Chapman, Anna. 2021. "How the pandemic has changed holidaymaking in Britain." *The Conversation*. Available at https://theconversation.com/how-the-pandemic-has-changed-holidaymaking-in-britain-168409, accessed on February 14, 2022.

Davenport, Alex et al. 2020 *The geography of the covid-19 crisis in England*, Institute for Fiscal Studies [Online]. Available at https://www.nuffield foundation.org/news/geographic-impact-covid-19-crisis-diffuse, accessed February 14 2022.

Drever, John Levack. 2013. "Silent soundwalking: An urban pedestrian soundscape methodology." Paper read at *AIA-DAGA 2013, the joint Conference on Acoustics, European Acoustics Association Euroregio, 39th annual congress of the Deutsche Gesellschaft für Akustik and the 40th annual congress of the Associazione Italiana di Acustica*, at Merano, Italy.

Elks, Sonia. 2021. "As covid-19 hits holiday plans, deprived UK coastal towns see opportunity." Thomson Reuters Foundation. Available at https://www. reuters.com/article/us-health-coronavirus-britain-tourism-tr-idUSKCN2D Q1ET, accessed February 14 2022.

Fincham, Ben, Mark McGuinness, and Lesley Murray. 2010. *Mobile Methodologies*. Basingstoke: Palgrave Macmillan.

Gallagher, Michael, and Jonathan Prior. 2014. "Sonic geographies: Exploring phonographic methods." *Progress in Human Geography* 38 (2): 267-284.

Gilchrist, Paul, Thomas Carter, and Daniel Burdsey, eds. 2014. *Coastal Cultures: Liminality and Leisure.* Vol. no. 123. Eastbourne: LSA.

Gray, Fred. 2014. "Foreword." In: Gilchrist, Paul, Thomas Carter, and Daniel Burdsey, eds. *Coastal Cultures: Liminality and Leisure.* Croydon: Leisure Studies Association.

Jarratt, David, and Sean Gammon. 2016. "'We had the most wonderful times': Seaside nostalgia at a British resort." *Tourism Recreation Research* 41 (2): 123-133.

Järviluoma, Helmi. 2017. "The art and science of sensory memory walking." In: Marcel Cobussen, Vincent Meelberg, Barry Truax, eds. *The Routledge Companion to Sounding Art.* Abingdon: Routledge.

Jenne, Ellen. 2021. "The beautiful seaside town named the most sought after place for second homes." My London. Available at https://www.mylondon. news/lifestyle/travel/salcombe-most-popular-second-homes-22592807, accessed February 13, 2023.

Joyner, Lisa. 2021. "20 best coastal towns to move to in the UK. Country Living." Available at https://www.countryliving.com/uk/homes-interiors/property/ a34038697/best-coastal-towns/, accessed February 13, 2023.

Kinney, Penelope. 2017. "Walking interviews." *Social Research Update* (67).

Lees, Loretta, and John McKiernan. 2012. "Art-led regeneration in Margate: Learning from moonbow jakes café and lido nightclub intervention." *Art & the Public Sphere* 2 (1-3): 17-35.

Lenzi, Sara, Juan Sádaba, and PerMagnus Lindborg. 2021. "Soundscape in times of change: Case study of a city neighbourhood during the covid-19 lockdown." *Frontiers in Psychology* 12: 570741.

McCann, Hannah, and William Tullett. 2021. "Our sensory experience of the pandemic." Pursuit: The University of Melbourne. Available at https:// pursuit.unimelb.edu.au/articles/our-sensory-experience-of-the-pandemic, accessed February 13, 2023.

Millington, Gareth. 2005. "Meaning, materials and melancholia: Understanding the palace hotel." *Social & Cultural Geography* 6 (4): 531-549.

Mitchell, Andrew et al. 2021. "Investigating urban soundscapes of the covid-19 lockdown: A predictive soundscape modeling approach." *The Journal of the Acoustical Society of America* 150 (6): 4474-4488.

Murray, Lesley and Helmi Järviluoma. 2019. "Walking as transgenerational methodology." *Qualitative Research*: QR 20 (2): 229-238.

Obrador-Pons, Pau. 2009. "Building castles in the sand: Repositioning touch on the beach." *The Senses & Society* 4 (2): 195-210.

Prosser, Bethan Mathias. 2022. "Listening to urban seaside gentrification: Living with displacement injustices on the UK south coast." PhD Thesis. Brighton: University of Brighton.

Shah, Preena. 2011. "Coastal gentrification: The coastification of St Leonards-on-Sea." PhD Thesis. Loughborough: Loughborough University.

Shields, Rob. 1991. *Places on the Margin: Alternative Geographies of Modernity.* London: Routledge.

Smith, Darren. 2012. "The social and economic consequences of housing in multiple occupation (HMO) in UK coastal towns: Geographies of segregation." *Transactions of the Institute of British Geographers* 37 (3): 461-476.

Steele, Jenny, and David Jarratt. 2019. "The seaside resort, nostalgia and restoration." In: Elaine Speight, ed. *Practising Place: Creative and Critical Reflections on Place.* Art Editions North.

Thibaud, Jean-Paul. 2013. "Commented city walks." *Wi: Journal of Mobile Culture* 7 (1): 1-32.

Walton, John K. 2000. *The British Seaside: Holidays and Resorts in the Twentieth Century.* Manchester: Manchester University Press.

Ward, Jonathan. 2018. "Down by the sea: Visual arts, artists and coastal regeneration." *International Journal of Cultural Policy* 24 (1): 121-138.

Ward, Jonathan. 2015. "Geographies of exclusion: Seaside towns and houses in multiple occupancy." *Journal of Rural Studies* 37: 96-107.

Westerkamp, Hilde. 1997. *Soundwalk from home*: Museum of Walking. Available at https://www.museumofwalking.org.uk/wp-content/uploads/2017/08/Soundwalk-from-Home.pdf, accessed February 13, 2023.

Westerkamp, Hilde. 2017. "The practice of listening in unsettled times." Paper read at *Invisible Places: Sound, Urbanism and Sense of Place*, at São Miguel Island, Azores, Portugal.

Chapter 9

Burning Tires, Sauerkraut and Dung: The (Classist) Boundaries of an Olfactory Landscape

Sara Nikolić

University of Belgrade, Serbia

Abstract

This chapter examines olfactory landscapes and othering practices reflected through the categorization of unpleasant smells in an urban environment, taking place in a middle-class socialist-era large housing estate in Belgrade. The data is drawn from two consecutive methodological steps: an online questionnaire and sensory walks conducted with residents of New Belgrade's housing estate. Olfactory claims made by middle-class inhabitants of the researched housing estate are divided into three categories referring to a three-stage series of distinctions and othering practices: external Others, internal Others, and double Others. Looking at the intersection of class and race, the chapter argues that olfactory constructions play a significant role in the way collective identities are tacitly (re)produced and puts forward the idea that the production of "otherness" of lower social classes is interwoven with the fabric of the middle-class white body epitomizing civility, culture, modernity, and propriety.

Keywords: olfactory landscape, sensory anthropology, urban poor, racialization, class distinction.

* * *

Introduction

The real secret of class distinction in the West (...) is summed up in four frightful words which people nowadays are chary of uttering but which were bandied about quite freely in my childhood. The words were: The lower classes smell.

(Orwell 1937, 159)

Not only does the odour symbolizes the qualities of the Other, but it also embodies the ability of those others to disrupt one's order. Throughout history, ideas about odorous women, the insensitive noses of the lower classes, and the foul odour of inferior races mutually reinforced each other (Tullett 2016). Moreover, all cultures distinguish between pleasant and unpleasant, attractive and repellent smells (Osborne 1977). These distinctions provide a "handy tool for social symbolism," and it is in this way that the nose is one's most delicate "instrument of social discrimination" (van Beek 1992, 52). As van Beek vividly describes in the case of the Kapsiki/Higi people, the nose may be our most delicate instrument for discriminating between "the in and the out, either as individuals or as groups" (van Beek 1992, 52). In the article on olfactory symbolism and cultural categories, Constance Classen points out that the primary negative olfactory characteristics ascribed to the Other in different cultures are foul, dangerously fragrant and inodorate (Classen 1992, 158). "The foul other is immediately and obviously repellent" (Classen 1992, 158). It is precisely that foul Other – or rather a notion of them – that is the subject of this chapter.

A broad multidisciplinary literature on odour, aroma and the senses suggests that in othering, boundary-drawing, and racialization processes, we might expect arguments based on smell to carry particular weight (Classen, Howes and Synnott 1994). Some scholarly explanations invoke environments, culinary choices, and cosmetic practices as explanatory factors for the difference in smell between Us and Others. In research on boundaries and distinctions, the social experience of scent is most well documented; those considered 'other' are generally perceived to smell bad, while one's social groups are perceived to smell good or not at all (Cerulo 2018; Classen 1993).

Anthropologists and cultural historians have long considered olfaction primarily a social, political, and cultural process (Manalansan 2006, 50). Howes and Lalonde (1991, 126) argue that where visual discrimination failed, the proximate senses of smell and taste could be mobilized in producing social distinction and their "own form of social power." This article builds on a range of recent empirical works, particularly that of Andrea Racleş and Ana Ivasiuc (2019) and Alison Gerber (2021), on the phenomenon of othering of disadvantaged social groups through olfactory categorizations and racialization, firmly anchored in the European tradition.

The first part of this chapter presents a brief contextual background on the housing estate – *blok 45* (sr) – where the research was conducted. It is necessary to acquaint the reader with the socialist-modernist design of this housing estate and the transitional transformations that abounded in its fate, as well as the fate of its inhabitants, in order to grasp the dynamics and tensions within and around this housing estate that is the subject of this chapter. This section is followed by a brief description of the methodological procedure used to collect the ethnographic data that, together with numerous theoretical and empirical materials on the topic of differentiation and othering through olfactory practices, is the basis for the discussion and argumentation of the chapter. This ethnographic material originated as a by-product of research for the needs of the doctoral dissertation on housing and the relationship to urban commons in New Belgrade after the privatization of public housing and thematically exceeded the scope of the dissertation.

In the second section of the chapter, attention is turned to the interpretation and contextualization of the material, focusing on the olfactory claims and the boundaries of the olfactory landscape of researched housing estate. In terms of hierarchy and inclusion/exclusion, the difference between 'full-fledged and civilized' citizens of new Belgrade and 'newcomers' and 'intruders' is less marked in the case of the urban poor, working-class and internally displaced persons who moved in during the 1990s than in the case of Roma in informal settlements bordering the apartment block. It is inevitable to consider the deep-rooted everyday racism that members of the Roma people in Europe have been facing for centuries to interpret this difference in marking. I argue that olfactory constructions play a significant role in the way collective identities are tacitly (re)produced, and put forward the idea that the production of 'otherness' of lower social classes is interwoven with the fabric of the middle-class white body epitomizing civility, culture, modernity and propriety.

Blok 45

Before moving on to the description of the methodological procedure and the unravelling of entangled narratives of race, class, and culturally conditioned olfactory categories among the inhabitants of New Belgrade's large housing estate, in the next section, I will present the essential features of this settlement, relevant for further interpretation.

New Belgrade was primarily conceived as the governing capital of the newly established state, with the primary function of being the seat of power of the new federal bureaucratic structure. The large housing estates are shaped in the spirit of modern functionalism, which implies an orthogonal urban matrix (Lukić 2010, 57); functional zoning of the city into four zones (housing, green areas and recreation, industry, management, and culture); separation of work from the housing; mono functionality of residential areas and standardized meeting places.

The large housing estate discussed in this chapter is located along the bank of the Sava, popularly known as Blok 45 is one of four symmetrically distributed housing estates along the left Sava riverbank. The architectural solution for this housing estate was selected, together with the solution for the identical block 70, at the all-Yugoslav competition in 1966.

With a population of approximately 17,000 inhabitants, blok 45 is located eight kilometres from the city centre and five kilometres from the centre of the municipality of New Belgrade. In a city with underdeveloped public transport, such isolation from the city centre makes this apartment block less valued in terms of real estate prices compared to other parts of New Belgrade. Inhabitants who grew up in this housing estate during the infamous 1990s and early 2000s and popular culture often represent this apartment block through ghettoizing narratives. However, the entire modernist landscape of New Belgrade, including the housing estate in question, has been going through a gentrification process (Backović 2010; Erić 2008; Petrović 2008) that is reflected primarily in the nearby construction of luxury housing and the rise in real estate prices of old buildings.

Research on the social structure of the inhabitants of New Belgrade gives us further insights into the material reality of New Belgrade and its inhabitants. Not only is the municipality of New Belgrade the wealthiest municipality in Serbia today, but sociological findings show that its class structure has always been highly homogeneous. According to sociological research (Backović 2010; Petrović 2008), the social structure of the population in New Belgrade has been extremely homogeneous from the very beginning. Before the 'giveaway' privatization of the public housing stock in 1991, as many as 87% of apartments were socially owned (Petrović 2008, 62), and families with employees in 'non-manual' activities – state and party administration, cultural institutions, business associations, banks, and the Yugoslav People's Army – inhabited these housing estates. Housing, economic, and social inequality deepened after the sale of the housing stock in 1991 and continued to decline under neoliberal housing policies that have been dominant ever since.

After the Yugoslav wars in the nineties, many ethnically Serbian families, regardless of their family history and background, immigrated to what is now called Serbia. According to the Municipality of New Belgrade assessment from 2008,[1] only about 30,000 internally displaced persons reside in the territory of

---

[1] *Lokalni akcioni plan za unapređenje položaja izbeglih i interno raseljenih lica u gradskoj opštini Novi Beograd za period 2009 - 2013.* Available at: https://novibeograd.rs/wp-

the entire municipality, whose total population is over 250,000. Even though there are no exact data on the number of displaced persons per housing estate in New Belgrade, it can be assumed that the number is around 10% per housing estate, including the one that is the subject of this chapter. In addition to the privatization of the public housing stock, another crucial component for further understanding the olfactory and class landscape of Blok 45 is its location. Being hunted from the city centre, in its immediate vicinity, only one-kilometre northwest, there are several smaller informal Roma settlements (slums) and a social housing complex. Somewhat further, about the third kilometre to the northwest, there are unplanned and semi-rural settlements on the edges of the city territory of Belgrade.

Method

Exploratory mapping

The first in a series of steps that led to creating the smell map of block 45 is a preliminary, exploratory "mapping." It was conducted in an online survey to which thirty residents of New Belgrade responded. A simple questionnaire compiled through the QuestionPro[2] platform contained three questions. The first question is closed and refers to the current residence of the respondents, while the other two are open. More precisely, the second question, with five possible open-ended answers, refers to pleasant odours or odours that evoke pleasant memories of the investigated settlements. The third question is structured similarly and refers to unpleasant smells or odours that evoke unpleasant memories of the researched blocks.

The data obtained in this way are presented in the format of a legend (Figure 9.1). Different colours are indicators of various 'sources' of odours. For example, odours of plant origin, chemical origin (i.e. pollution), animal origin, et cetera. Colour intensity is a symbolic indicator of the frequency of responses, so the most intense indicates a high frequency of odour specificity in

---

content/uploads/2016/07/lokalni_akcioni_plan_izbeglice_irl.pdf. Acessed on February 14, 2023.

[2] This online survey was shared through closed Facebook groups of researched settlements and further through pages whose content is related to New Belgrade blocks, such as Blokovi.com, Brutalizam i renesansa, Blok 45 INFO, and others. The answers were collected in the period from December 17, 2019, to January 31, 2020.

respondents' answers. In contrast, the palest shade of a particular colour indicates idiosyncratic reactions given by individual respondents.

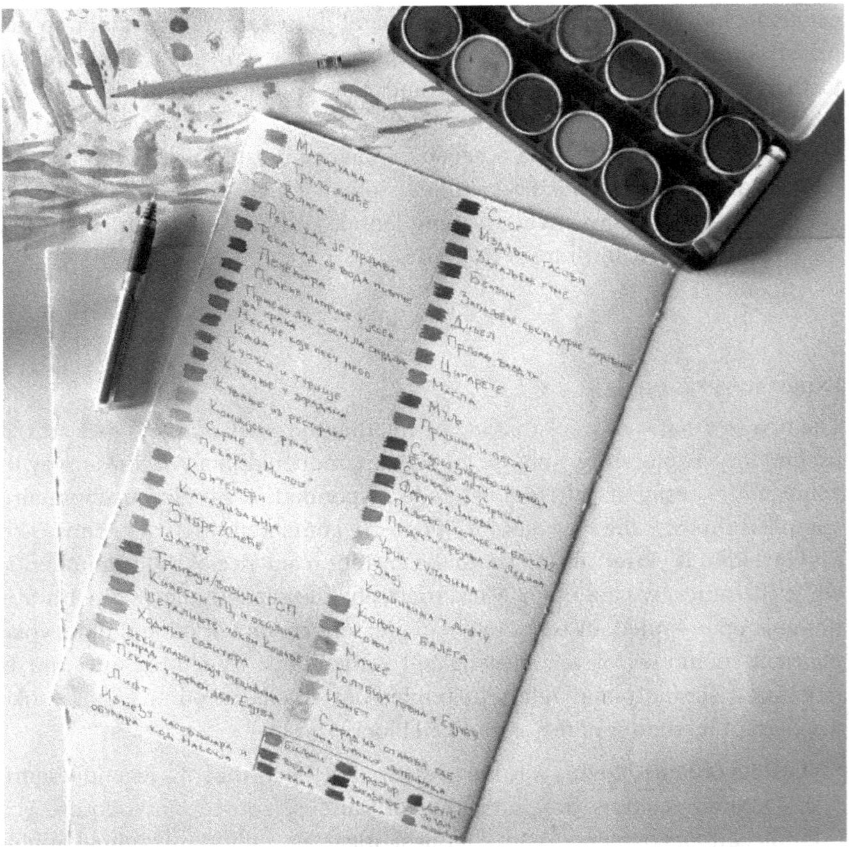

Figure 9.1: Legend. The legends of both pleasant and unpleasant odours were later used for elicitation during the smell walk. Photo by Sara Nikolić.

Smell-walking

Thirteen residents of Blok 45 (8F, 5M) aged 22 to 65 participated in this phase of research. These research participants can be classified into a broad middle-class category according to their level of education, occupation, and income level per household member. Data was collected between May 2020 and December 2021.

Firmly anchored in phenomenological approaches to ethnographic research, this research phase was designed around one everyday practice – walking. A rich ethnographic material was created while walking with the respondents through the spaces where they spend their free time, circling the invisible borders of what they perceive as a home territory or "third place" (Oldenburg 1989) or observing them proudly take on the role of tour guide through the "concrete dormitory." This material consists primarily of interviews recorded in motion (walk-along), which abound in graphic descriptions of olfactory sensations and memories evoked by the described scents (first kiss, summer vacation, NATO bombing). The second layer of ethnographic material comprises photographs of essential spaces, ambiences, and objects taken during a joint walk.

During the walk, the respondents referred to their everyday *"fragrant experiences,"* to the ubiquitous and 'typical' smells of the block in which they live, and the sensory landscapes in which they are immersed. Respondents were asked pre-determined and ad-hoc questions to examine experiences, interpretations, spatial practices (Carpiano 2008, 264) and relationships with other residents of the research block.

Discussion

Nothing can prevail against aversion to smells.
(Corbin 1986: 210)

In the wake of the "sensory turn" and the growing academic interest in sensory studies in the past two decades, anthropologists and cultural historians have shown how crucial olfactory pretexts are in constructing and upholding boundaries (Drobnick 2006; Eliassi 2017; Smith 2006; Tullett 2016) and in the construction of the 'other' across cultural contexts (van Beek 1992; Hazel 2014).

The following section will present narratives and practices through which the residents of New Belgrade's Blok 45, themselves members of the dominant social group, construct boundaries that exclude and abject their neighbours – members of lower social classes and disadvantaged social groups. To a certain extent, this refers to refugees, more precisely families from Croatia, Bosnia and Kosovo, who, in negligible numbers, immigrated to this settlement during the 1990s, beneficiaries of social housing, and residents of nearby semi-rural settlements. Most of these othering, abjecting and often racializing practices and narratives refer to the Roma population living in informal settlements in the immediate vicinity of Blok 45.

As a rule, the dominant group in a society ascribes to itself a pleasant or neutral smell within the system of olfactory classifications (Classen 1992, 159). Relying on claims based on individual experiences of smell, the middle-class inhabitants of this housing estate set boundaries that exclude those they consider inferior, threatening, or foreign. Such olfactory claims "have unique properties that can allow them to be weaponized in social and political life" (Gerber 2021, 2). As research shows, the shortcomings of smells as evidence – their ephemeral nature and the predicament of independent confirmation – can allow claimants to leverage cultural structures that link olfactory experience with urgent public concerns. Such olfactory claims might be particularly viable when they "interact with other categorical distinctions that are imprecise and deeply felt" (Gerber 2021, 5).

In this sense, it is possible to determine three types and levels of distinction – external others, internal others, and double others. Each of the three individual stories of distinction, which varies in intensity from landscape boundaries as the mildest, through collective stereotyping narratives to neo-racist political engagement and neighbourhood self-organizing as the most intense, will be analysed in detail and illustrated with examples in the following sections.

Dung: External others

Data on this level of differentiation and othering are read from the exploratory mapping phase. Namely, when the respondents answered the third question[3] enumerating odours of animal origin and odours related to agricultural work (e.g., manure, horse dung, pigsty), as well as odours of air pollution that do not originate from traffic (e.g., domestic wood and coal burning) the presumed location of the stench always supplemented the answers. It is irrelevant how successfully they located these unpleasant odours. What is exciting and led me to think about othering practices through olfactory claims is that only in this context does the presumed location appear in the respondents' answers. And not only that, the assumed location is always marked explicitly outside this housing estate's cadastral and mental boundaries.

Out of the 54 mentioned unpleasant odours or odours that evoke unpleasant memories, the need to ascribe location only to the odours mentioned above – at the cost of doing so inaccurately – testifies to the need to establish a clear boundary between two types of settlements. On the one side is Blok 45, aerated "Ville radiouse" on the banks of the Sava: an urban housing estate built on utopian ideas, in whose spatial matrix modernist ideas, knowledge and values are woven. This settlement also has its stench. These malodours need not be explicitly localized as they befit such a modern urban settlement – sewage,

---

[3] Unpleasant odors or odors that evoke uncomfortable memories.

exhaust fumes, cigarettes, marijuana, smog, greasy street food, and garbage. On the other side, only a few kilometres northwest (twice closer than the city centre) are Ledine, Bežanija, Surčin and Jakovo. These are suburban and unplanned settlements whose inhabitants are still partially engaged in agriculture, settlements that are not attached to the city sewerage and heating plant. In the backyards of these settlements are pigsties, manure, and septic tanks. In fall and winter, small mounds of coal and firewood are stacked under the eaves inside those yards. In short, these are settlements inhabited by the poor working class. They are too far away for Blok 45 residents to consider them neighbours and part of their community. They are external others.

As such, they are not a 'threat' to Block 45 residents. Nevertheless, the stench associated with their daily practices necessary for existence is a special kind of pollution:

> You can feel it when the pressure drops and the stench from the village rises. That's it. Bank directors live here. You have such people living in such a city, such a beautiful settlement, and everything stinks of manure. I have nothing against manure when I'm in the countryside, but I have when I'm here. That's not normal. But well, there are worse things ... (m, 62, retiree)

When Košava[4] brings the smell of coal in autumn or when a steamy summer day reeks of manure, even just for a moment, a rupture in the olfactory landscape of the modernist settlement arises. Hence the need to emphasize that the smell of the village, which has no place in the deodorized modernist settlement, does not belong to it. It is not the stench but its displacement that pollutes and disturbs the order.

The borders between Block 45 and these working-class settlements are clearly inscribed in the physical space. However, the stench, just like the landscape, "refuses to be disciplined" (Benediktsson and Lund 2012) or to respect boundaries one has built – whether tangible like those in a built environment, visible to the naked eye like class, or utterly intangible like cognitive and emotional.

---

[4] Cold, squally southeastern wind found in parts of East Europe and the Balkans.

Sauerkraut: Internal others

Different varieties of otherness tend to be typed according to an olfactory chart whereby the repulsive aspect of the Other is conveyed through the symbolism of corrupting stench. "Only insofar as the other is perceived as complying with cultural norms it can be attributed a pleasant, relatively innocuous odour" (Classen 1992, 148). This section refers to the internal others. The residents of the housing estate Blok 45 are separated not by kilometres but by partition walls from the Others who live in apartments just like theirs, look almost like them and speak the same language. More precisely, this section refers to the olfactory claims middle-class residents of Blok 45 use for othering and social distancing from their neighbours belonging to the lower classes.

In these olfactory claims, the collective identity of 'refugees' (*izbeglice*, srb.) or 'newcomers' (*došljaci*, srb.) was often attributed to members of the lower classes. However, this discourse of exclusion is not reduced to idiosyncratic responses but appears as a widespread stereotype that, as such, is not unique to the residents of Block 45. The majority of such othering olfactory claims indicate the *newcomers'* backwardness and "lack of will to modernize":

> Worst smell? Roasted peppers, of course. I personally do it on the grill at home. But not the way they do, in bulk. You must have had some unpleasant experiences in your building because many people... today's date[5] is perfect for this story in general, many people came from the "Storm," and so on. They were there, it's actually the question that today is the day that determines the fate of both the country and this part of Belgrade. Because it's incredible how all these people did not escape across the river,[6] but here and up there in the villages behind Batajnica, Surčin, Ledine, and whatever else is there. I think that is it. Many things here are related to that, they brought that kind of culture from their village. I don't blame them for anything, do not get me wrong, but it is a kind of rural culture that this is it... It is unnatural for them! When you say, "Man, you pickled like 20 kilos of cabbage in the basement, the whole building stinks!" he is angry and looks at you grimly as if you have something personal against him. (M, 28, journalist)

---

[5] August 4th 2020, anniversary of the Opperation Storm of Croatian War of Independence in 1995 that resulted in the displacement and evacuation of thousands of Serbs from Croatian teritory.

[6] In the city centre.

Cabbage and pickled vegetables in the basement. This problem is much deeper than cabbage and pickles. And it's never young people who do that. I have never met someone who is born in the 90s, lives alone and has sauerkraut on their balcony. Do you have sauerkraut? Well, neither do I, and I wouldn't ever have it. I like to eat it very much and am a little hypocritical about where it comes from. But somehow, I think it's that moment of people coming from the countryside in their later years. Fuck that, I'm leaving Serbia at some point – not because the state is forcing me, even though it is forcing me – but because I would like to try something somewhere else. You assimilate with New York, with Vancouver, no matter what city in the world. But those people that came here, I think it's people who can't, they are too old to assimilate with any environment, it's just that. (f, 26, student)

In the case of internal others, similarly to the external others, it is not the body that is foul but the 'lifestyle.' More precisely, it is primarily the culinary practices that are foul. These vivid and affective interview segments illustrate that the differentiation between 'clean' and 'dirty,' 'civilized' and 'savage,' citizens and 'refugees' is based predominantly on culinary practices. The culinary practices do not apply to the type of food consumed since both are bound by traditional Serbian cuisine, but to the manner and place of preparation. When they want sauerkraut or roasted peppers, the middle-class residents of this housing estate visit traditional cuisine restaurants or buy ready meals in supermarkets, as the codes of conduct of their class dictate.

Unlike the *melu* and *rerhe* people, van Beek vividly describes (1992), the distinction here is not based on the idea that unclean food like fish 'pollutes' the eater. On the contrary, it is based on the idea that 'traditional, peasant, stinky' food is prepared where it does not belong – in a middle-class, deodorized, modernist housing estate. In the case of 'newcomers,' the distinction between 'visual' and 'actual' citizens is blurred. The smell distinguishes 'real citizens' who do not smell from those whose non-affiliation is revealed by gastronomic and cultural practices. Such a view is neither new nor typical of the participants in this study. On the contrary, it has long been supported in the anthropological literature that civility requires olfactory neutrality (Bauman 2002, Cohen 1988). Furthermore, the domestic space is infused with meanings of one's industriousness, commitment to the community values, and virtue and merit of deserving to be recognized as a righteous citizen – both locally and nationally.

Burning tires: Double others

Roma is discursively relegated to backwardness, laziness and, thus, 'smelliness' (Racleş and Ivasiuc 2019, 26; see also Ivasiuc 2019). Along the class dimension, the focus on the poverty of Roma groups has been a fundamental principle of racialization (van Baar 2017), interlaced with the processes of criminalization. As Racleş and Ivasiuc point out, the latter is often concretely transferred in policies focused on the segregation of Roma (Racleş and Ivasiuc 2019). This section illustrates how in the case of Roma as 'double others,' olfactory claims of some of the middle-class Blok 45 inhabitants, from the narrative level and neighbourhood gossip, grow into action and discriminatory practice.

For their nomadism, the Roma are othered as perpetually out of place and, hence, dangerous. The impure elements are the ones that have heterogeneous characteristics problematizing their belonging to one or another category (Douglas 1966). However, the Roma settlement near Blok 45 is not nomadic. On the contrary, due to the lack of a coherent housing policy, non-investment in public housing, insufficient social housing construction, and the inadequacy of other forms of housing support, many Roma families live in unsanitary, substandard, improvised settlements on the outskirts of the cities. Such settlements, often close to landfills and polluted areas, in an 'urbanism of contempt' (Brunello 1996 in Racleş and Ivasiuc 2019, 29) begot double territorial stigmatization – "not only did the land taint the bodies that inhabited it, but it became tainted through the presence of those abject bodies" (Racleş and Ivasiuc 2019, 29).

Due to a mixture of neglect by the public waste services, economic activities of metal extraction performed by some of the Roma and cost-reducing strategies of non-Roma individuals and companies disposing of bulky waste illegally near such settlements, many of them are surrounded by heaps of waste. Periodically, these are burnt, generating large amounts of smoke and social alarm in Blok 45 and surrounding housing estates. In addition to waste burning, other activities that emit air pollution are melting plastic cables to reach copper wire (that is later sold) and heating by burning car and truck tires. Almost identical to the examples from Romania and Italy, Racleş and Ivasiuc (Racleş and Ivasiuc 2019) refer to the narrative unravelling around this phenomenon, making use of the olfactory repertoire by emphasizing the *acrid stench* of the smoke spilling over a considerable distance and the fact it endangers one's health when inhaled:

> Literally, number one for me is those burning tires. I feel suffocation by that. Gipsies set them on fire, Roma, to be politically correct. The Roma

burned their tires in the summer for some unknown reason, I don't know if they drive away mosquitoes or are just jerks. In winter, I understand – you're warming up. I don't understand the summer. It smelled so bad. I had a headache for four days. (m, 36, architect)

You have nowhere to run, so you have to run to the city centre. You cannot see each other. It's not constant, I've experienced it a couple of times, but I have to throw all my clothes into the laundry basket every time. Not to be harsh, but it's so embarrassing. That is perhaps the most unacceptable thing to me here. People are complaining like "NATO bombed us, people are dying of cancer, blah blah blah." I'm not sure this is anything less harmful than that. Those burned tires, and secondary raw materials don't know what they burned there, but it is as if you were in the ghetto movie. You go up to the window and see a barrel burning. Postapocalyptic New York, motherfucker. (m, 28, journalist)

These complaints are neatly slotted into a specific and well-established set of cultural beliefs about smell: 'bad air' that endangers health can be identified by smell and requires ongoing management and amelioration. Moreover, "adherence to hygienic norms is necessary to be considered a good citizen" (Gerber 2021, 2). Of course, most respondents were careful in their choice of words and gave socially acceptable answers. However, many justified themselves by saying "*that they do not think that the Roma stink, but that their way of life stinks,* objectively." All of the informants who complained about "*Roma-related air pollution*" (f, 26, student) "centred their vulnerability in their complaint" (Gerber 2021, 11). In all olfactory claims and complaints about air pollution "*originating from the Gypsy settlement*" (f, 60, municipal clerk), the dominant motive is the self-victimization of a privileged group through socially acceptable racist narratives.

In addition to health and respiratory hazards, environmental concerns were also commonly cited in complaints (significantly more often by women) – in these olfactory claims, "a foul smell was often presented as proof of an environmental hazard" (Gerber 2021, 12). Concern for the environment was often connected in these complaints with concern that local regulations were not being followed:

Let's face it, I am someone who has been completely removed from any kind of racism and nationalism to the extent that I do not truly feel even an iota of national identity. My only identity is who I am – ****'s mother,

****'s wife. I have no other identity. So, when I'm telling you this, it's really experiential. I have nothing against Roma, but I say that all summer long, we cannot open the windows at night because they steal the cables and then burn the plastic parts because they can only sell copper. In block 45, the Roma are seriously threatening me, and if I could, I would strongly advocate that they be sanctioned, punished, or even driven away. You can't tolerate their work when you see horses walking, horse dung remaining behind, windows unable to be opened because tires and cables are burning, the fountain working for three days, and then not working anymore because they are filling canisters to carry to their slums and so on, and so on. Nothing has changed much since I have lived here except for pollution from the Roma, which burn cables that no one can do anything about them. It's like they are untouchable. The law does not apply to them. (f, 47, copywriter)

In the context of growing air pollution in Belgrade and the increased interest of the media and political movements in environmental issues, complaints about the stench coming from informal settlements become understood as legitimate concerns regarding public and environmental health hazards. As such, local activist groups and individuals often use them on social media to justify demands for mass eviction and the destruction of informal housing settlements (Gerber 2021, 15). Many Blok 45 inhabitants, including several respondents, have founded the Facebook group *BLOKada SMRADA* (Block the Stench). These so-called activists send organized complaints to the communal militia about the stench of Roma settlements. Furthermore, these 'activists' do not only sign petitions demanding the forced eviction of Roma families who live there by force of circumstances but also harass, mistreat and, without permission, film the 'untouchable' Roma children who collect electronic waste in the neighbourhood. In their words, they point out the *danger* Roma represents to order and the environment from an early age.

I don't know if you saw it in the Facebook group. I write about these burning tires almost every Saturday. These are some things where you have facts about what happens to the ozone layer when plastic is burned. Either you're an idiot or don't care, but I'm really sorry – we have to do something about it. Let the state punish them or move them elsewhere, but my children will not breathe this air. (f, 35, teacher)

In the context of Serbia, the historical segregation of Roma is noticeable, both through informal housing and the construction of social housing exclusively for them. These social housing complexes are large in scale and often quite far from the city's infrastructure and adequate services (Ćurčić and Timotijević 2022; Vilenica 2019). Neglect of segregation, poverty and everyday racism faced by Roma families from these settlements have been made possible thanks to depoliticized discourses on the poverty of the Roma. In addition, Roma families are often victims of forced evictions that leave them on the streets, opening a new circle of their social exclusion. From 2009 to 2012 alone, over three thousand Roma were evicted from informal settlements in Belgrade (Amnesty International 2010; Petrović et al. 2013). The most massive evictions occurred in New Belgrade – in the immediate vicinity of Blok 45.

Moreover, demands "*to do something about it,*" illustrated in the quote above, reinforce racial difference whilst "expunging the less tasteful qualities" (Tullett 2016, 318) of everyday racism and segregation. Pollution of the public sphere by such harmful discourses "facilitated the slippage to neo-racist imaginaries and squalor, forging victim-blaming representations of undeservingness" (Racleş and Ivasiuc 2019, 22). In comparison, classical racism operates by relying on "external signs (physical or not) to infer internal, biological or inherited essences to explain behaviour, culture, and social position" (Lemon 2000, 63), statements of residents of Blok 45 testify that 'everyday racism' (Essed 1991) relies on imaginaries of how *others* engage, in specific ascribed ways, in everyday practices and with material objects. Furthermore, those ways are assumed to make detectable *their* failure to 'follow "decent human standards"' (Largey and Watson 2006, 31).

Concluding remarks

This chapter presented the insights and attitudes of the part of the middle-class inhabitants of housing estate Blok 45 in New Belgrade towards members of the lower classes from their and nearby settlements. These insights were gained through two successive methodological steps – exploratory olfactory mapping through an online survey of 30 respondents and smell-walks involving 13 respondents. The research was realized over two years, from December 2019 to December 2021. Apart from the coronavirus pandemic, which is a topic beyond the scope of this chapter, no other significant qualitative changes have been observed related to the researched housing estate (blok 45) and its immediate surroundings, both in terms of demographic trends, the built environment, and the political context.

The results indicate three levels of distinction and othering practised by the middle-class inhabitants of the New Belgrade blok 45. The layers of distinction were interpreted based on olfactory claims made by the respondents. Odour can form a productive angle for the classification inquiry, serving as a social symbol of dirt and pollution, inclusion and exclusion (van Beek 1992). Following Mary Douglas (1966), the strategy of olfactory perception can be a strategy of social discrimination through cultural definitions of dirt and cleanliness, civility, and savagery.

The first level refers to the 'external others,' that is, the inhabitants of the surrounding semi-rural suburbs. Residents of Blok 45 do not meet them every day, nor do their scents infuse the olfactory landscape of the block too often. According to the residents of Blok 45, the scents that come from there are the scents "that have no place in the city." In this way, by bringing rural and animal-related scents into the urban environment, the order and mental landscapes of Block 45 are disturbed by a whiff. However, since these scents are brought by the wind and do not arrive by direct encounter with the bearers of the *stench*, there is no pronounced and value-coloured distinction, neither at the level of the narrative nor the level of practice. In this case, class differences are implied. Respondents refer to them as an "objective fact" without needing to fence themselves off or use rhetorical means to strengthen the existing boundaries.

The second level refers to 'internal others,' i.e. other residents of the same housing estate who are members of the lower classes and to whom the collective identity of *newcomers, refugees,* or displaced persons who immigrated to Belgrade after the wars of the 1990s in Yugoslavia, is often ascribed. In this case, the borders are more porous. Thus, the respondents feel the need to affectively point out their existence and tangibility, which is reflected primarily in the 'backward' and 'uncivilized' culinary practices. Similar to the previous case, the frequent trope indicates the odours that do not belong to the modern city and apartment building – the odours that stink of poverty. This narrative often appears in the dominant, elitist discourse in urban areas in Serbia, on which there is still not enough academic literature.

These practices of distinction and othering exist primarily at the level of narratives and mocking stereotypes. They are not (yet) a threat to those made objects of ridicule. However, in the third level of differentiation, the class dimension is intertwined with a racial one. Therefore, the third case is about the 'double others.' For the residents of New Belgrade's Blok 45, these 'double others' are Roma, who live primarily in a nearby informal, substandard settlement or a complex of social housing right behind it. When talking about Roma, residents of Blok 45 position their own (often overemphasized) vulnerability at the centre of their olfactory claims under the auspices of health and environmental concerns, thus neglecting the material reality of their Roma neighbours. This is not an attempt to relativize the danger posed by air pollution caused by burning rubbish, cables and tires but to shed light on the fact that such practices are, of course, never an expression of 'innate nature' or 'culture' or 'Roma lifestyle' but only existential coercion. In this case, therefore, it is not a stench that has no place in the city but a stench that is explicitly marked as detrimental to health. Such olfactory claims, when directed towards the Roma, lead to collective action and institutional response in the form of punishment by the communal militia, requests for forced evictions, and bullying of children and young adults by so-called eco-activists. For now, these collective, self-organized actions never produced solidarity and a request to the state to provide adequate living and housing conditions so that Roma neighbours would not be forced to heat on burning tires and suffocate in someone else's garbage.

A deeply ingrained notion of the olfactory as 'the most denigrated sensory domain of modernity' (Howes 2006, 169) locates the olfactory dimension of the domestic space at the centre of a discussion about racializing processes of othering that are intrinsically interlinked with those of 'selfing' (cf. Baumann and Gingrich 2004). In contrast to the unclean, uncivilized, unindustrious, and undisciplined bodies and, more importantly, the 'lifestyles' of the working class, newcomers and Roma – the middle-class body and self are constituted as conspicuously clean, civilized, industrious and disciplined. Nevertheless, considering the "poorly trained noses, impoverished language, and emotion-laden interpretations" (Gerber 2021: 3), the scentful experience might seem a flawed premise for social action.

This article, therefore, suggests that looking at the intersection between class and race might reveal some of the reasons for the ways middle-class residents of Blok 45 feel only 'quiet contempt' for one group of their 'stinky' neighbours while wholeheartedly trying to keep others away from their concrete utopias – regardless of the conditions and the material reality in which these foul bodies live. The abject body of the poor, especially when racialized, "threatens the subject with contamination and defilement, inducing violent reactions, repulsions and convulsions" (Hepworth 2012, 433). Visceral of these actions signify the intimacy of the act (Racleș and Ivasiuc 2019, 33), through which the class subject is both constituted and disrupted.

References

Amnesty International. 2010. "Serbia: Stop the forced eviction of Roma settlements." London: AI.

Backović, Vera. 2010. *Socioprostorni razvoj Novog Beograda.* Beograd: Institut za sociološka istraživanja Filozofskog fakulteta.

Bauman, Zygmunt. 2002. "The sweet scent of decomposition." In: Rojek C. and Turner B., eds. *Forget Baudrillard?* Abingdon: Routledge. Pp. 22–46.

Baumann, Gerd, and Andre Gingrich, eds. 2004. *Grammars of Identity / Alterity. A Structural Approach.* New York: Berghahn.

Benediktsson, Karl, and Katrín Anna Lund. 2012. *Conversations with landscape.* London: Routledge.

Carpiano, Richard M. 2008. "Come take a walk with me: The 'Go-Along' interview as a novel method for studying the implications of place for health and well-being." *Health & Place* 15: 263-272.

Cerulo, Karen. 2018. "Scents and sensibility: Olfaction, sense-making, and meaning attribution." *American Sociological Review* 83(2): 361–389.

Classen, Constance, David Howes and Synnott Anthony. 1994 *Aroma: The Cultural History of Smell.* London and New York: Routledge.

Classen, Constance. 1992. "The Odor of the Other: Olfactory Symbolism and Cultural Categories." *Ethos.* 20(2): 133-166.

Classen, Constance. 1993. *Worlds of Sense: Exploring the Senses in History and across Cultures.* London and New York: Routledge.

Cohen, Erik. 1988. "The broken cycle: Smell in a Bangko soi (lane)." *Ethnos* 53(1–2): 37–49.

Corbin, Alain. 1986. *The Foul and the Fragrant: Odor and the French Social Imagination.* Cambridge, MA: Harvard University Press.

Ćurčić, Danilo and Jovana Timotijević. 2022. December 30. "U Jabučki rit ne stižu novine." *Peščanik.* Available at https://pescanik.net/u-jabucki-rit-ne-stizu-novine/, accessed on February 15, 2023.

Douglas, Mary. 1966. *Purity and Danger.* London: Routledge.

Drobnick, Jim. 2006. *The Smell Culture Reader.* Oxford and New York: Berg.

Eliassi, Barzoo. 2017. "Conceptions of immigrant integration and racism among social workers in Sweden." *Journal of Progressive Human Services* 28(1): 6–35.

Essed, Philomena. 1991. *Understanding Everyday Racism: An Interdisciplinary Theory.* Newbury Park: Sage.

Gerber, Alison. 2021. "'Everyone's Annoyed': Leveraging Uncertainty in the Smell of Others." *Cultural Sociology,* 1-20.

Hazel, Yadira. 2014. "Sensing difference: Whiteness, national identity, and belonging in the Dominican Republic." *Transforming Anthropology* 22(2): 78–91.

Hepworth, Kate. 2012. "Abject Citizens: Italian 'Nomad Emergencies' and the Deportability of Romanian Roma," *Citizenship Studies,* 16 (3–4): 431–449.

Howes, David, and Marc Lalonde. 1991. "The Histoy of Sensibilities: Of the Standard of Taste in Mid-Eighteen Century England and the Circulation of Smells in Post-Revolutionary France." *Dialectical Anthropology* 16(2): 125-135.

Howes, David. 2006. "Charting the Sensorial Revolution," *The Senses and Society* 1, no. 1: 113-128.

Ivasiuc, Ana. 2019. "Reassembling Insecurity: The Power of Materiality." In: R. Kreide and A. Langenohl, eds. *Conceptualizing Power in Dynamics of Securitization: Beyond State and International System.* Baden-Baden: Nomos, 367–394.

Largey, Gale Peter, and Rodney Watson. 2006. "The Sociology of Odors." In: J. Drobnick, ed. *The Smell Culture Reader.* Oxford: Bloomsbury. Pp. 29–40.

Lemon, Alaina. 2000, *Between Two Fires: Gypsy Performance and Romani Memory from Pushkin to Postsocialism.* Durham: Duke University Press.

Lukić, Ivana. 2010. "Mogućnosti i ograničenja ortogonalne urbane matrice Novog Beograda sa aspekta vizuelnih efekata." In: *Nauka i praksa,* vol.13. Niš: Institut za građevinarstvo i arhitekturu. Pp. 57-61.

Manalansan, Martin, F. 2006. "Immigrant lives and the politics of olfaction in the global city." In: J. Drobnick, ed. *The Smell Culture Reader.* Oxford and New York: Berg. Pp. 41–52.

Oldenburg, Ray. 1989. *The great good place: cafés, coffee shops, community centers, beauty parlors, general stores, bars, hangouts, and how they get you through the day.* New York: Paragon House.

Orwell, George. 1937 [2018]. *The Road to Wigan Pier.* London: Penguin Books.

Osborne, Harold 1977. "Odours and appreciation." *British Journal of Aesthetics* 17: 37-48.

Petrović, Mina, Caterina Berescu, and Nora Teller. 2013. "Housing exclusion of the Roma: Living on the edge." In: Jozsef Hegedus, Martin Lux, and Nora Teller, eds. *Social housing in transition.* London: Routledge. Pp. 98–115.

Petrović, Mina. 2008. "Istraživanje socijalnih aspekata urbanog susedstva: Percepcija stručnjaka na Novom Beogradu." *Sociologija,* L (1): 55-78.

Racleş, Andreea, and Ana Ivasiuc. 2019. "Emplacing Smells: Spatialities and Materialities of 'Gypsiness.'" *Anthropological Journal of European Cultures* 28(1): 19–38.

Smith, Mark M. 2006. *How Race is Made: Slavery, Segregation, and the Senses.* Chapel Hill: University of North Carolina Press.

Tullett, William. 2016. "Grease and Sweat: Race and Smell in Eighteenth-Century English Culture." *Cultural and Social History* 13 (3): 307-322.

Van Baar, Huub. 2017. "Evictability and the biopolitical bordering of Europe." *Antipode* 49(1): 212–230.

Van Beek, W. E. A. 1992. "The dirty smith: smell as a social frontier among the Kapsiki/Higi of north Cameroon and north-eastern Nigeria." *Africa* 62: 38-58.

Vilenica, Ana. 2019. "Contradictions and Antagonisms in (Anti-) Social(ist) Housing in Serbia." *ACME: An International Journal for Critical Geographies* 18(6): 1261-1282.

Chapter 10

Worn-out and Wanted:
Footwear and its Temporalities

Veronika Zavratnik

University of Ljubljana, Slovenia

Abstract

Based on ethnographic fieldwork in Ljubljana, this chapter focuses on the practices and lived experiences of people regarding their footwear and the ways in which they negotiate their lives through their footwear choices. By understanding footwear as an integral part of bodily engagement with the world, the aim is to highlight footwear as a significant part of contemporary life, a part of important events and transitions, and its ability to traverse the present and connect it to the past and the future. Using the metaphor "footwear landscape" (Hockey, et al. 2014, 257) and a sensori-social approach (Howes 2022), the chapter describes people's imaginings of the past and the future through their footwear.

Keywords: material culture, footwear, past, present, future, Ljubljana

* * *

Prologue: Red Converse shoes

If I had to choose my favourite pair of shoes, I'd have no problem. Although I have not worn them for many years because they are practically unwearable, [my] red Converse shoes immediately come to my mind. The ones I begged my dad for in my second year of high school – just as I begged for Superstars a few years earlier. Both pairs, I remember, at that time embodied exactly what I wanted to be(come): rebellious, independent, rocker. /.../ Well worn, with cracked rubber, wrinkles, and tears in the fabric, inscribed with slogans and names and with a hole in the sole. At some point, I also changed the laces: yellow on the right side and Rastafarian colours on the left. I remember well how a friend of a friend untied his ponytail, pulled them out of his hair one summer evening and gave them to me. I also remember well most of the occasions when the inscriptions were made, the friends who wrote them and the conversations we had. Occasionally my Converse [shoes] would get a new decoration, usually part of a beer can – called 'sntnt' in slang – while we were drinking late at night at a nearby flea market. Three festivals, four summers, cold winter days (when it was highly indecent to admit you were cold in canvas shoes), countless jumps through a student dorm window (at forbidden hours, of course!), secretly made tongue piercing, arguments, first loves. After four years and several failed attempts, I finally realised that the sole was beyond repair and packed them up and put them in a box that sits on top of the wardrobe. The red Converse shoes helped me through a period of identity questioning, they introduced me to new friends in a new era of my life, and because they were the ultimate choice, they also solved many of the typical fashion dilemmas of adolescence. Of course, I could not throw them away!

/... / When I feel like the combination of first-world problems and the hardships of adulthood are moulding me too much, red Converse shoes soothe the heaviness of those feelings. They remind me of a (now) almost vanished 'rebellious' streak, of stubbornness, determination, optimism. They remind me of my father. They remind me of friendships and of an infinite sense of power. Red Converse shoes are not just a pair of my favourite shoes. They are a part of who I am and how I became who I am. /.../ Sometimes I even wish I was like a Converse shoe – universal and durable. But, actually, we are most similar in that we both remember the same events and keep the same memories. (Field Diary, January 2019)

Figure 10.1: A memory packed in the box with red Converse shoes. Martina Zavratnik, ferry on the way to the island of Korčula, Croatia, summer 2008.

Introduction

A short, autoethnographic excerpt from a field diary introduces this chapter for three reasons. Firstly, it aims to emphasise footwear as a significant part of contemporary life, as a part of important events and life transitions, as being responsive to change in (social) environments and identification processes, and their ability to connect the past and the present (Hockey et al. 2014, 257). Secondly, the excerpt suggests the importance of understanding clothing not only as significant in constituting one's appearance, but also – recognizing that it is "worn on the body" (Woodward 2007, 25) – constituting the "sensual experience of wearing" (Bernes and Eicher 1993, 3 in Woodward 2007, 25). And thirdly, I have decided to begin this chapter with a personal narrative also for a very non-academic reason, simply to share the story of my favourite pair of shoes with the people who will read it and to begin this chapter with some "warmth" (Miller 2008, 296). Daniel Miller (2010, 41) makes a similar point in his studies of clothing: studies of clothing should not be "*cold*" (emphasis in original), devoid of any intimate and emotional details, but instead should aim to evoke "the tactile, emotional, intimate world of feelings" to convey to the reader how it feels to wear a specific piece of clothing or – as in this case – a particular pair of shoes. For this reason, I employ, in what follows, an approach to material culture studies as represented in the work of Daniel Miller, Chrisopher Tilley, Victor Buchli and others who have contributed to what David Howes (2022, 321) terms the paradigm of "the sensori-social life of things." In other words: I employ a sensori-social approach (Howes 2022) that posits things as "bundles of social relation[s]" as well as "bundles of sensory qualities or sensual relations" (Howes 2022, 322).

Miller's thoughts on clothing, however, are to be understood in parallel with his call to see things not (only) as representations – as "messages" – but as part of material culture, as "one part of a process of objectification, or self-alienation" (Miller 2010, 58; cf. Miller 1987, 19-33). Drawing on Erving Goffman and Ernst Gombrich, he suggests that through the social process of objectification, objects become taken for granted and thus powerful:

> [O]bjects are important not because they are evident and physically constraint or enable, but often precisely because we do not 'see' them. The less we are aware of them, the more powerfully they can determine our expectations by setting the scene and ensuring normative behaviour, without being open to challenge. They determine what takes place to the extent that we are unconscious of their capacity to do so. (Miller 2005, 5)

He terms this capacity of things to fade out of our attention as the "humility of things" (Miller 2005, 5; Miller 2010, 51). Despite (or, as Miller and Woodward (2012, 16-17) would have it, because of) the ubiquity of footwear, it seems quite unusual to inquire why people wear the shoes they do. I have had numerous conversations starting with sentences such as: "*No, I really don't care about shoes, I'd just wear anything.*" Or: "*No, I never think about what shoes I am going to wear, I always wear just one model.*" Sometimes these conversations ended hours later, after an odyssey in shopping malls and shoe shops. 'Anything' – as it turned out – was nevertheless carefully chosen by taking into consideration the colour, the model, the materials, and the brand, and when the 'one same model' could not be found in Ljubljana, it was finally bought online and delivered by expensive express shipping from Spain. The question I want to pose, then, is a simple one: Why go to all this trouble if shoes are just something we put on our feet to protect us from cold, rain or other unpleasant conditions if they are just a means to facilitate our walking? As Mike Michael (2000) suggested in his paper on the role of mundane technologies, only a few people might choose their footwear purely for their function – it will also be chosen for its meaning (or lack thereof). This chapter, hence, explores footwear by paying attention to material and semiotic affordances shoes can engender (Sherlock 2014; 2016).

The role footwear plays in our experiences of the world has been interpreted in different ways; either as a tool that complicates our experiences of the environment (Michael 2000), a device imposing a separation "between the activities of a mind at rest and a body in transit, between cognition and locomotion, and between the space of social and cultural life and the ground upon which that life is materially enacted" (Ingold 2004, 321), or an aid in inquiries into how people live out their identities (Hockey et al. 2013, 9). These perspectives notwithstanding, it holds true that, as Giorgio Riello and Peter McNeil (2006) summarize, the relationship between a person and footwear is one that could be described with the phrase 'from the cradle to the grave,' as footwear is present in people's life events and transitions (Hockey et al. 2013) and is an important part of popular culture.[1] Understanding the (physical)

---

[1] However, in popular culture and daily life, shoes are often "discussed in terms of what they *stand* for" in terms of fashion, femininity, or gender (see, for example, Huey and Kenny 2014; Riello and McNeil 2006; Shawcross 2014; Steele and Hill 2012; Small 2014) "rather than what they are and how they are subjectively perceived and consumed" (Sherlock 2014, 26). It is, however, important to acknowledge that "what they stand for" influences – as it is visible also in this chapter – the consumption and use of the footwear.

body as socially and culturally constructed (Entwistle 2000), I approach footwear by using the metaphor of "footwear landscape" proposed by Hockey et al. to describe the "situated, perspectival nature of human beings' temporal orientations and therein people's scope for re-imagining what was or what might be" (Hockey et al. 2014, 257) through their footwear. This chapter then discusses footwear as part of the material culture central to our bodily engagements with the world and through which we experience the world. Space, time, body, and social contexts indeed give the footwear an active role in shaping identities, affiliations, and our personal attitudes. Shoes can thus offer a nuanced insight into "who we are and how we engage with the world" (Sherlock 2014, 26). The aim of this paper is, to paraphrase Daniel Miller (2005, 38), to show how shoes make people.

The material presented in this chapter was collected over the course of eight years, beginning in 2014.[2] My fieldwork took place mostly in Ljubljana, Slovenia. Part of the research was done in collaboration with the students of ethnology and cultural anthropology when, in 2019, we worked together with the Slovene Ethnographic Museum to prepare the exhibition on footwear *Bosi, obuti, sezuti* (Eng: *My feet. My shoes. My way,* Žagar 2020) which included people from different parts of Slovenia. It included people from nine to eighty-two years of age, occupied as a singer in a rock band, a nurse, a lawyer, a saleswoman and salesmen, a pensioner, a therapist, an astrological psychologist, and many others. My own research work was carried out using semi-structured interviews, informal conversations, and observation of the role footwear play in people's daily life – during our meetings, in shoe shops, and in public places. Part of the fieldwork was carried out in the homes of my interlocutors while going through their shoe wardrobes. Many of the interviews were carried out during walking, a practice that started spontaneously, mostly due to the suggestion made by my interlocutors, as it was easier for them to discuss some aspects of 'shoe lives' by not sitting down.

Shoes that are

As part of material culture, footwear stands at the intersection of the physical and social environment (Sherlock 2014, 47), the body, and the ability to participate in and shape the wearer's experiences. In her study of women's clothing choices in two British cities, London and Nottingham, Sophie

---

[2] The focus of my master thesis research was Converse All Stars shoes (Zavratnik 2014; 2016; 2019); later – in my doctoral research – I turned my attention to footwear in general.

Woodward (2007, 24) argues that a crucial part of understanding material culture is to understand its materiality as "lived and embodied"; how a fabric feels on the skin, how it holds the body, how it conceals or reveals, what it affords to the body. She shows how choosing clothes is a complex activity connected to the social contexts we expect to enter, our daily schedules, planned activities, the places we plan to visit, and the obligations that await us during the day. In this sense, clothing should be understood as a kind of framework chosen with daily obligations and individual and societal expectations in mind: "*I already think in the morning about what awaits me during the day – will I have time to go home* [to change] *or not?*" An interlocutor of mine, a young woman whose job included having meetings with her clients, many times online, sometimes in person, explained how at her previous job, she had an extra pair of "*slightly nicer shoes*," i. e., pumps, in her drawer to reduce the stress of being poorly prepared for the occasion and having to plan whole day already in the morning. According to Mike Michael (2000), footwear can be understood as a mundane technology that mediates and complicates our relationship with the environment. That is, footwear can be seen as a kind of framework that helps us encounter the environment beneath our feet. The materiality of footwear, then, engenders how we will feel (about) this same world. For example, feeling too close to the ground can lead to not only unpleasant but also painful experiences. As one of my interlocutors explained:

> You know, when I walked [with Camper shoes], it was as if there was nothing between my feet and the ground. I mean, [as if] there was nothing between the asphalt and my feet. And because I walked a lot, of course, I felt the consequences – my feet hurt.

The experience of being close to the ground and feeling its texture can, on the other hand, also opens diametrically different kind of sensations:

> Once you start wearing barefoot shoes, there's no going back because the [normal] shoes from before do not fit you anymore. /.../ Your feet expand. You know, it's like when you go barefoot for the summer, and then you wonder why your trainers feel so weird. Because they are [weird], aren't they? Of course, your feet were free all summer and now you force them back into something so tight. /.../ [When you wear barefoot shoes] the way you walk changes, you [start to] move like a cat. A little more elegant because you have to amortise.

Footwear, as we can see, influences and (co-)shapes the relationship (Michael 2000, 115) between the body and the environment depending on individual preferences and social contexts. When planning a trip to the Alpine mountains, visiting a family on a Saturday morning, trekking the Cuban moist forests region, or going bouldering, one will most probably choose a different type of footwear for each of these activities. Wearing different types of shoes enables different affordances, enables us to navigate different territories, and illuminates different aspects of our identities, such as being a mountaineer, a member of a family, a world traveller, or a climber. Understanding shoes as material and semiotic resources (Sherlock 2014, 47) for navigating our natural, cultural, and social environments means that changing one's shoes or taking them off can therefore mean a shift between different aspects of one's identity. This is reflected in one of the conversations on how playing football barefoot triggered a change in how one of my interlocutors positioned himself towards his colleagues, enabling him to become a fearless football player:

> Well, only once [did I play sports barefoot] when we had a sports day at our work /.../ and then I took off my Teva sandals /.../ and here I was playing tough again: here I am, playing barefoot. We were playing on a macadam, the stones were sharp, and there I go barefoot, 'I will try to outplay you, you can't touch me!' And you know, that's how it is, that's how you show – right from the beginning you show that you're not afraid of them.

As suggested earlier, it is crucial to understand footwear in use, in action, on people's feet and in different social contexts. However, our footwear wardrobes do not usually consist only of the shoes we wear on a regular basis. Often, when going through our wardrobe of shoes, we come across shoes that we have worn in the past but no longer wear for various reasons, as well as shoes that we bought with the plan to wear them but have not (yet) found the 'right' opportunity to put them on. Looking at a collection of shoes in the wardrobe, a sense of the past and the present can be materialized through "landmark pairs" (Hockey et al. 2014). Such shoes, moreover, can inform the future (Hockey et al. 2014, 257). As indicated in the introductory reflection, landmark pairs of shoes connect us to the past, and, on the other hand, imagining ourselves wearing a particular pair can also inform our visions of the future. In other words, the footwear landscape (Hockey et al. 2014) is a temporal landscape.

Shoes that were

Life itself is as much a long walk as it is a long conversation, and the ways
along which we walk are those along which we live.

(Ingold and Vergunst 2008, 1)

As a particular pair of shoes is "worn habitually over a period of time /.../ it
comes to define a person during a particular period of one's life" (Woodward,
2007, 25). Shoes help us remember the past, the events, and experiences when
we wore them, and the people we were with at the time, and thus enable us to
travel in time, revive memories, and retrieve our past identities. Exploring how
footwear can be used to inquire into the ways in which people live out their
identities, Jenny Hockey et al. (2013, 9) observe that "[k]nowing who we are
partly derives from knowing who we have been," a point echoed by Sophie
Woodward's (2007) description of clothes as means to remember our former
selves and to construct who we are here and now. Following the social lives (cf.
Kopytoff 1986) of shoes, when they go from being a wished-for pair to being
shoes worn daily, and finally to becoming a memory object or a worn-out pair
to be discarded, can, for a researcher, "make salient what might otherwise
remain obscure" (Kopytoff 1986, 67), namely provide insights into people's
past identities and experiences.

Wearing a pair of shoes is also a bodily practice. Through use, the shoes
"merge" with the wearer's body, assume the shape of the foot, respond to
environmental influences, and thus form an especially intimate relationship
with the wearer. This relationship is especially durable as the person's footprint
on the sole of the shoe, and the adjustments in other materials of the shoes can
remind of the person's presence even after he or she has stopped wearing them
(or the person is gone), meaning that our identity construction acquires a
bodily and sensory dimension. As shown in one of the conversations on
second-hand footwear, the shape assumed by footwear through its use can
remind of the events and paths walked in the shoes, that is to say, experiences
one has had. Questioned as to why she never buys used, second-hand shoes,
even though she buys second-hand clothing, one of the interlocutors
responded: "*Because I think that... I don't wanna walk in someone else's shoes*
[Author's note: English in original]. *I also attribute a symbolic meaning to this. I
want to walk these paths on my own.*" It is interesting to note here that an
English idiom has been used to express an empathetic attitude toward
footwear that has already been used by someone else. As the English idiom
acknowledges, the connection between shoes and their wearer is accelerated
through use; by showing signs of use and retaining the shape of the foot, shoes
come to embody events and experiences of a person's life. In Slovenian,

perhaps the most similar idiom is 'Everyone knows where his shoe pinches' (*Vsak sam ve, kje ga čevelj žuli*), which refers to undesirable events, discomfort, or worries. In a similar way, one of the students noted in her reflexive writing on the pair of shoes she likes to wear the most: "I see my two shoes as my companions who listen to me without prejudice. They are friends who support and comfort me, but they still pinch me here and there just to bring me back to reality." For her, too, a shoe that pinches reminded her of the difficulties of "reality."

A particular pair of shoes a person wears throughout his or her life can embody experiences and memories of certain events, even of periods of one's life and can thus be interpreted as kind of (auto)biographical object (Hoskins 1998; Hockey et al. 2013). In a way, certain pair of shoes can serve as a kind of anchor that reminds a person or a certain time and place:

> I have some strange memories of my childhood and adolescence, of the time when I was trying to gain my independence. And for me, my Converse shoes are a kind of emotional symbol, representing hanging out with my friends and, well, of consolation. I'd say that. /.../ And also, they have always been with me: my first kisses and other important events in my life – I have always worn them. And they connect me to those memories, to those first-time events, which were completely new and unique at the time, and maybe that [is why] I still keep them: because they are a pleasant reminder of how it felt when you were infinitely naïve and convinced of who knows what ideals and you were a good example of what you can do [if you want to], which [now you know] you cannot, ever. An example of a perfect, I'd say, perfect idea of what can be done with an energy, willingness, proactivity, exactly what I still wish people had more of, me included, more initiative. And it seems to me that this coincides exactly with the time when I was wearing my Converse shoes.

One of my interlocutors explained to me that she could not part with her almost completely worn-out Reebook trainers, which in a way became even a memory object, a pair that has lost its functionality but preserves memories of her grandmother, who was also the original owner:

> At the moment, my favourite shoes are white Reebok sports shoes that my grandmother gave me some time ago. I have them for at least two years and have worn them every day, but now I cannot because the sole is falling off. The shoes are old because my grandmother had bought

them about 30 years ago, but the quality is good, and they have lasted. They have a special meaning for me, and I am not ready to throw them away yet. I doubt I ever will, because they remind me of someone very important to me and all the memories I shared with her. Now they are stored in a box in my room. I don't want to wear them anymore because I don't want to destroy them completely.

Due to their evocative power (Vogrinc 2005), a pair of shoes can, then, also act as a beholder of a memory, a reminder – as the following account on Converse All-Star shoes suggests – of personal history and of social norms expected in certain life periods:

Oh, yes, now I remember something else. I stopped wearing Allstars back then [in 1994 or 1993] /.../ you could buy them, but they weren't that popular anymore. And then they started [becoming popular again] sometime around 2010, and I wasn't interested in them anymore. Because I knew – well, they were good [shoes] from that time when I was young and stuff, teenager in my late years – but I didn't want to wear them anymore, mainly because of their sole. And, I mean, it wouldn't be appropriate either.[3] /.../ I'd rather have them remind me of a certain time in my life than wear them again. They're something – yes, they are to remind me of my personal history. /.../ I don't want to make a big, nostalgic thing out of them. That time is over now. Well, I still dress the same, but I don't want to wear the same haircut anymore.

Certain types (and brands) of footwear are associated with certain music genres or even subcultures. Alexandra Sherlock, for example, wrote about how Clark's Originals have become synonymous with "masculine style, authenticity, coolness" (Sherlock 2014, 30) and their connection to the Manchester indie music scene (Sherlock 2014; Sherlock 2016). Similarly, discussing Dr Martens' branding strategies, Cath Davies noted their connections to New Age Travellers, punk, grunge, and indie music (Davies 2014, 3). And in my research on Converse All Stars, as shown already in the prologue, I noticed connections to punk, grunge, and rock music (Zavratnik 2014; Zavratnik 2016); All Stars

---

[3] Similarly, another interlocutor explained, why he stopped wearing Converse All Stars shoes: *"We had to grow out of that phase, and now we're at the point in life where we want people to take us seriously, right /.../ we want to prove that we can be professional."*

were many times discussed as *"this one accessory /.../ in rock and roll that kind of represented you. If you have All-Stars, then you're a real rocker /.../."*

In the case of Converse All Stars, too, it is crucial to acknowledge the cultural importance of the way in which materials react to the practice of walking, how they adjust to the foot, and how the traces of use are shown through time – cracked white rubber that turns yellowish, holes in the upper part of the shoe that is made of canvas, the dirt that cannot be washed away even by a washing machine. With "age and interactions with people" (Miller 2009, 162), they acquire patina (cf. McCracken 1988; Appadurai 1996; Miller 2009), but only for those with specific (sub)cultural knowledge. Thus, in line with Arjun Appadurai's thoughts, All Stars shoes acquired their full meaning only in a proper context, i.e., only in and for those "assemblies of objects and people who know how to indicate, through their bodily practices, their relationship to these objects" (Appadurai 1996, 75). As one of the interlocutors explained, it was wrong to have *"clean, nice* [All Stars] *shoes, where the white* [rubber] *was really white and you could see one's mother was cleaning them"* as it was just *"too fancy."* Traces of wear became "a sign of the right sort of duration in the social life of things" (Appadurai 1996, 75). For him, these were especially important as he noted that Converse All Stars were becoming more and more *"commercialised"* and were worn by the people who wear them only because they were *"popular."* Cacked rubber and holes in the canvas, then, became essential in shaping his (past) identity as a rocker. We can see how a particular pair of shoes imbued with the memories of the past can become essential in how memories of events, periods, and past identities materialize.

Shoes that will be

/.../ sometimes I think to myself, 'What if you beautified yourself?' But then I think: 'Who will walk in these shoes?!'

Our footwear choices in the present are not only engendered by the past and the present. Buying a new pair of shoes inevitably addresses the question of the future, as imagining what a pair of shoes can help us be(come) in the future is ingrained in the very act of choosing. For example, one of my interlocutors asked me to go shoe shopping with her, as – as she said – I seem to have a lucky hand when it comes to finding a pair that 'fits.' She needed a new pair of shoes for the christening of a family friend's daughter. For her, buying shoes is a nightmare. She wears size 41-42, has a narrow foot, and has a very picky taste. She told me that it has often happened to her that she had to buy shoes in the men's department because, for many women's models 41 is the largest size. Normally she would just wear her usual 'everyday shoes,' but she was going to be a godmother, so she wanted to buy shoes that were nice enough to match her chosen outfit – a long floral skirt, a white shirt, and a denim jacket – but not too fancy so she could still wear them with her usual outfits. She already knew which brands suited her ergonomics, and after five pairs, she found shoes that were narrow enough and nice enough. She put both shoes on, looked in the mirror and asked: *"How will I look in front of the altar with a baby in my hands?"*

In other words, my interlocutor imagined herself wearing specific shoes. One can see how a godmother-to-be imagined herself in a specific situation, in a specific context, with a specific role on her hands and specific shoes on her feet. A similar process was reflected on another occasion in the opinion of another interlocutor when, while shopping, she said:

> For example, I love colours and patterns and things like that on my shoes, but it's not my style. And if I had shoes like that, I couldn't combine them with anything, and it doesn't make sense. I mean, I'm always thinking about how I'm going to wear them – am I? It's not a problem to buy them, but why just leave them standing there then. /.../ With these things, if I'm not sure, I can just go [to the shop] and look at a pair of shoes many times before I decide. /.../ In that sense, maybe I'm thinking more practically [and ask myself]: 'Are you going to wear them?'

Orientation towards the future is part of how we experience our every day, and imagining (short-term) futures influences how we construct our daily outfits (Woodward 2007), footwear included, as we choose them carefully according to our daily obligations. However, the influence of media and popular culture should not be overlooked. It is beyond the scope of this chapter to explore how popular culture and fashion influence our footwear choices, yet it should be noted that there is a connection between commercially produced imaginaries and teleoaffects that promise recognisable futures. Building on the work of Theodore Schatzki, Rebecca Bryant and Daniel M. Knight (2019, 140) refer to all futural orientations as teleoaffects, dispositions that "mobilize[s] a set of practices that encompass a number of associated actions and ends which people acceptably pursue." We can see specific teleoaffective structures (cf. Schatzki 2002, 80 in Bryant and Knight 2019, 18) in the introductory reflexive excerpt on Converse All-Star shoes or in Alexandra Sherlock's research on Clarks Originals (Sherlock 2016) mentioned earlier. A similar observation can be made regarding one of my interlocutor's experiences. He told me about one of the first pairs of shoes he bought when he started his university studies in the nineties and wanted – as he put it – to become part of the folk-rock music scene. At the time, the duo Simon and Garfunkel were something he looked up to. He explained how his imaginaries affected his fashion choices:

These are Paul Simon and Art Garfunkel, right. This is the record of their greatest hits. /.../ When I saw the cover of the record – this is the back of the record – wow! 'I want to have shoes like that. I want those shoes! These, from Paul Simon. /.../ These shoes. I want to have them.' And I had a sweater like this, I asked my grandma to knit me one. And then I bought a pair of trousers like these, and in between there were [these shoes] – this is a scene from New York, and I wanted them badly. But that was, I saw this photo in 1990, and that wasn't even the fashion of New York in the 90s. But I really wanted to go to New York and dress like that.

Shortly after seeing the record cover, he bought a pair of shoes similar to the ones worn by Simon in Spain, where he was visiting with a friend. He spent the last of his money to buy those shoes, even if it meant that he could not afford a train ticket to get home afterwards and instead had to hitchhike and travel as a stowaway. He slept with the new shoes in his sleeping bag just to make sure they were not stolen in case someone tried to chase him away from their improvised sleeping places. If, as Maurice Halbwachs (1992, 25) had it, we always remember important events, then, in this case, remembering the exact experiences and misadventures suggest the importance of pursuing an imagined future identity that would materialise through a particular pair of shoes.

When considering orientations towards the future through footwear, however, one must distinguish between the act of selecting a pair of shoes from the already existing footwear wardrobe in order to construct one's daily wardrobe, something Janja Žagar has called a "fragmentary order" (Žagar Grgič 2011), and the purchase of a new pair of shoes. While the first involves a short-term vision of the future, usually related to the schedule of the day, a purchase involves a longer temporal perspective in which one imagines oneself in (more) situations or even in new social roles. Rebecca Bryant and Daniel M. Knight's (2019) theorization of different orientations to the future (i. e., anticipation, expectation, speculation, potentiality, hope, destiny) is particularly helpful in discussing the ability of footwear to traverse the present and connect it to the future, as for our understanding of how the future "awakens the present" (Bryant and Knight 2019, 192). In this way, we can better understand the quotidian. For instance, buying a new pair of shoes, expectation of wearing them one day in the future is implicitly present – we buy new shoes because we expect we will most probably wear them in a (near) future. One can, for example, buy shoes with the expectation of wearing them to a certain event (e.g., a wedding) or for a particular activity (e.g., mountain climbing), or one may even expect to wear them in specific places (e. g. in the mountains). Bryant and Knight (2019, 58) label expectation as a "conservative teleology" because of its implicit and assumed reliance on the past; we expect what we expect because we rely on our past experiences.

The futural orientation that seems most pertinent here, however, is hope. Bryant and Knight (2019, 134) write about hope as "a form of futural momentum, a way of pressing into the future that attempts to pull certain potentialities into actuality." In other words, "[h]ope is about something that doesn't presently exist but potentially could" (Bryant and Knight 2019, 134). For example, every time one of my interlocutors buys his shoes, he imagines himself wearing those shoes in one of the cities he has visited in the past. While drawing on his past experiences of visiting these cities, he simultaneously acknowledges that the imagined future may or may not realise. Visiting a certain city with a specific pair of shoes is what he hopes for, a possibility, a disposition that "motivate[d] his activity" of buying a pair of shoes "here-and-now" (Bryant and Knight 2019, 157), but the outcome of this futural orientation is "uncertain" (Bryant and Knight 2019, 142):

> You know, when I buy my shoes, I always imagine, 'Okay, I am going to buy these shoes now,' and then I imagine a city, a foreign city, where I am going to go [with them]. /.../ I wear some clothes, depending on the weather, a camera, [shoes] and that's it! Every time I look at those shoes – and I imagined the shoes I am wearing now in the same way! I thought 'Wow, I am going to wear these in Belgrade,' I imagined Belgrade very clearly. Then, I never went to Belgrade with these shoes.

On another occasion, the same interlocutor explained how he 'prepared' himself for a newly expected social role and the obligations and responsibilities that would come with it:

> Do you know when I bought the first [Birkenstock slippers]? /.../ I bought the first Birkenstock sandals when my [first] son was born, and I assumed I will have to carry him around to blurb him. And at that time my feet kind of [hurt] when I walked barefoot in a certain rhythm. And [I assumed] that would bother me. And I bought a pair of Birkenstock slippers, they were notoriously expensive /.../ even though our family

didn't have money to afford much. But I bought [a pair], I still have them at home, they are clogs. And I only wore them at home, they were my slippers,[4] and it was really much easier to carry him around.

The decision to buy this pair of clogs was made in the hope that he would become a good, attentive, and caring father. To achieve what he hoped for, he actively took care of his own feet by giving them enough support to walk comfortably for a long period of time. Following Stef Jansen's (2016, 448 in Bryant and Knight 2019, 139-140) analytical distinction between transitive and intransitive modalities of hope, the ability to walk for longer periods of time can be interpreted as a transitive object of hope that generates intransitive hopefulness to be a good father in general. In this sense, the future was brought into the family home even before the child was born. The relationship with a son was established and materialized even before he was born, namely through this pair of Birkenstock clogs.

Conclusion

> Oh hey, I put some new shoes on
> and suddenly everything is right.
> I said Hey, I put some new shoes on
> and everybody's smiling, it's so inviting.
> Oh short on money but long on time,
> slowly strolling in the sweet sunshine
> and I'm running late, and I don't need an excuse
> 'cause I'm wearing my brand-new shoes.
>
> (Paolo Nutini, New Shoes)

In his ethnography *The perfect fit: Creative work in the global shoe industry*, Claudio E. Benzecry looks at the process of globalization from the perspective of the women's shoe industry. Using the "follow the thing approach" (Benzecry 2022, 14), he traces the process of shoe production through his work with designers, developers, production managers, fit models, and others. Although his primary aim is to provide an insight into an example of how global production works from the ground up, he implicitly shows that the process of shoe production is one of creativity, selection, and negotiation between drawing on previous experience, producing something new, and predicting

---

[4] In Slovenia, it is very common to have a special pair of sleepers that one only wears inside the house.

future (fashion) trends. The leitmotif of this chapter, which focuses instead on the practice of choosing and wearing shoes, was in some ways similar: to show how shoes, when approached analytically and by employing what David Howes (2022) termed the sensori-social approach, can help us understand how people negotiate their lives, understand the(ir) past (identities) and imagine the(ir) future. By understanding footwear as significant to bodily engagements with the world (Hockey et al. 2013) and by employing the metaphor of "footwear landscape" (Hockey et al. 2014) this chapter also showed how by choosing our footwear we navigate not only our natural but also cultural and social environments (Sherlock 2014, 47).

We can see how a pair of shoes can come to embody memories and experiences by association with a particular place, a particular time, and particular people. Through continuous wearing, a pair of shoes can become imbued with memories of the past, acquiring an affective dimension and becoming what Jonas Frykman and Maja Povrzanović Frykman (2016, 24) have called sensitive objects. One could, in fact, take this point even further, holding, for example, that by throwing away the pair of shoes that embodies a memory of a certain event, the significance of the event is also reduced or that by throwing away the shoes one can also throw away (hurtful) memories. This was also reflected in the conversation about the wedding shoes: "*If I were divorced, I'd most probably throw them away.*"

In the final section of this chapter, I draw on the work of Rebecca Bryant and Daniel M. Knight (2019) and their conception of futural orientations, specifically hope, to show how a person can hope for and even prepare for their future (identities) by choosing a particular pair of shoes. By drawing the "not-yet into the present" and by "motivat[ing] activity in the here-and-now" (Bryant and Knight 2019, 157), hope as a futural orientation is "awakening the present" (Bryant and Knight 2019, 198; Bryant 2020) – also through our footwear.

To conclude this chapter, I would like to return to the introductory section and to the "humility of things" (Miller 2005, 5; Miller 2010, 51). In a short reflection, one of the students with whom we prepared the abovementioned exhibition on shoes reflects on the fact that she only ever wears one pair of shoes – because they fit so well that she does not even notice they are there. And it is exactly this good fit, this invisibility, that makes her feel – safe.

Why do I wear only one [pair of shoes]? Because they are the most comfortable and functional, because I know they will not let me down.

I know they will not let me down wherever I go, because they are the most universal of all shoes [I have] /.../.

It is this humility of our shoes that enables us to sense and make sense of ourselves and our environments in the past, the present and the future.

References

Appadurai, Arjun. 1996. *Modernity at large: Cultural dimensions of globalisation.* Minneapolis: University of Minnesota Press.

Benzecry, Claudio E. 2022. *The perfect fit: Creative work in the global shoe industry.* Chicago, London: University of Chicago Press.

Davies, Cath. 2014. "Smells like teens spirit: Channeling subcultural traditions in contemporary Dr Martens branding." *Journal of consumer culture* 16(1): 192-208.

Entwistle, Joanne. 2000. *The fashioned body: Fashion, dress and modern social theory.* Cambridge, Malden: Polity Press.

Halbwachs, Maurice. 1992. *On collective memory.* Chicago, London: University of Chicago Press.

Hockey, Jenny, Rachel Dilley, Victoria Robinson, and Alexandra Sherlock. 2014. "The temporal landscape of shoes: A life course perspective." *The sociological review* 62(2): 255-275.

Hockey, Jenny, Rachel Dilley, Victoria Robinson, and Alexandra Sherlock. 2013. "Worn shoes: Identity, memory and footwear." *Sociological research online* 18(1): 1-14.

Hoskins, Janet. 1998. *Biographical objects: How things tell the stories of people's lives.* New York, London: Routledge.

Howes, David. 2022. "In defense of materiality: Attending to the sensori-social life of things." *Journal of material culture* 27(3): 313-335.

Huey, Sue, and Kathryn Kenny. 2014. *Shoetopia: Contemporary footwear.* London: Laurence King Publishing Ltd.

Ingold, Tim. 2004. "Culture on the ground: The world perceived through the feet." *Journal of material culture* 9(3): 315-340.

Ingold, Tim, and Jo Lee Vergunst. 2008. "Introduction." In: Tim Ingold and Jo Lee Vergunst, eds. *Ways of walking: Ethnography and practice on foot.* London, New York: Routledge. Pp. 1-20.

Kopytoff, Igor. 1986. "The cultural biography of things: Commodization as process." In: Arjun Appadurai, ed. *The social life of things: Commodities in cultural perspective.* Cambridge, New York: Cambridge University Press. Pp. 64-92.

McCracken, Grant. 1988. *Culture and consumption.* Bloomington: Indiana University Press.

Michael, Mike. 2000. "These boots are made for walking...: Mundane technology, the body and human-environment relations." *Body & Society* 6(3-4): 107-126.

Miller, Daniel. 1987. *Material culture and mass consumption.* Oxford, Cambridge: Blackwell.

Miller, Daniel. 2005. "Materiality: An introduction." In *Materiality*, Daniel Miller, ed. 1-50. Durham, London: Duke University Press.

Miller, Daniel. 2008. *The comfort of things.* Cambridge, Malden: Polity Press.

Miller, Daniel. 2009. "Buying time." In: Elisabeth Shove, Frank Trentmann, Richard Wilk, eds. *Time, consumption and everyday life: Practice, materiality and culture.* Oxford, New York: Berg. Pp. 157-170.

Miller, Daniel. 2010. *Stuff.* Cambridge, Malden: Polity Press.

Miller, Daniel, and Sophie Woodward. 2012. *Blue jeans: The art of the ordin*ary. Berkley, Los Angeles, London: University of California Press.

Riello, Giorgio, and Peter McNeil. 2006. "A long walk: Shoes, People and Places." In: Giorgio Riello and Peter McNeil, eds. *Shoes: A history from sandals to sneakers.* Oxford, New York: Berg. Pp. 2-28.

Riello, Giorgio, and Peter McNeil. 2006. *Shoes: A history from sandals to sneakers.* London, New York: Berg.

Shawcross, Rebecca. 2014. *Shoes: An illustrated history.* London, New Delhi, New York, Sydney: Bloomsbury.

Sherlock, Alexandra. 2014. "'It's kind of where the shoe gets you to, I suppose': Materializing identity with footwear." *Critical studies in Fashion & Beauty* 5(1): 25-51.

Sherlock, Alexandra. 2016. *'This is not the shoe.' An exploration of the co-constitutive relationship between representations and embodied experiences of shoes.* Unpublished doctoral thesis. Sheffield: University of Sheffield.

Small, Lisa. 2014. *Killer Heels: The art of the high-heeled shoe.* Munich, London, New York: Brooklyn Museum.

Steele, Valerie, and Colleen Hill. 2012. *Shoe obsession.* New Haven, London: Yale University Press.

Tilley, Christopher. 2006. "Objectification." In: Christopher Tilley, Webb Keane, Susanne Küchler, Michael Rowlands and Patricia Spyer, eds. *Handbook of material culture.* Los Angeles, London, New Delhi, Singapore: SAGE. Pp. 60-73.

Vogrinc, Jože. 2005. "Kako so predmeti omrtveli in kaj jim danes vdihuje življenje? Sociologove opazke." *Argo* 138-141.

Woodward, Sophie. 2007. *Why women wear what they wear.* Oxford, New York: Bloomsbury.

Zavratnik, Veronika. 2014. "Ko stvari postanejo pomembne, niso več naključne": Pomen materialne kulture pri tvorbi identitete posameznika. Master thesis. Ljubljana: Department of ethnology and cultural anthropology.

Zavratnik, Veronika. 2016. "Alstarke so pa malo dlje ostale': Čevlji kot del materialne kulture." *Etnolog* 77: 147-163.

Zavratnik, Veronika. 2019. "'O, čevlji, kako vas ljubim!'" In: Andrej Studen, ed. *Mimohod blaga: materialna kultura potrošniške družbe na Slovenskem.* Ljubljana: Inštitut za novejšo zgodovino. Pp. 199-210.

Žagar, Janja. 2020. *Bosi. Obuti. Sezuti. Vodnik po razstavi Slovenskega etnografskega muzeja.* Ljubljana: Slovenski etnografski muzej.

Žagar Grgič, Janja. 2011. '*Osebni videz: Izbira in komunikacija.*' Unpublished doctoral thesis. Ljubljana: University of Ljubljana.

Contributors

Editors

Blaž Bajič is an Assistant Professor and a researcher at the Department of Ethnology and Cultural Anthropology, Faculty of Arts, University of Ljubljana, where, in 2017, he received his PhD. As a post-doctoral researcher in cultural studies at the School of Humanities of the University of Eastern Finland, he participated in SENSOTRA - Sensory Transformations and Transgenerational Environmental Relationships in Europe, 1950–2020 project (ERC-2015-AdG 694893; 2017-2021). His areas of interest include anthropology of the senses, popular culture and leisure, everyday life, anthropology of space and place, urban anthropology, globalization, anthropology of art and creativity, digitization, ecology, epistemology, etc. He also participated in the TRACES - Transmitting Contentious Cultural Heritages with the Arts (H2020-EU.3.6.-693857; 2016-2019) and DSI Digital Social Impact (KA226-050D8E8E; 2021-2023).

Recently, he co-edited the Senses of Cities: Anthropology, Art, Sensory Transformations (with Rajko Muršič and Sandi Abram; University of Ljubljana Press, 2022), Views of the Three Valleys (with Ana Svetel and Veronika Zavratnik; University of Ljubljana Press, 2021), and Close-ups: Youth, the Future and Imagining Development in Solčavsko (with Ana Svetel and Veronika Zavratnik; University of Ljubljana Press, 2022)

In 2021, Bajič was awarded the Emerging Scholar Award for outstanding early-career researchers by OnSustainability Research Network. He is also the current president of the Slovenian Ethnological and Anthropological Association KULA.

Ana Svetel is a teaching assistant and a researcher at the Department of Ethnology and Cultural Anthropology, Faculty of Arts, University of Ljubljana, where, in 2023, she received her PhD. In the dissertation, based on ethnographic fieldwork in Northeast Iceland, she focused on weather, seasonality, light and darkness in social dimensions of the Icelandic landscape. Her areas of interest include anthropological studies of landscape, environment, and language, with a regional specialization in the Slovenian Alps and Northern Europe.

Since 2021 she has participated in the following projects: HAPPY – Qualitative research methodology in Higher education teaching APProaches for sustainabilitY and well-being in Bhutan, Anthropological study of rural-urban and urban-rural migrations in Central Europe – The case of Slovenia and Hungary, and DigiFREN – Digital Aestheticization of Fragile Environment. She is also an assistant of the Learning Community Epistemology of everyday life within the EUTOPIA network.

Recently, she co-edited two volumes, Views of the Three Valleys (with Blaž Bajič and Veronika Zavratnik; University of Ljubljana Press, 2021) and Close-ups: Youth, the Future and Imagining Development in Solčavsko (with Blaž Bajič and Veronika Zavratnik; University of Ljubljana Press, 2022). She is the editor-in-chief of the Bulletin of the Slovene Ethnological Society Library series and serves as an editorial board member of the journal Svetovi/Worlds. In 2022, Svetel was awarded the Emerging Scholar Award for outstanding early-career researchers by OnSustainability Research Network. She is the co-chair of the Young Scholars Working Group at the International Society for Ethnology and Folklore (SIEF).

Authors

Rajko Muršič is a Professor of ethnology and cultural anthropology at the University of Ljubljana, Faculty of Arts, Department of Ethnology and Cultural Anthropology. His research focuses on the anthropology of popular music, theories of culture, epistemology, urban anthropology, methodology of anthropological research, sensory studies, digital ethnography, the use of algorithms, etc. His regional interests comprise Slovenia, Central and South-Eastern Europe (fieldwork in Slovenia, Poland, North Macedonia, Germany, and Japan).

He published eight monographs (all in Slovene) and co-edited eleven collections (six in English). He served as a member of the Executive Committee of the IUAES and a president of the Slovenian Ethnological and Anthropological Association Kula. He was the initial editor of the monograph series Zupanič's Collection.

As the principal researcher, he completed two national research projects. Recently, he was engaged as an expert researcher in the ERC project Sensotra (Sensory Transformations and Transgenerational Environmental Relationships in Europe, 1950-2020) at the University of Eastern Finland (2016-2021), and he is active in the project B-Air (Art Infinity Radio - Creating Sound Art for Babies, Toddlers and Vulnerable Groups) led by Radio Slovenia (2020-2023). He is as well the leader of the partner's team in the Erasmus+ project Happy (Qualitative Research in Higher Education Teaching Approaches for Sustainability and Well-being in Bhutan), led by the Free University in Amsterdam. Since 2022, he has participated in two projects financed by the Chanse Programme: Reimagining Public Values in Algorithmic Futures and Digital Aestheticization in/of Fragile Environments.

His recent works include Glasbeni pojmovnik za mlade (Music Glossary for the Youth), 2017; Sounds of Attraction: Yugoslav and Post-Yugoslav Popular Music (co-editor Miha Kozorog), 2017; Občutki mest: antropologija, umetnost, čutne transformacije (Feelings of Cities: Anthropology, Art, Sensory Transformations; co-editors Sandi Abram and Blaž Bajič), 2022.

Linda Lapiņa (pronouns she/they/it) works as an Associate Professor of Cultural Encounters at Roskilde University, Denmark. Linda is also a dancer and a psychologist. They grew up in Rīga, Latvia, and have been living in Copenhagen, Denmark, since 2004. Their work at the university is dedicated to making space for more bodies and forms of knowing, including arts-based, sensuous, affective, and more-than-human knowledges; and to contributing to generous and nourishing academic communities. Linda has published on a variety of topics, including racialisation, differentiated whiteness, and shifting migrant positions in the context of mobility between Eastern and Western Europe; Danishness and Danish exceptionalism; urban change and gentrification; temporalities and affectivity in urban space; and more-than-human memory. In addition to fieldwork and interviews, they work with autoethnography, arts-based, and affective methodologies. They are co-heading the research group Interkult and the departmental network in Environmental Humanities at the Department of Communication and Arts at Roskilde University. They have also been a visiting artist/researcher with the performance collective Sisters Hope (since 2021). Linda's recent research interests include urban-rural food encounters and alternative food systems; and affective dimensions of climate disaster.

Helmi Järviluoma is a Finnish sound, music, and cultural scholar and writer. She is Professor Emerita of Cultural Studies at the University of Eastern Finland. As a sensory and soundscape ethnographer, Järviluoma has developed the mobile method of sensobiographic walking. Her research and art span the fields of sensory remembering, qualitative methodology (especially regarding gender), environmental, cultural studies, sound art, and fiction writing. In

2016, she received an Advanced Grant from the European Research Council (ERC-2015-AdG 694893 SENSOTRA) in order to study Sensory Transformations and Transgenerational Environmental Relationships between the years 1950–2020 in three European cities. Among her 180 publications, co-authored Gender and Qualitative Methods (2003/2010) and Acoustic Environments in Change (2009) continue to draw attention. She has written and directed six radio features for the Finnish Broadcasting Company. In 2019, the Finnish Union of University Professors selected Helmi Järviluoma as professor of the year 2019, and she was awarded the decoration of Knight First Class of the Order of the White Rose in Finland. In 2018, the Finnish Academy of Science and Letters invited her as a member.

Inkeri Aula is a post-doctoral researcher in the Visual Communication Design research group (AVCD) in the School of Arts, Design, and Architecture at Aalto University, Finland. Currently, her research focuses on creativity, particularly on the effect of creative environmental relationships on well-being in later life, and on combining sensory and narrative methods for the fields of art and design with older adults. Previously, she has researched how the sensing of the environment has changed in European cities in ERC AdG-funded project SENSOTRA (2017-2021). Her doctoral thesis investigated Afro-Brazilian 'worlding' in the trans-local fight-dance-art of capoeira (University of Eastern Finland, 2020), based on multi-sited ethnography in Brazil and in Finland.

Artist collaborations and research creation are part of Aula's practice. In the artist group Aula, Niskanen & Salo, she has participated in the creation of site-responsive and immersive new media art installations that have been displayed in different countries, mainly in the USA and Finland. She collaborated with comics artist Sanna Hukkanen in the creation of a graphic book about Finno-Ugric mythical stories about trees and forests, *Metsänpeitto*, which received the North Karelia Art Prize in 2018, and has since been translated into three more languages.

Aula has published diverse research articles in the fields of anthropology and cultural studies in English, Finnish, and Portuguese. She is a member of several scientific societies, including a vice member board of the Finnish Anthropological Society. Her versatile research interests include environmental relationships, relational onto-epistemologies, cultural imaginaries, forest myths, anthropology of the senses and multisensory ethnography, artist collaborations, and research creation.

Sonja Pöllänen (MSSC) is a sensory anthropologist writing her PhD on affect theory, likenessing, and people's sensorial relationship with digital technology. Her PhD is based on fieldwork done for an ERC adv. grant (GA 694893) project SENSOTRA. The project aimed to produce new understandings of the changes in people's sensory environmental relationships in three European cities during a particular period in history, 1950–2020. Currently, Sonja works as a digital ecosystems and communications manager at Nokia.

Eeva Pärjälä is a grant researcher and doctoral student in the Social and Cultural Encounters doctoral program at the University of Eastern Finland. She is currently working as a grant researcher both at the University of Eastern Finland and at the University of Turku, combining working on her PhD research with data analysis and visualization in the New Economies of Artistic Labour – from Entrepreneurship to Sustainable Collectives project (funded by the Kone Foundation 2020–2024). She started her PhD research as a Junior Researcher at SENSOTRA - Sensory Transformations and Transgenerational Environmental Relationships in Europe, 1950–2020 project (ERC-2015-AdG 694893; 2017-2021). Her research focuses on transgenerational place attachment combining sensory anthropology, human geography, and urban studies.

Milla Tiainen is a Senior Lecturer in Musicology at the University of Turku, Finland, and Associate Professor (title of Docent) of Musicology at the University of Helsinki. She has published nearly 70 scientific articles in peer-reviewed journals and edited books in the areas of musical performance studies, cultural studies of music and sound, interdisciplinary voice studies, sensory studies, and new materialist and posthumanist research approaches to the study of arts and gender. She has co-edited special issues on these topics for such journals as Body & Society (2014), Cultural Studies Review (2015), and The Polish Journal of Aesthetics (2020). She is also co-editor, among other volumes, of Musical Encounters with Deleuze and Guattari (Bloomsbury Academic, 2017), Mattering Voices (Routledge, forthcoming in 2024), and New Materialism and Intersectionality (Routledge, forthcoming in 2024). Tiainen has worked as a researcher in a number of funded projects, including SENSOTRA (the University of Eastern Finland, ERC-funded, 2016–21, https://uefconnect.uef.fi/en/group/sensotra/) and Localizing Feminist New Materialisms (the University of Turku, Academy of Finland-funded, 2017–21). She was also one of the four main applicants and a working group leader of the Europe-wide research network, New Materialism: Networking European

Scholarship on 'How Matter Comes to Matter' (EU-funded COST Action IS1307, 2014–18). Tiainen is currently co-lead, with art historian Dr. Katve-Kaisa Kontturi, of the interdisciplinary project New Economies of Artistic Labor (funded by the Kone Foundation, 2020-24). She is also the Chair of the Finnish Musicological Society which received the annual science award of the Federation of Finnish Learned Societies in 2023, given in recognition of the society's long-term work in advancing music scholarship and its contributions to Finnish culture.

Juhana Venäläinen is an Associate Professor of Cultural Studies at the University of Eastern Finland, Joensuu, where he received his PhD in 2015. His research areas include commons theory, sensory studies, cultural economy, transformations of work, discourses of economic change, and everyday economic moralities. Currently, Venäläinen leads a research project on "Post-ownership as an interpretation and experience of economic change" (2022–2025, funded by the Kone Foundation) as well as a work package and the research team at the University of Eastern Finland in the research consortium "DigiFREN" (Digital Aestheticization of Fragile Environment, 2022–2025, funded by CHANSE ERA-NET co-fund programme, grant agreement 101004509). He has also recently participated in the ERC AdG project "SENSOTRA" (Sensory Transformations and Transgenerational Environmental Relationships in Europe, 1950–2020) with a special focus on developing the notion of the sensory commons and on devising the methodology of sensobiographic walks together with Helmi Järviluoma. Venäläinen has published and edited volumes and special issues about employment precarity, the experience economy, and financial cultures. His research articles have received awards such as "Academic Pen of the Year 2016" for the Best Finnish Article in social sciences in 2013–2015, together with Tero Toivanen) and "Best Article of the Year" (in Oikeus journal, 2011). Venäläinen holds the title of Docent (Adjunct Professor) in Cultural Studies of Work and the economy at the University of Jyväskylä.

Sandi Abram holds a PhD in Social and Cultural Anthropology from the University of Eastern Finland. Between 2017 and 2021, he participated as a Doctoral Researcher in the ERC-funded project SENSOTRA – Sensory Transformations and Transgenerational Environmental Relationships in Europe and currently works as a Post-doctoral Researcher at the Peace Institute, Ljubljana, and at the Department of Ethnology and Cultural Anthropology, University of Ljubljana. In 2022 he co-edited (with Blaž Bajič and Rajko Muršič) the book Senses of Cities: Anthropology, Art, Sensory

Transformations (University of Ljubljana Press). His main research interests are aestheticization, sensory and urban studies, non-institutional creative practices, multimodal and collaborative ethnography.

Katja Hrobat Virloget is an Associate Professor at the Faculty of Humanities of the University of Primorska, Slovenia, where she is currently Vice-Dean for Research and Head of the Department of Anthropology and Cultural Studies.

Her research interests include, on one side, migration and population movements, anthropology of memory, and, on the other side, intangible heritage, narrative tradition, mythical landscapes, and interdisciplinary research.

She has written a book V tišini spomina / In the Silence of Memory, on the so-called "Istrian exodus" after World War II with its divided memories and contested heritages. For its version in Slovenian, the latter translated to English in Silences and Divided Memories. The Exodus and its Legacy in Post-War Istrian Society by Berghahn books (2023), she received a nomination for the Excellence in Research Award 2022 by the Slovenian Research Agency and the Murko Award – the national ethnological prize (2021). In her second research area of intangible heritage, she successfully applied her research knowledge in the creation of The Mythical Park of Rodik. For the idea and realization of The Mythical Park, she received the Prometheus of Science for Excellence in Communication (2020) from Slovenian Science Foundation. The Mythical Park was awarded by Slovenian Museum Association (2021) for the innovative presentation of a narrative tradition in the landscape and as the second-best thematic route in Slovenia by the Tourist Association of Slovenia (2021). For her scientific work, she has received the Award for scientific excellence from the University of Primorska (2021) and the Bartol Award for Scientific Excellence at the Faculty of Humanities UP (2020).

Saša Poljak Istenič is a Research Associate at the Research Centre of the Slovenian Academy of Sciences and Arts (ZRC SAZU), Ljubljana, and an Assistant Professor at the Faculty of Tourism, University of Maribor, Slovenia. She received her PhD in ethnology at the University of Ljubljana in 2012. She led a post-doctoral project Surviving, Living, Thriving: Creativity as a Way of Life, funded by the Slovenian Research Agency (Z6-6841; 2014-2016), and a bilateral research project Urban Futures: Imagining and Activating Possibilities in Unsettled Times, co-funded by the Slovenian Research Agency and Croatian Science Foundation (J6-2578, IPS-2020-01-7010; 2020–2023). She also participated in several nationally funded research projects and international applied research on urban life, creativity, sustainability, social inclusion, and heritage. Her areas of interest derive from urban anthropology, anthropology of space and place, and anthropology of futures.

She published a monograph Tradicija v sodobnosti / Tradition in a contemporary world (Založba ZRC, 2013) and co-authored a book Družbeni učinki urbanega kmetijstva / Social Impact of Urban Agriculture (with Jani Kozina, Mateja Šmid Hribar, Jernej Tiran and Nela Halilović; Založba ZRC, 2019). She is a co-editor of Glasnik Slovenskega etnološkega društva / Bulleting of the Slovene Ethnological Society and was a guest editor of several thematic issues of Slovenian and Croatian journals, most recently of the issue on urban futures in Traditiones (2022).

As part of the AgriGo4Cities project team, she won the Diploma of Excellence for the Black Sea – Danubian Social & Economic Innovator (the European Commission – DG MARE, Romania) in 2019. She is also a member of the Executive Board of the Slovene Ethnological Society, the Expert Council of the Slovene Ethnographic Museum, and the Expert Committee on Intangible Cultural Heritage at the Ministry of Culture.

Jaka Repič is an Associate Professor of cultural and social anthropology at the Department of Ethnology and Cultural Anthropology, Faculty of Arts, University of Ljubljana. He completed his PhD thesis in 2006 with a study of transnational migrations between Argentina and Europe, with a special focus on the Slovenian diaspora in Argentina and returned mobilities. He teaches courses on the methodology of ethnology and cultural anthropology, current debates in social and cultural anthropology, urban anthropology, and ethnology of Australia and Oceania.

He was a visiting professor at Universidad Autónoma de Barcelona (2019-20) and Universidad de Buenos Aires (2010-11, 2015, 2017, 2023). He is currently the leader of a research programme, Ethnological Research of cultural knowledge, practices and Forms of Socialities (2022-2027).

Jaka Repič's research interests include diaspora studies, social memories, urbanisation and spatial studies, and anthropology of art. He has published two books in Slovenian ("Tracing Roots": Transnational Migration between Argentina and Europe and Urbanization and Constitution of Ethnic Communities in Port Moresby, Papua New Guinea). His recent publications include an edited volume Moving Places: Relations, Return, and Belonging (co-edited with Nataša Gregorič Bon, Berghahn books, 2016), and a special issue on Art and Migration in the journal Two Homelands. In the past years, he has also focused on the environmental changes and spatial practices in the Slovenian Alps.

Bethan Mathias Prosser is a researcher and listening practitioner, spanning roles across higher education and the community/voluntary sectors. Bethan lectures in the School of Humanities and Social Sciences at the University of Brighton, where she was awarded her PhD in 2022. Developing a form of participatory listening research, her PhD used listening methods to investigate residential experiences of urban seaside gentrification and displacement injustices on the UK south coast. She has recently been awarded an Economic and Social Research Council Post-Doctoral Fellowship by the South Coast Doctoral Training Partnership. Through this Award, she will continue to bring academic and practice-based listening approaches together to creatively understand and engage residents in issues of social justice and place. During her PhD, she also worked as a Research Assistant on the SENSOTRA - Sensory Transformations and Transgenerational Environmental Relationships in Europe, 1950–2020 project (ERC-2015-AdG 694893; 2017-2021). Alongside research, Bethan works with a community music social enterprise and eco-musicology collective, developing interactive listening walks, sound foraging, and music-making activities.

Sara Nikolić is an anthropologist and activist who, through her research practice based on critical, visual and sensory ethnography, explores housing cultures and practices after the "give-away" privatization of the public housing stock in Yugoslavia. She is a doctoral student at the Department of Ethnology and Anthropology of the Faculty of Philosophy in Belgrade. Nikolić has been a research assistant at the Institute of Philosophy and Social Theory (IFDT) in Belgrade since 2018. At the IFDT, she is taking part in the work of the Laboratory for Active Citizenship and Democratic Innovations (ActiveLab) and Laboratory for Theory, Creation and Politics of Space (PerspectLab), through which she has been a part of research teams that conduct interdisciplinary qualitative research on new social movements, cultures of rejection (Volkswagen Foundation: 94765), trust in governance (H2020: 870572) and residential satisfaction. Since 2021 she has been an editorial board member and host of the IFDT Podcast Zvuk misli. In 2019 she has been awarded the IJURR Foundation scholarship to attend the RC21 Doctoral School in Comparative Urban Studies in Delhi, thanks to whom most of her inspiration for applying a sensory approach to housing research originates. In 2020 and 2021, she was awarded the Young Leaders Fellowship for PhD research on housing cultures transformation by the SYLFF Foundation. She presented the findings from the work that is part of this collection in 2023 at the Uncommon Senses IV conference at Concordia University in Montreal.

Veronika Zavratnik is a teaching assistant and researcher at the Department of Ethnology and Cultural Anthropology, Faculty of Arts, University of Ljubljana, where she is currently completing her PhD on footwear in everyday life. Since 2021, she also works as a researcher at the Institute for Innovation and Development of the University of Ljubljana (IRI UL). Previously, she worked at the Faculty of Electrical Engineering, Laboratory for Telecommunication.

Her broader research interests include material culture, digitalization, environment, sustainability, and applied anthropology. She is currently involved in several projects related to digitalization (DSI Digital Social Impact (KA226-050D8E8E; 2021-2023); DigiFREN (CHANSE-657; 2022-2025)), energy (INFINITE building renovation (GA 958397; 2020-2025)) and innovative teaching approaches (Active8-Planet (621436-EPP-1-2020-1- SI -EPPKA2- KA).

Recently, she co-edited Handicrafts in Slovenia: Contemporary Challenges and Perspective*s* (with Mateja Habinc; University of Ljubljana Press, 2022), Views of the Three Valleys (with Blaž Bajič and Ana Svetel; University of Ljubljana Press, 2021), and Close-ups: Youth, the Future and Imagining Development in Solčavsko (with Ana Svetel and Blaž Bajič; University of Ljubljana Press, 2022). She is the managing editor of Svetovi/ Worlds: Journal for Ethnology, Anthropology, and Folkloristics, published by the University of Ljubljana Press. In 2020, she was awarded the Emerging Scholar Award for outstanding young scholars in the field of sustainability by the OnSustainability Research Network.

www.ingramcontent.com/pod-product-compliance
Lightning Source LLC
Chambersburg PA
CBHW072124020426
42334CB00018B/1698